Yale Near Eastern Researches, 6

# Oh Angry Sea

(a-ab-ba hu-luh-ha):

The History of a Sumerian

Congregational Lament

RAPHAEL KUTSCHER

New Haven and London
Yale University Press
1975

Designed by Sally Sullivan
and set in Monotype Imprint type.
Printed in the United States of America by
The Murray Printing Company, Forge Village, Mass.

Published in Great Britain, Europe, and Africa by
Yale University Press, Ltd., London.
Distributed in Latin America by Kaiman & Polon,
Inc., New York City; in India by UBS Publishers'
Distributors Pvt., Ltd., Delhi; in Japan by John
Weatherhill, Inc., Tokyo.

To my mother
Mrs. Edith T. Kutscher
and to the memory of my father
Professor Eduard Yechezkel Kutscher ז"ל

# Contents

List of Plates   viii

Acknowledgments   ix

List of Abbreviations   xi

Introduction:  Sumerian Congregational Laments over the Destruction of
  Cities   1

Chapter 1   The Individual Texts of a-ab-ba  hu-luh-ha: External
           Data   8
      2   Textual Questions   15
      3   The History of the Reconstructed Text in the Light of the
           Separate Recensions   19
      4   Syllabic Orthography   32
      5   The Epithets of Enlil   44
      6   The Texts   52

Glossary   154

Plates   167

Selective Indices   177

# List of Plates

Plate 1   YBC 4659 Text A Obverse: copy by R. Kutscher

Plate 2   YBC 4659 Text A Reverse: copy by R. Kutscher

Plate 3   CNM 10051 Text B: Upper Edge

Plate 4   CNM 10051 Text B: Obverse and Right Edge

Plate 5   CNM 10051 Text B: Reverse and Right Edge

Plate 6   VAT 7824 Text Ea: Obverse

Plate 7   VAT 7824 Text Ea: Reverse

Plate 8   Recension A (Yale), Recension B (Copenhagen)

Plate 9   Recension C (British Museum)

# Acknowledgments

This study grew from a doctoral dissertation which I prepared at Yale University under the guidance of William W. Hallo. I should like to express my deepest thanks to him for his advice, interest, and untiring help in its preparation; it is impossible to footnote each of his many contributions. My thanks are also due to Thorkild Jacobsen of Harvard University for having generously devoted so much of his time to discussing with me problems in the texts treated here.

Ferris J. Stephens (died 1969) and Jacob J. Finkelstein offered much advice and help in reading tablets. William L. Moran kindly permitted me to quote from his unpublished "Canonical Temple List." I am grateful to them.

I am indebted to Jørgen Laessøe and to the Copenhagen National Museum for the photographs of tablet CNM 10051 and for their kind permission to publish them; to Gerhard Rudolf Meyer, Generaldirektor of the Staatliche Museen zu Berlin, for the photographs of tablet VAT 7824 and for permission to publish them; to Edmond Sollberger of the British Museum for collating tablet BM 132095; and to Joachim Krecher for an advance copy of his *Sumerische Kultlyrik*.

I am grateful to the Graduate School of Yale University and to the Department of Near Eastern Languages and Literatures for their financial support of my studies in the years 1962–67. The hospitality I was shown at Yale was duplicated everywhere in the United States; surely it is only a small indication of the greatness of this country.

RAPHAEL KUTSCHER

*Cambridge, Massachusetts*
*May 1969*

The manuscript of this book went to press essentially as completed in 1969 and has been delayed for technical reasons. Only minor additions and corrections have been made since then.

I wish to express my appreciation of funds provided me by the National Endowment for the Humanities which enabled me to travel to the United States in 1972 to complete the manuscript.

I wish to express my gratitude to Jane Isay for her careful and meticulous editorial supervision, and to Florence Stankiewicz for her editorial assistance.

My wife Carol read the manuscript and corrected my English style. I am greatly obliged to her.

R.K.

*Tel Aviv University*
*July 1973*

# Abbreviations

*For symbols of lexical texts, see CAD; for titles of Sumerian literary compositions, see separate list.*

AASF B      Annales Academiae Scientiarum Fennicae Series B.

*AcOr*       *Acta Orientalia.*

*AfO*        *Archiv für Orientforschung.*

*AHw*        W. von Soden, *Akkadisches Handwörterbuch*, Wiesbaden, Harrassowitz, 1959——.

*AJSL*       *American Journal of Semitic Languages and Literatures.*

*ANET*[3]    J. B. Pritchard, ed., *Ancient Near Eastern Texts Relating to the Old Testament*, 3d ed. with Suppl., Princeton, Princeton University Press, 1969.

*AOTU*       *Altorientalische Texte und Untersuchungen*, Leiden, Brill, 1917.

AS          Assyriological Studies, Chicago, University of Chicago Press.

*ASKT*       P. Haupt, *Akkadische und Sumerische Keilschrifttexte*, Leipzig, Hinrichs, 1881–82.

*BA*         *Beiträge zur Assyriologie.*

*BaghMitt*   *Baghdader Mitteilungen.*

*BASOR*      *Bulletin of the American Schools of Oriental Research.*

*BAW*        B. Meissner, *Beiträge zum assyrischen Wörterbuch*, *1*, 1931 (= AS 1), *2*, 1932 (= AS 4).

BE          The Babylonian Expedition of the University of Pennsylvania, Series A: Cuneiform Texts, Philadelphia.

*BiOr*       *Bibliotheca Orientalis.*

*BL*         S. Langdon, *Babylonian Liturgies*, Paris, Geuthner, 1913.

BM          Tablets in the collections of the British Museum.

BRM         A. T. Clay, ed., Babylonian Records in the Library of J. P. Morgan, New Haven, Yale University Press, 1912——.

*CAD*                A. Leo Oppenheim, ed., *The Assyrian Dictionary of the Oriental Institute of the University of Chicago*, Chicago, The Oriental Institute, 1956——.

*CAH*[2]             *The Cambridge Ancient History*, rev. ed. of vols. 1 and 2, Cambridge University Press.

*Catalogue*          C. Bezold, *Catalogue of the Cuneiform Tablets of the British Museum*, London, 1889–96.

CNMA                 Copenhagen National Museum, Antiksamlingen.

*Corpus*             E. Sollberger, *Corpus des inscriptions "royales" présargoniques de Lagaš*, Geneva, E. Droz, 1956.

*CT*                 British Museum, Department of Egyptian and Assyrian Antiquities, *Cuneiform Texts from Babylonian Tablets, etc., in the British Museum*, London, British Museum, 1896——.

CTL                  W. L. Moran, "Canonical Temple List" (in manuscript).

"Die Musik"          H. Hartmann, *Die Musik der sumerischen Kultur* (University of Frankfurt a/Main, 1960).

*Eames Collection*   A. L. Oppenheim, *Catalogue of the Cuneiform Tablets of the Wilberforce Eames Babylonian Collection* (= American Oriental Series 32), New Haven, The American Oriental Society, 1948.

*Ellil*              F. Nötscher, *Ellil in Sumer und Akkad*, Hanover, Lafaire, 1927.

Emesal Voc.          Emesal Vocabulary, *MSL 4*, 1–44.

*Glossar*            C. Bezold, *Babylonisch-Assyrisches Glossar*, Heidelberg, Carl Winter, 1926.

*Götterepitheta*     K. Tallqvist, *Akkadische Götterepitheta* (= Studia Orientalia 7), Helsinki, Societas Orientalis Fennica, 1938.

*GSG*                A. Poebel, *Grundzüge der sumerischen Grammatik*, Rostock, 1923.

*GSGL*               A. Falkenstein, *Grammatik der Sprache Gudeas von Lagaš, 1–2* (= Analecta Orientalia 28–29), Rome, Pontifical Biblical Institute, 1949–50.

*HUCA*               *Hebrew Union College Annual.*

*IEJ*                *Israel Exploration Journal.*

*JAOS*               *Journal of the American Oriental Society.*

*JCS*                *Journal of Cuneiform Studies.*

*JNES*        *Journal of Near Eastern Studies.*

*JRAS*        *Journal of the Royal Asiatic Society.*

K             Tablets in the Kuyunjik Collection of the British Museum.

*KAR*         Erich Ebeling, *Keilschrifttexte aus Assur religiösen Inhalts*, *1–2* (WVDOG 23, 34), Leipzig, Hinrichs, 1919–20.

*Königshymnen*  W. H. Ph. Römer, *Sumerische "Königshymnen" der Isin-Zeit*, Leiden, Brill, 1965.

*Kultlyrik*   J. Krecher, *Sumerische Kultlyrik*, Wiesbaden, Harrassowitz, 1966.

*LKU*         A. Falkenstein, *Literarische Keilschrifttexte aus Uruk*, Berlin, Staatliche Museen, 1931.

LSS           Leipziger Semitistische Studien, Leipzig, Hinrichs, 1903–1932.

*MAD 2²*       I. J. Gelb, "Old Akkadian Writing and Grammar," *Materials for the Assyrian Dictionary*, *2*, 2d ed., Chicago, University of Chicago Press, 1961.

MDP           Mémoires de la délégation en Perse, Paris, Leroux, 1900——.

*MIO*         *Mitteilungen des Instituts für Orientforschung.*

*MSL*         B. Landsberger et al., *Materialen zum sumerischen Lexikon*, Rome, Pontifical Biblical Institute, 1937——.

MVAG          Mitteilungen der vorderasiatisch-aegyptischen Gesellschaft, Berlin-Leipzig, 1896–1944.

*Namengebung*  J. J. Stamm, *Die akkadische Namengebung*, (= MVAG 44), Leipzig, Hinrichs, 1939.

*Nanna–Suen*   Å. Sjöberg, *Der Mondgott Nanna-Suen in der sumerischen Überlieferung*, I. Teil: Texte, Stockholm, Almqvist & Wiksell, 1960.

NBC           Tablets in the Nies Babylonian Collection, Babylonian Collection, Yale University.

NBGT          Neo-Babylonian Grammatical Texts, *MSL 4*, 129–202.

*NG*          A. Falkenstein, *Die neusumerischen Gerichtsurkunden*, *1–3*, Bayerische Akademie der Wissenschaften, philosophisch-historische Klasse, Munich, 1956–57.

OBGT          Old Babylonian Grammatical Texts, *MSL 4*, 45–128.

OECT 6        S. Langdon, *Babylonian Penitential Psalms* (= Oxford Editions of Cuneiform Texts, vol. 6), Oxford, 1927.

*OLZ*         *Orientalistische Literaturzeitung.*

| | |
|---|---|
| *Or NS* | *Orientalia*, New Series. |
| *Pantheon* | A. Deimel, *Pantheon Babylonicum*, Rome, Pontifical Biblical Institute, 1914. |
| *PAPS* | *Proceedings of the American Philosophical Society*. |
| *PBS* | *Publications of the Babylonian Section, University Museum, University of Pennsylvania*, Philadelphia, The University Museum. |
| *PSBA* | *Proceedings of the Society of Biblical Archaeology*. |
| *IV R²* | H. C. Rawlinson, *The Cuneiform Inscriptions of Western Asia*, 4, 2d ed., ed. T. G. Pinches, London, Bowler, 1891. |
| *RA* | *Revue d'assyriologie et d'archéologie orientale*. |
| *RLA* | E. Ebeling et al., *Reallexikon der Assyriologie*, Berlin, de Gruyter, 1932——. |
| *Royal Titles* | W. W. Hallo, *Early Mesopotamian Royal Titles* (= American Oriental Series, 43), New Haven, American Oriental Society, 1957. |
| *SAHG* | A. Falkenstein and W. von Soden, *Sumerische und akkadische Hymnen und Gebete*, Stuttgart, Artemis, 1953. |
| *Šamaš* | A. Schollmeyer, *Sumerisch-babylonische Hymnen und Gebete an Šamaš*, Paderborn, Schöningh, 1912. |
| *SBH* | G. A. Reisner, *Sumerisch-babylonische Hymnen nach Thontafeln griechischer Zeit*, Berlin, Spemann, 1896. |
| *SBP* | S. Langdon, *Sumerian and Babylonian Psalms*, Paris, Geuthner, 1909. |
| *SEM* | E. Chiera, *Sumerian Epics and Myths*, Chicago, University of Chicago Press, 1934. |
| *SGL* | *Sumerische Götterlieder*, *1*, ed. A. Falkenstein, Heidelberg, 1959; *2*, ed. J. J. A. van Dijk, Heidelberg, 1960. |
| *SK* | *Sumerische Kultlieder* (= Vorderasiatische Schriftdenkmäler 2 and 10), 1912 and 1913. |
| *ŠL* | A. Deimel, *Šumerisches Lexikon*, 2. Teil, Rome, Pontifical Biblical Institute, 1928–33. |
| *SLTN* | S. N. Kramer, *Sumerian Literary Texts from Nippur*, (= Annual of the American Schools of Oriental Research, 23), New Haven, 1944. |
| *STT* | O. R. Gurney, J. J. Finkelstein, and P. Hulin, *The Sultantepe Tablets, 1–2*, London, 1957–64. |

| | |
|---|---|
| *Sumer* | *Sumer: A Journal of Archaeology in Iraq.* |
| *Système verbal* | E. Sollberger, *Le Système verbal dans les inscriptions "royales" présargoniques de Lagaš*, Geneva, Droz, 1952. |
| *Tākultu* | R. Frankena, *Tākultu, De sacrale Maaltijd in het assyrische Ritueel*, Leiden, Brill, 1953. |
| *Tammuz* | Thorkild Jacobsen, *Toward the Image of Tammuz and Other Essays on Mesopotamian History and Culture*, ed. William L. Moran, Harvard Semitic Series 21, Cambridge, Mass., Harvard University Press, 1970. |
| TCL | Textes cunéiformes du Louvre, Paris, Geuthner, 1910——. |
| TCS | Texts from Cuneiform Sources, *1*, ed. E. Sollberger, *The Business and Administrative Correspondence of the Kings of Ur*, Locust Valley, N.Y., Augustin, 1966. |
| *Thésaurus* | R. Jestin and M. Lambert, *Contribution au Thésaurus de la langue sumérienne*, AK, Paris, 1955. |
| TMH | Texte und Materialen der Frau Professor Hilprecht Collection of Babylonian Antiquities, Berlin, Akademie Verlag. |
| *TRS* | H. de Genouillac, *Textes religieux sumériens du Louvre* (= TCL, 15–16), Paris, Geuthner, 1930. |
| UET | Ur Excavation Texts, London, British Museum. |
| *UVB* | *Vorläufiger Bericht über die … in Uruk-Warka unternommenen Ausgrabungen*, Berlin, 1930——. |
| VAS 17 | J. J. A. van Dijk, *Nicht-kanonische Beschwörungen und sonstige literarische Texte*, Vorderasiatische Schriftdenkmäler der staatlichen Museen zu Berlin, neue Folge, Heft 1 (Heft 17, Berlin, 1971). |
| VAT | Tablets in the collections of the Staatliche Museen, Berlin. |
| *WO* | *Die Welt des Orients.* |
| WVDOG | Wissenschaftliche Veröffentlichungen der Deutschen Orient-Gesellschaft. |
| *WZKM* | *Wiener Zeitschrift für die Kunde des Morgenlandes.* |
| YBC | Tablets in the Yale Babylonian Collection, Yale University. |
| YNER | Yale Near Eastern Researches, 3, ed. W. W. Hallo and J. J. A. van Dijk, *The Exaltation of Inanna*, New Haven, Yale University Press, 1968. |
| *ZA* | *Zeitschrift für Assyriologie.* |

*ZwZw*        D. O. Edzard, *Die "Zweite Zwischenzeit" Babyloniens*, Wiesbaden, Harrassowitz, 1957.

*For titles of Sumerian literary compositions see the catalogue of W. W. Hallo in JCS 20, 1966, 90 f. The following additions and editions should be noted:*

"Coronation of Ur-Nammu"      W. W. Hallo, *JCS*, *20*, 1966, 139 ff.

"The Curse of Agade"      A. Falkenstein, *ZA*, *57*, 1965, 43 ff.

"Enki and the World Order"      I. Bernhardt and S. N. Kramer, *Wissenschaftliche Zeitschrift der Friedrich-Schiller Universität, Jena, 9*, 1959/1960, 231 ff.

*The Exaltation of Inanna*      W. W. Hallo and J. J. A. van Dijk (= YNER 3), New Haven, Yale University Press, 1968.

"Hymn to Šulpae"      A. Falkenstein, *ZA*, *55*, 1963, 11 ff.

*Two Elegies*      S. N. Kramer, *Two Elegies on a Pushkin Museum Tablet: A New Sumerian Literary Genre*, Moscow, Oriental Literature Publishing House, 1960.

"Ur-Nammu"      Å. Sjöberg, *Orientalia Suecana*, *10*, 1961, 3 ff.

# Sumerian Congregational Laments over the Destruction of Cities

Sumerian congregational laments over the destruction of cities can be divided into two major categories: the neo-Sumerian ones (which exist in Old Babylonian copies) and the late ones (which exist in neo-Assyrian and Seleucid copies). Of the former category, no copies dating from the late periods are known. Some of the late city laments, on the other hand, are presumed to be redactions of earlier literary works (other than city laments) which are known from Old Babylonian copies, but this has not been established beyond doubt. At any rate, there seems to be no connection between the neo-Sumerian congregational laments over cities and their late counterparts. The two categories represent two distinct literary genres and consequently differ in their *Sitz im Leben* in the religion of Ancient Mesopotamia.

Three major laments are known from Old Babylonian copies: *Lamentation over the Destruction of Ur, Lamentation over Sumer and Ur,* and *Lamentation over the Destruction of Nippur.* To these can be added now, with the publication of UET 6 part 2, two more laments: over Sumer and Uruk (no. 141), and over Eridu (no. 142). To this roster may be added a lament over the é-ki-mar (M. Lambert, *RA,* 55 [1961], 191 no. 41). *The Curse of Agade,* although touching upon the same subject, namely, the destruction of a city, treats it from a different vantage point. According to S. N. Kramer (*The Sumerians* 62) it is an historiographic composition and is thus also classified by M. Lambert, *RA, 56* (1962), 81 no. 75. This view is rejected by A. Falkenstein, who interprets the composition as a piece of political propaganda (*ZA,* 57 [1965], 47 f.).[1]

Although the neo-Sumerian laments were not composed for historiographic purposes, they contain historical information, implicit and explicit, of no negligible value. In a fine historical analysis of the *Lamentation over the Destruction of Ur,* Th. Jacobsen (*AJSL, 58* [1941], 219 ff.) shows quite

---

1. Be that as it may, the scribe certainly did not lament the fall of Agade; the composition is concluded with "Agade is destroyed, praise Inanna!"

convincingly that this composition was written to commemorate the fall of
the city to the Elamites in the well-known historical event which marked
the downfall of Ibbi-Suen and the end of the Third Dynasty of Ur. The information contained in this lament is, however, indirect; the blame for des-
troying the city is laid to the Elamites, the Halam and the Su peoples, but no
names of individual personages are mentioned. The second lamentation over
Ur, now called *Lamentation over the Destruction of Sumer and Ur*, contains
more explicit information. It states specifically that Ibbi-Suen was taken
(prisoner) to Elam (*WO, 1* [1950], 378 l. 33), and it names as the peoples
who took part in the devastating of Sumer the Elamites, Su, Amorites,
Halma and the Gutians. It also refers to other cities which shared Ur's fate
(see Kamer, UET 6/2 p. 1). Likewise, the *Lamentation over the Destruction of
Nippur* mentions that Nippur and a number of other cities were attacked by
the Amorites (ti-da-nu-um) and that the city was restored by Išme-
Dagan[2] (Edzard, *ZwZw* 86 ff.; Kramer, UET 6/2 p. 2). The two new laments,
although not yet investigated, will probably also yield information of historical significance once subjected to close analysis.

These laments were composed relatively soon after the events on which
they concentrate. The catastrophe had great and lasting impact upon the
collective memory of the nation, and perhaps also upon the individual
memories of those who had experienced it. The compositions include vivid
scenes of the bloodshed and destruction which prevailed. Jacobsen (*AJSL,
58*) dates the composition of the *Lamentation over the Destruction of Ur* to
the time of Lipit-Ištar, i.e. not later than four generations after the fall of Ur.
Edzard (*ZwZw* 57) dates it to one generation after the event. The destruction
of Nippur and Babylon, described in the *Lamentation over Nippur*, he sets
in the time of "Išme-Dagan or his predecessors" (ibid., 90). The laments
resemble the texts designated by the native term balag.[3] This term is known
mostly from the late periods. In the Old Babylonian period balag-compositions can be recognized primarily by their outer characteristics, but only
four compositions are expressly labeled as such (Krecher, *Kultlyrik* 30 f.).
Balag is that genre of Sumerian literature which centers mainly on laments for
major public disasters. Th. Jacobsen, who made this observation (*AJSL, 58,*
222), adds that recitation of a balag was an indispensable part of the ritual
accompanying the demolition and rebuilding of temples. *The Lamentation
over Ur*, he suggests, was composed for and used at the restoration of Ur by
the Isin kings (ibid., 223).

2. Edzard suggests (*ZwZw*, 91 f.) that the Amorite (or beduin) attack was carried
out as part of the attack on Babylonia by Ilušuma of Assur, but this is rejected by van
Dijk, *JCS, 19* (1965), 24 f.

3. On balag see H. Hartmann, "Die Musik," 52 ff., 210 f.; *CAD, B*, 38 f. s.v.
*balaggu*; Krecher, *Kultlyrik*, 19 ff., 30 f.

If this is so, one need not wonder why most of the balag-compositions of the Old Babylonian period are not labeled as such, for to the scribes who designated the "genre" of compositions the term was not generic at all, but functional, implying that such a composition was to be recited or chanted, accompanied by the balag-instrument, at the particular ceremony for which it was composed, and then it was returned or given over to the scribal school to be incorporated into the curriculum. By that time, perhaps, it did not need the functional label balag any more since it was not to be assigned to any ceremony again. The lamentations discussed earlier had the same function: having fulfilled their task at the ceremony celebrating the rebuilding of the cities concerned, they became an integral part of the curriculum of the scribal schools. This is evident from the fact that all three major laments mentioned above are entered in the literary catalogues from Ur (Hallo, *JCS*, *20* [1966], 90 nos. 38–40). Even more suggestive, of course, is the simple fact that these laments were found in so many copies. Furthermore, they were not confined to the school of the city of their origin, but were also distributed to other scribal schools. The *Lamentation over Ur* was originally published (AS 12) from copies originating in Nippur, while the *Lamentation over Nippur* exists in copies not only from Nippur but also from Ur.

The unique use of the lament during the dedication of a new temple may also explain why there exist two (and perhaps more) laments over the destruction of Ur: presumably a new lament was composed for the restoration of each temple and, once used, was put into circulation in the scribal schools (cf. also Hallo's hint concerning royal hymns, *JCS*, *20* [1966] 139 n. 82).

From a literary point of view these laments display a masterful use of the classical Sumerian language, freshness of style and a sincere creative effort. In the *Lamentation over Ur* (which is the only one so far fully edited), refrains are limited to certain sections of the composition and are meant primarily to stress the desolation and agony prevailing in the city after its destruction. Except for a few sections (at least in the *Lamentation over Ur* and in the *Lamentation over Nippur*) written in Emesal, these laments are written in the main Sumerian dialect, Emegir. We shall later see the significance of this point.

With the Kassite period, a new era of Mesopotamian literature began. Akkadian became the main language in which the output of the schools was written.[4] A handful of compositions from the body of neo-Sumerian belles-lettres, whose messages appealed to the Middle Babylonian scribes, were translated and edited only in Akkadian (most notably, the Gilgameš cycle).

4. See Falkenstein, "Die babylonische Schule," *Saeculum*, *4* (1953), 134 ff. and, more recently, Hallo, "New Viewpoints on Cuneiform Literature," *IEJ*, *12* (1962), 13 ff.

Others were copied in Sumerian, with an interlinear Akkadian translation introduced (e.g. the hymn to Ninisinna, *KAR*, 15 and 16; [see Falkenstein, *SAHG*, 363] or *The Exploits of Ninurta*). But the overwhelming majority of the neo-Sumerian belles-lettres disappeared from the scene. Such genres as royal hymns, disputations, school essays, and the lamentations over cities did not leave decisive impressions upon the later cuneiform literature. These genres were retrieved from Old Babylonian copies only by modern Sumerology.

In the neo-Assyrian, neo-Babylonian, and especially in the Seleucid periods, a new type of Sumerian city lament emerges. But this new type is markedly different from the neo-Sumerian one. The neo-Sumerian type had displayed a truly original effort and superb poetic qualities: creative language, fresh style, and balanced rhythm. In contrast, the late city laments are repetitive, unimaginative, composed to a large extent of clichés, and devoid of poetic rhythm. This is due, in part, to the extensive use made of epithets of Enlil and also to the mechanical enumerations of cities, temples, city gates, etc. As examples one can quote the series mu-tin nu-nuz$_x$(nunuz)-gin$_x$, edited by Langdon, *Sumerian and Babylonian Psalms* (1909), 130 ff., which is a lament in which Nippur, Isin, Lagaš, Kiš, Dilbat, and some of their temples are mentioned. The Seleucid text Rm IV 97, published by Pinches, *PSBA May 1901*, is a lament recounting the Gutian attack on certain cities in Babylonia. The text is in Akkadian, but it may well be of Sumerian origin. From a literary point of view it is insignificant, since it centers around the theme "The daughter of x (name of city) is crying . . ." On the basis of the exclusion of some cities from the list and the arrangement of those included, Sidney Smith drew some significant historical conclusions about the Gutian period (*JRAS* [1932], 301 ff.). *SBH* 29, which is a Nippur lament (see below p. 8), contains a list of some of the important structures of that city. Over one third of the text of the second tablet of the neo-Babylonian version of a-ab-ba hu-luh-ha (a lament over Nippur and Babylon which is here edited; the title is known from the colophon, see p. 12 below), is occupied by three strings of the twelve heroic epithets of Enlil. A refrain is repeated *after every single line throughout the text* and many lines contain an "inner" refrain as well. The text *SBH* 13, which is part of a Seleucid edition of a-ab-ba hu-luh-ha, consists in its major part of the twelve heroic epithets of Enlil— each followed by a refrain—and a list of Enlil's ancestors.

The late city laments tend to generalize in their description of violence. They usually limit themselves to stereotyped terms of destruction and mourning, repeating these terms again and again. References to historical events or to names of personages, such as sometimes appear in the neo-Sumerian laments, are lacking. One major neo-Sumerian city lament which bears some of the characteristics of the late laments is *SK* 25, which is a lament over Isin.[5] Like their ancient counterparts, the late laments belong to the native balag genre (see above); unlike them, however, they are written in the Emesal dialect. Although this is no proof, it is at least a strong hint that they functioned in religious services (see *Kultlyrik* 26 f.). Similarly, the neo-Sumerian letter-prayers, which were the literary form used in private prayer to a god or in a petition to a king, and were written in Emegir, were replaced in the post-Sumerian period by the Emesal literary genre ér-šà-hun-gá (cf. *RLA 3* 160). In fact most, if not all, of the non-archival output of the Seleucid scribes was in the domain of liturgical literature. Some of the city laments appear in the neo-Assyrian catalogue *IV R* 53, which contains titles from the repertory of the *kalû* priests, who specialized in Emesal (cf. W. G. Lambert, *JCS, 16* [1962], 68 and, in detail, *Kultlyrik*, 20 n. 9). The lament over Nippur and Babylon a-ab-ba hu-luh-ha which is edited here is entered in the catalogue once as a balag of Enlil (i 18) and once as a balag to Marduk (20; for details of titles in the catalogue see chap. 2). Since the composition deals with Nippur and Babylon, it is natural that it be described as dedicated to Enlil and to Marduk, the respective patron gods of the two cities.

Direct evidence about the role which a-ab-ba hu-luh-ha played in the ritual is obtained from Assur and Uruk calendars (Langdon, *AJSL, 32* [1926], 115 ff.). In the former, obv. 21 f., its recitation as a litany to Marduk is prescribed for the twenty-fifth (?) day of a month whose name is broken. In the Uruk calendar TCL, 6, 48 (from the Seleucid period), the same litany is prescribed for recitation to Anu, the patron deity of the city, in the mornings of the second and fifteenth of the month of Nisan (obv. 9 ff.) and on the eighteenth of Arahsamna (rev. 9 f.). The possibility cannot be excluded that in the Uruk ritual it was Nippur and Uruk which were the subjects of the lament and not Nippur and Babylon as in the neo-Babylonian text; this would also explain how the litany came to be recited to Anu. Be that as it may, the significance of these findings lies in the fact that the composition bewailing the destruction of a city could be adjusted for different cities and be employed in the worship of their respective patron deities.

There are some hints which point to a possible Old Babylonian origin of the late congregational city laments (e.g. the connection between the reverse of the Old Babylonian [?] text NBC 1315 and the neo-Assyrian *STT* 155, both closely associated with a-ab-ba hu-luh-ha [see pp. 17 f.]). But whereas the former is a litany to Enlil, the latter is described in its colophon as an eršemma to Marduk. The first ten lines of NBC 1315 are duplicated in an expanded form in the reverse of a-ab-ba hu-luh-ha (see chap. 6, lines *49 ff.); and its incipit line, e-lum gud-sún appears twice in the neo-Assyrian catalogue

---

5. Edited by J. Krecher, *Sumerische Kultlyrik*, 53 ff.

IV R 53. In i 13 it refers to a balag composition which is represented by NBC 1315 (see in detail pp. 17 f.).

The Old Babylonian origin of the neo-Babylonian series a-ab-ba hu-luh-ha (and the closely associated am-e bára-an-na-ra) can now be established on a firm basis. Tablet 4659, of the Yale Babylonian Collection, dated to the first year of Samsu-iluna, is the second tablet of the Old Baby-lonian version of this series. It contains stanzas IV–XIII of that composition, after which a catchline follows. The colophon, however, contains only the date, and no information about which series the tablet belongs to. Stanzas IV–VI of the Yale text are paralleled, in a much expanded form, in the second tablet of the neo-Babylonian recension of a-ab-ba hu-luh-ha from obv. 41 to the end of the text. The catchline of *CT 42* 1 leads to stanza VIII of the Yale text. Up to obv. 41, the neo-Babylonian text is divided into two sections which, we believe, parallel stanzas, II–III in the Yale series (lost with the first tablet). Stanzas VIII–XIII of the Yale text are presumably paralleled in the third (lost) tablet of the neo-Babylonian series.

From a literary point of view, the Old Babylonian recension can be charac-terized in almost the same words as its late counterparts: it contains numerous repetitions, it makes extensive use of refrains, and it regularly quotes the attributes of Enlil. Most important is the fact that, like its late counterparts, the Yale text does not yield any information leading to the identification of the events it commemorates. It refers to destruction and mourning in very general terms, and it contains none of the detailed descriptions found, for example, in the *Lamentation over Ur*. In one significant point, however, it does differ from its late counterparts: it is a lament composed only for Nippur, and it addresses itself only to its patron deity, Enlil.

The dissimilarity between the neo-Sumerian city laments and a-ab-ba hu-luh-ha is a dissimilarity in ritual function. The former were written to be recited in a ceremony marking the restoration of ruins, of temples or other structures, or even of whole cities, destroyed during a major disaster. Their detailed description of the disaster which caused the destruction, and their allusions to peoples and personages involved, bear directly upon the occasion for which they were written. But their use in the liturgy was limited: having fulfilled their unique purpose at the particular ceremony for which they were written, they were scrapped from cultic use and were retained as secular literary works, appreciated for their belletristic values only.

Not so a-ab-ba hu-luh-ha. We suggest that very early in its history it was adapted for use as a standard balag to be chanted at ceremonies marking the demolition and rebuilding of temples.[6] The second half of the composition (from stanza XIV on) consists of a hymn and a prayer to Enlil (see pp. 23

6. The prescripiton of a-ab-ba hu-luh-ha for certain days in the Assur and Uruk calendars may signify that these days were propitious for these ceremonies.

and 28 below). It may well be that the first half, namely, the lament (stanzas I–XIII) was recited during the ceremonies marking the demolition of the old temple, while the hymn and the prayer were recited during the ceremonies marking the laying of the foundation to the new temple.

The composition of a-ab-ba hu-luh-ha might have been motivated by an actual event which brought destruction upon Sumer or part of it. In chapter 3 p. 19 we suggest that originally the composition did not center around Nippur, but that that city was introduced as its subject at a later stage in the development of the lament. In other words, the lament was edited in Nippur for use there. In order to preserve its universal appeal, all details or allusions to any particular events or personages had to be suppressed. a-ab-ba hu-luh-ha was composed, so to speak, as a multiple-use balag, to be utilized whenever necessity arose.

This limitation of the composition to temple ceremonies may explain why it is absent from the Old Babylonian literary catalogues (see Hallo, *JAOS, 83* [1963], 169 for bibliography). Unlike the "historical" laments, which are included in the catalogues (see above), a-ab-ba hu-luh-ha was not considered classical literature to be studied; it was copied primarily for cultic use.

From the very function of this lament at the restoration of temples, it is obvious that it was recited in congregational services; the explicit reference to the first person plural (see chap. 6 line *191) and the excessive use of refrains are further proofs. The last mentioned feature suggests, perhaps, recitation by two choruses: one for the text, the other for the refrain (see in detail chapter 3).

# The Individual Texts of a-ab-ba hu-luh-ha: External Data

The Sumerian congregational lament a-ab-ba hu-luh-ha has so far been recognized in nine texts. These texts represent nine different recensions dating from the Old Babylonian, neo-Assyrian, neo-Babylonian, and Seleucid periods. Each of the texts constitutes one tablet (or a part thereof) of a multiple-tablet recension. It is obvious, then, that we do not have the entire composition preserved in any given recension. To the best of our knowledge, none of the texts exists in more than one copy (with the possible exception of VAT 7824 which may be a duplicate of *SBH* 29). Yet, except for the Yale (A) and Copenhagen (B) texts, parts of all the other texts are duplicated by parts of other compositions.

The text of a-ab-ba hu-luh-ha is presented in transliteration, translation, and with notes in chapter 6 in the form of a composite text, reconstituted from all the individual texts. This is done for methodological expediency, to show the development of the text throughout the ages. The lines of the composite text are assigned successive numbers preceded by an asterisk *; references to these lines are also preceded by asterisks. A hand copy of the only unpublished text, YBC 4659, is presented on plates 1–2.

In this study, the individual texts which are used to reconstitute the composite text are assigned the sigla A–I. Passages in other texts which duplicate any parts in these texts are marked by lower case letters suffixed to the respective capital letters. Four of these duplicating passages are parts of duplicate texts; they are further marked "a" and "b" respectively. Three texts used to reconstitute the composite text exist only as parts of other compositions; they are Ea, Haa/Hab and Ia.

Following is a list of the texts; it includes museum number, date of the text, place of publication, and the section in the composite text in which it appears.

| Text | | Museum no. | Date | Place of Publication | Lines in Composite Text |
|------|-----|------------|------|---------------------|------------------------|
| A | | YBC 4659 | Old Babylonian | Plates 1–2 | *41–*192 |
| B | | CNMA 10051 | Old Babylonian | JCS, 8, 82 f. | *28–*184 |
| C | | BM 132095 | Neo-Babylonian | CT, 42, 1 | *1–*118 |
| | Ca | VAT 8243 | Middle Assyrian | KAR, 375, ii 21–32 | *32–*37 |
| | Cb | VAT 283 + | Seleucid | SBH, 22, rev. 1–22 | *49–*72 |
| | Cc | VAT 288 + | Seleucid | SBH, 21, obv. 1–15 | *49–*61 |
| | Cd | VAT 246 | Seleucid | SBH, I, obv. 50–53 | *103–*107 |
| | Ce | AO 3924 | Old Babylonian | TRS, 2, ii 9–13 | *103–*107 |
| | Cf | K. 4613 | Neo-Assyrian | IV R, 11, rev. 39–46 | *34–*37 |
| | Cg | BM 96933 | Old Babylonian | CT, 36, 35 i 25–31 | *13–*20 |
| | Ch | VAT 248 + | Seleucid | SBH, 14, rev. 19–22 | *34–*37 |
| | Ci | VAT 321 + | Seleucid | SBH, 40, ovb. 16–21 | *103–*106 |
| | Cj | NBC 1315 | Old Babylonian(?) | RA, 16, 208 | *49–*63 |
| | Ck | VAT 609 + | Old Babylonian | SK, 25, viii 19–22 | *34–*37 |
| D | | VAT 214 | Seleucid | SBH, 13 | *128–*200 |
| | Da | K. 1296 | Neo-Assyrian | IV R², 21* no. 2 obv. 30–33 | *140–*141 |
| | Db | VAT 8243 | Middle Assyrian | KAR, 375, ii 50–53 | *142–*143 |
| Ea | | VAT 7824 | Seleucid | Nötscher, Ellil pl. I–II | *153–*187 |
| | Eb | VAT 370 + | Seleucid | SBH, 29, obv. 19–rev. 24 | *153–*178 |
| F | | BM 85204 | Old Babylonian | CT, 42, 26 | *185–*237 |
| | Fa | VAT 246 | Seleucid | SBH, I, obv. 38–43 | *206–*211 |
| | Fba | VAT 410 + | Seleucid | SBH, 58, obv. 13–22 | *207–*211 |
| | Fbb | K. 2875 | Neo-Assyrian | BA, 5, 617 f. | *207–*208 |
| | Fc | VAT 4112 | Old Babylonian | SK, 101, 4–13 | *217–*223 |
| | Fd | BM 13963 | Old Babylonian | CT, 15, 10:15–21 | *218–*223 |

| Text | Museum no. | Date | Place of Publication | Lines of Composite Text |
|------|-----------|------|---------------------|------------------------|
| G | BM 29623 | Old Babylonian | CT, 15, 12–13 | *237–*295 |
| Haa | K. 2003 + | Neo-Assyrian | IV R², 28* rev. 5–70 | *237–*296 |
| Hab | VAT 245 | Seleucid | SBH, 46, rev. 27–30 | *237–*296 |
| Hb | VAT 37 + | Seleucid | SBH, 70, obv. 1–14 | *287–*296 |
| Hc | VAT 14490 | Neo-Babylonian | LKU, 14, ii 28–32 | *288–*291 |
| Ia | VAT 6427 | Neo-Assyrian | VAS, 17, 55: 2–7 | *253–*278 |

Text Hab duplicates the first and last lines of text Haa; the intervening lines were "skipped" by the scribe.

Different parts of the same text have been given different sigla if they duplicate different texts of the composition. These are Ca and Db (from KAR, 375, ii) and Cd and Fa (from SBH, I, obv.).

For Cj, see also below, chapter 2, note 5.

TEXT A

Text A is a tablet from the Yale Babylonian Collection, marked YBC 4659. It is 159 mm long, 70 mm wide and has a maximum thickness of 30 mm. The obverse is inscribed with 39 lines of the text in one column plus 5 rubrics for stanzas[1] (IV–VIII). The reverse contains lines 40–70 of the text, a catchline, five rubrics for stanzas (IX–XIII), and a colophon. One line, mistakenly omitted by the scribe and not counted in the colophon, is inscribed on the left edge. A ruled line shows where it is to be inserted (see chap. 6, notes to line *155).

The tablet is in very good condition (broken, but almost completely rejoined from the fragments). Some signs are broken, and some were erased by mistake, the scribe having pressed his finger—or his stylus—vertically across the last three lines of the written text (l. 70, kirugu XIII and the catchline). Nearly all the lost signs can be restored on the basis of internal or external evidence.

1. For convenience, we have substituted the English word stanza for the Sumerian ki-ru-gú throughoul this work without insisting that this is always a precise equivalent. On the reading and possible meaning "prostration" of the term ki-ru-gú see Falkenstein, ZA, 49 (1949), 105.

The colophon of text A reads as follows:

70 mu-bi-im
iti zíz-a u₄ mina-kam
mu *sa-am-su-[i-lu-na]* lugal

Translation: "Its lines are seventy. Month of Shabaṭu, second day; year: Samsu-iluna (became) king" (ca. 1749 B.C.E.). The figure 70 in the line count does not include the line inscribed on the left edge; see notes to line *155.

The colophon is significant in two aspects: first, it provides a definite Old Babylonian date for the text; second, the very presence of a date on a Nippur tablet is an uncommon phenomenon (Hallo, *JCS*, *20* [1966], 92 n. 31). That the origin of this tablet is indeed the Nippur school cannot be decisively proved, but it is unlikely to be any of the other schools. Nippur boasted one of the finest schools in the Old Babylonian period (most recently Hallo, *JCS*, *20*, 91 f., especially nn. 23, 31, and 32). The carefully executed signs, the straight ruled lines and the well formed tablet are further credits to this school.

## TEXT B

This text was copied by Th. Jacobsen from a broken four-column tablet in the Copenhagen National Museum, Antiksamlingen, marked 10051. The script is Old Babylonian but the origin of the tablet is unknown. Judging by a photograph of the right edge of the tablet, we estimate that about one third of the original tablet is missing on the right side and, because the break is not even, more is missing on the left side.[2] Accordingly, each column originally contained about 24 lines, but since the surviving part of the fourth column is uninscribed, and the missing part contained no more than ten lines, the original length of the text did not exceed 82 lines. The last paragraph of the text, namely col. iii 5 ff., is unintelligible.

## TEXT C

Text C is published in *CT*, *42* as text no. 1. Dr. E. Sollberger examined the tablet and suggested to us in a private communication that its date is neo-Babylonian. Its provenance is unknown. The lower edge of the tablet is missing, but little is broken on the surface of the existing text. The existing part, obverse and reverse, consists of 92 lines. A duplicate shows that the last

2. I am indebted to the National Museum, Copenhagen, Department of Oriental and Classical Antiquities, and to Jørgen Laessøe for providing me with the excellent photographs of the tablet, and for permission to publish them; see plates 3–5.

part contained six lines at the top of the reverse (and, presumably, at the bottom of the obverse). Thus the original length of the tablet was slightly more than one hundred lines. According to the colophon, the text is the second tablet of the series a-ab-ba hu-luh-ha, and the catchline and colophon imply that the series included at least one more tablet. The colophon of the text reads as follows:

rev.   45: dub mina-kam a-ab-ba hu-luh-ha nu-al!³-til
rev.   46: ᵐTIL.NU.GAR

Translation: "It is the second tablet of a-ab-ba hu-luh-ha; unfinished."

It is doubtful whether the last line contains the name of the scribe, BE-ṣalma-iškun, as Figulla thought (CT, 42, p. 4).

## TEXT D

This text was published by Reisner, in *Sumerisch-Babylonische Hymnen* (1896) as no. 13. Its most probable provenance is either Babylon or Uruk, and its date may be Seleucid or Arsacid. The tablet is broken and the surviving part contains over fifty partial or whole lines, with the colophon and catchline (if there was any) broken.

## TEXT Ea

Like text D, this text is very late. Here, however, we are more fortunate, for the existing part of this broken tablet preserved the colophon with the precise date and location. On the obverse there are over twenty lines, and on the reverse over ten lines in addition to the two-line colophon are preserved. The colophon of Ea reads as follows:

Rev.   12. IM ᵐᵈ*na-na-a*-MU DUMU *šá* ᵐᵈ6[0-x-x] A ᵐᵈ30.TI.ᵘⁱÍR GIŠ
          ᵐᵈ60.TINⁱᵗ DU[MU x-x]
       13. UNUGᵏⁱ ITI GUD U₄ 27.KAM MU ÉŠ.7.KAM ᵐ*si-lu-ku* LUGAL

Translation: Tablet of Nanâ-iddin son of A[nu?-x] descendant of Sin-leqe-unninni, hand of (GIŠ for ŠU, i.e. the scribe) Anu-uballiṭ son of [xx]: Uruk, month of Ayaru, 27th day, 67th year of the Seleucid era (=245 B.C.E.).

The traces of the name of Nanâ-iddin's father, as seen in a photograph[4]

3. E. Sollberger, in the above communication, states that the sign is AL. My thanks are due to him for his help. See now S. N. Kramer, *JCS, 23* (1970), 10.

4. I wish to thank Prof. Dr. G. R. Meyer, Generaldirektor of the Staatliche Museen zu Berlin, for supplying me with photographs of the tablet, VAT 7824, and for permission to publish them; see plates 6–7.

do not allow us to identify him. The phonetic indicator *ú* in the name of Sin-leqe-unninni is, so far as I know, unique, but cf. $^d$30.TI-*un-nin-nu*, TCL 6, 57 rev. 17. On Sin-leqe-unninni and the Uruk scribes boasting to be his descendants, see W. G. Lambert's discussion in *JCS*, 11 (1957), 3 f. and, among his references, especially Neugebauer, *Astronomical Cuneiform Texts*, *I*, 13 ff.

## TEXT F

Text F contains no information as to its date or place of origin. The few lines erased at the end of the text are not believed to have been a colophon (see notes to *237). The script, nonetheless, is Old Babylonian.

The 35-line obverse is defaced in some places but most of the broken sections can be restored on the basis of duplicates. The reverse contained about 13 lines, none of which survived in complete form. A few more lines were erased, and the rest, marked "space for 12 more lines" by the copyist, remained uninscribed.

## TEXT G

Text G, *CT*, *15*, 12–13, (collated by S. N. Kramer, *RA 65* [1971] 24) is inscribed on a two-column tablet, obverse and reverse, and contains 34 lines. The script is Old Babylonian but the provenance is unknown. The colophon reads:

34 ér-šèm-ma $^d$en-líl-a-kam
i.e. "34 (lines), it is an eršemma of Enlil."

### TEXTS Haa AND Hab

Text Haa is from the library of Assurbanipal. It is the last section of a larger composition and is followed by a catchline—largely broken—and, presumably, a colophon, also broken. Its duplicate, Hab, is perhaps the latest copy in our roster. Its colophon bears a double date:

MU 157-KAM *šá ši-i* MU 221-KAM $^m$*Ar-šá-ka-a* LUGAL LUGAL.MEŠ.
Translation: "Year 157 (which is the 221st year [of the Seleucid era]) of Arsaces, King of Kings," i.e. 91 B.C.E.

Only the first and last lines of the text are inscribed (the former is accompanied by an Akkadian translation). The intervening lines were skipped by the scribe; see notes to *238.

## TEXT Ia

Text Ia, which has been called to our attention by W. Hallo, was published too late to be included in the Composite Text; for transliteration see p. 64. It is a shorter version of text Haa, and it mentions only Nippur (and the Ekur and Kiur) and Babylon (and the Esagila). This is the only text which has an Akkadian translation for line *253. Notice the mistake in the Akkadian translation of line 6: *a-lum šá na-ak-ru ú-šá-an-[nu-ú]* "The city which the enemy flooded(?)." For the correct transliteration and translation see line *273.

# Textual Questions

## PROPORTIONS

The six different recensions of a-ab-ba hu-luh-ha are of unequal propor-
tions. They range in size from the two-tablet recension B to the six(?)-tablet
recension D. In this part of Chapter 2 we shall try to establish the size of five
of the recensions which lend themselves to this kind of scrutiny; recension Ea
does not offer enough material for an evaluation.

We mentioned above (chap. 1) that the existing part of text B is approxi-
mately two-thirds of the original size of the tablet, the remaining third
having been lost. On this basis, and considering that the surviving portion
of the fourth column is uninscribed, we estimated that text B was originally
no more than 82 lines long.

Comparison of the existing parts of text B with their parallels in text A
suggests that the former originally contained stanzas IV, VI, VIII, X, XI, and
XII, but not the refrain stanzas V, VII, and IX. The first section of text B,
namely i 1–5 (which is followed by a division line) is paralleled in text C by
the section obv. 28–40 (composite text *28–*40), which is also followed by a
division line.[1] In the A recension this section was presumably paralleled by
stanza III in the lost tablet I. The first section in text C, namely, 1–27
(*1–*27), which is also followed by a division line, is presumably stanza II,
which was included in the A and B recension in the first (lost) tablets respectively. Stanza I is lost in all three recensions. In the C recension it occupied
the entire first tablet.

Assuming that tablets in a series are of equal length, it is very likely that
tablet I of the A series, with stanzas I–III, was about 70 lines long, tablet I of
the B series, with stanzas I and II, was about 96 lines long, and tablet I of the
C series, with stanza I, was about 110 lines long.

---

1. The discrepancy in the number of lines between B (5) and C (13) results from the
fact that the latter elaborates and expands on subjects treated more briefly in text A and
B, and from the incorporation of the epithets of Enlil in text C. In stanzas IV–VI,
which exist in both A and C, the ratio between them is 24:ca. 60.

Texts A, B, and C are the second tablets of their respective series. Comparing text A with text F (they have only three lines in common: *185, *186, and *190), one may assume that text A was succeeded by no more than one tablet. As to text B, the surviving portion of its fourth column is uninscribed, so we can assume that it is the last in its series. Text C was probably followed by two more tablets. It contains the neo-Babylonian stanzas II–VI; stanza VII (and perhaps also stanza IX) was not included in the lost third tablet of the C series (see Introduction). It is possible that stanzas VIII and X–XIII (and perhaps also stanza XIV) were included in the third tablet, and the fourth tablet included the remaining part of the balag (preserved in its Old Babylonian form in text F) and the eršemma.

Summing up this part of the discussion, we can tentatively conclude that text A is the second tablet of a three-tablet recension (210 lines, or less than that if the third tablet was not fully inscribed); text B is the second tablet of a two-tablet recension (96 + 82 = 178 lines), and text C is the second tablet of a four-tablet recension (420–440 lines). For graphic illustration see Plates 8–9.

It is more difficult to assess the size of the D series, as the existing part offers little to go by. At one point we observe that the six-line-long stanza X in text A is inflated into a twenty-three-line-long section in text D. But we also observe that although text D contains the late parallels of stanzas IX, XIII, and XIV of the A series, it is not likely to have contained all three of the intervening sections X–XII in its missing part. Calculating the original size of the series on the basis of these scant data would be too risky; by general analogy, however, one might assume a series of about six tablets.

Text Ea offers too little material for any sound evaluation. Text F is the last tablet of a presumably three-tablet series.

### CATALOGUES AND TITLES

We stated in the Introduction that a-ab-ba  hu-luh-ha is a balag composition. This is true of both the Old Babylonian and the late redactions. According to Krecher (*Kultlyrik* 30), only four Old Babylonian texts bear the "genre"-designation balag. All of them are multiple-column compositions and three are divided into stanzas. A few other Old Babylonian texts which do not bear a native designation are described by him as "seemingly" balag. The compositions designated ér-šèm-ma, on the other hand, are not divided into stanzas and they normally lack the appeal for the pacification of the heart (ibid. 29 f.).[2] These characteristics rule out the possibility that the Old Babylonian texts (A, B, and F) belong to the eršemma category on

---

2. For a deviating case see *Kultlyrik,* 31 n. 67.

the one hand (the appeal for the pacification of the heart appears in *126 ff.), and suggest that they belong to the balag on the other.[3]

By the neo-Assyrian period balag compositions regularly include an eršemma as their last section; this feature is already encountered, however, in the Old Babylonian period.

In the Introduction we mention that a-ab-ba hu-luh-ha does not appear in the literary catalogues of the Old Babylonian period. It does appear, however, in the neo-Assyrian catalogue of liturgies *IV R* 53 (+*RA*, *18* [1921], 158). Following observations by Langdon (*Analecta Orientalia*, *12* [1935], 202 f.) and by Jacobsen (*AJSL*, *58* [1941], 222 n. 15) that in column i of that catalogue balag compositions are arranged opposite their respective eršemma sections in col. ii, Krecher (*Kultlyrik* 19 ff. n. 9) identified some of the compositions. M. E. Cohen has suggested the possible restoration of the middle Babylonian literary catalogue TMHnF 3 53:21 as [a-ab-ba]-hu-luh-ha[d]en-líl-lá.

a-ab-ba hu-luh-ha is entered twice in the catalogue. It appears in i 18 with the addition *šá* [d]en-líl and its eršemmaš (ii 18-19) are entitled [x]-dam kur-ra mú-a and dilmun[ki] nigin-na. The incipit a-ab-ba hu-luh-ha is also to be restored in i 20 before [d]AMAR.UD and the eršemma šà-ba-ni ga-an-hun on the basis of K 8207 + 2724 (Langdon, Calendars of Liturgies, *AJSL* *42*:116; copy p. 126, "The Assur Calendar") obv. 22: [a-ab-ba] hu-luh-ha *ša* [d]AMAR.UD ÍR šà-ba-ni ga-an-hun ír-šèm-ma *ana* AN.ŠÁR *ina* É [d]*Da-gan*. The balag with which a-ab-ba hu-luh-ha še-ša₄ (ii 21) aligns is lost.

The incipit line of our composition may be identical to the incipit in col. ii 20[4] a-ab-ba-hu-luh-ha še-ša₄; however, see TMHnF 3 53:21 for the incipit, possibly being a-ab-ba hu-luh-ha [d]en-líl-lá.

In line 13 of the catalogue is entered the balag e-lum gud-sún-n[a?] (see notes to *49). The eršemma section of that entry reads umun-mu za-e. This entry was identified by Krecher (*Kultlyrik*, 20 n. 9, 31 n. 67) as referring to the late redaction of the Old Babylonian text NBC 1315 (*RA*, *16* [1919], 208[5]) and to its eršemma respectively. The former is a composition dedicated to Enlil. Its last stanza appears in the neo-Assyrian period on a

---

3. In text B the stanza division is replaced by ruled lines; the reason lies, perhaps, in the fact that the text is non-canonical (see chap. 3).

4. This line was renumbered 21 by Langdon in his recovery of the missing portion of the catalogue in *RA*, *18* (1921), 158, after having restored a line between the original lines 15 and 16; cf. also *IV R²* Additions and Corrections p. 10.

5. Krecher refers to *Babyloniaca*, *III*, pl. XV, apparently unaware of Langdon's improved copy in *RA*, *16*. In this improved copy, however, Langdon left out the penultimate line which reads: ki-šú-bi-im. By our estimate, the fragment (now at the Yale Babylonian Collection), which preserves the beginning and conclusion of the text, is about one-quarter to one-sixth of the tablet.

separate tablet (*STT*, 155) identified by its colophon as an eršemma of
e-lum[xx][6] (thus corroborating the evidence of the catalogue) but also as
an eršemma of Marduk!

In line 14 of the catalogue, e-lum gud-sún e-lum gud-sún is entered
as the eršemma (!) of the series am-e bára an-na-ra (edited by Langdon,
*SBP*, 95 ff.). This statement, too, can be corroborated from published texts:
the eršemma, 22 lines long, is duplicated by stanza V of the neo-Babylonian
recension C of a-ab-ba hu-luh-ha (see *49 ff.).

In other words, a literary piece starting with the words e-lum gud-sún
is used in the beginning of an Old Babylonian composition (NBC 1315),
thus giving it its title, in the middle of another composition (text C kirugu V),
and as an eršemma of a third (*SBH*, 22 = text Cb in our edition of a-ab-ba
hu-luh-ha).

Another example of the multiple use of a literary work: the eršemma of
a-ab-ba hu-luh-ha is found as an independent text in text G, but in text
Haa/Hab it is incorporated in a larger composition.

e-ne-èm-ma-ni i-lu i-lu, which appears syllabically in text B iii 4 as
an incipit line for a refrain section (see *182 and notes ad loc.), is entered in
the catalogue in line 9 as a balag whose eršemma is a [še-eb?] é-kur-ra.

The incipit line of the eršemma of a-ab-ba hu-luh-ha, namely,
dilmun[(ki)] nigin-ù (see *237) is entered in the catalogue three times in the
eršemma column: ii 23, 24, and 38 (with slight variations). In 38, the balag
line reads umun še-er-ma-al-la an-ki-a BAR-ú.[7]

We have seen, then, that in the neo-Assyrian catalogue, four lines from
a-ab-ba hu-luh-ha, all of them at the beginning of stanzas (*1, *49,
*184 [cf. notes ad loc.], and *237) are quoted as being the incipit lines of
independent compositions. From the multiple use of e-lum gud-sún shown
above, we can assume that the other three lines quoted in the catalogue refer,
in fact, to the relevant sections of a-ab-ba hu-luh-ha which were incorporated in other compositions.

6. e-lum gud-sún is prescribed for recitation to Anu on the first day of the month
of Nisan; see the Uruk calendar obv. 8 (Langdon, *AJSL*, *42* [1926], 121).

7. For BAR-*ú* = *ahû* "non-canonical" see *Kultlyrik*, 20.

# CHAPTER 3

# The History of the Reconstructed Text in the Light of the Separate Recensions

## ESTABLISHING A TYPOLOGY OF THE TEXTS

A superficial reading of the nine major texts of the composition suggests that they have a common origin. A basic stock of recurrent expressions, set in the same order and employed in identical themes, appears in the body of the composition. Yet no two texts can be recognized as identical duplicates. When bringing up identical themes, the various texts elaborate on them in different ways, emphasizing different aspects. Individual motifs appear with differing frequencies in the respective texts. Among the eight recensions there are no less than four different treatments of the attributes and epithets of Enlil. In short, then, the nine texts represent nine different recensions—from four distinct periods—of the same composition.

Regardless, however, of the chronological order of the copies, we have to determine the typology of the texts. Just as late copies can originate directly from an ancient tradition (as does text Ea), so can two or more different recensions, representing different stages in the development of the text, originate in the same period. Certain criteria should be used for typology. An important feature by which a text can be characterized is its size. In the process of numerous re-editings, texts do not normally shrink; on the contrary, they expand. Thus, as we have shown, the ratio of the Old Babylonian A to the neo-Babylonian C is $1:2\frac{1}{2}$. The six-line stanza X of A has expanded in D (Seleucid) into a section over 23 lines long (*126–*149), roughly four times the original length. Texts are expanded through the addition of refrain lines, creation of various combinations from a common stock of expressions,[1] or extensive elaboration on a theme. Enlil's attempts to ignore the plight of his people are treated in A and B in two lines respectively.

---

1. For example, a two-line theme in A is expanded to four in the parallel passage in C simply by the construction of one more combination from the common lexical stock at hand, and the addition of one single lexical element, *65–*68.

In text C this theme is treated in five lines (*103–*106). The source from which text Ea was copied contained a long list of temple attributes and of structures in Nippur and the scribe of text Ea informs us that he "skipped" 34 lines from this list. Part of that list can be retrieved from the duplicate text Eb (*161). Most common of all devices used, however, is the recurrent enumeration of Enlil's attributes and epithets. From one-, two-, or three-line treatments of these in our Old Babylonian texts (A, B, and F), the subject developed into seven- and twelve-line canonized strings of epithets (see in detail chap. 5). Other means of expansion, involving devices of a more substantial character, will be discussed presently.

Different redactions of the text do not simply mean outright artificial expansion, or even divergent literary arrangements. Some involve the introduction of changes of a different character. Text B is a syllabic version of text A, with some elementary literary changes. In the late texts D and Ea, a partial Akkadian translation had been inserted. Another factor governing changes from one recension to the other is the circumstances, geographical and historical, under which the individual copies were written. This factor, however, is not very prominent, and is found in only two cases. Text A mentions the power of Enlil prevailing over the mountain of Elam, whereas the parallel passage in C omits it, although, as we have already mentioned, text C normally elaborates on the themes treated by A. For the reason for this deviation from normal practice see the notes to line *64. Another case in point is the mention of Babylon in C 23 (line *23). Presumably, the text was edited (or copied) in Babylon or in another place under Babylonian influence, and that city was incorporated into the composition which originally centered around Nippur (cf. also the Introduction).

Applying the criteria described above, we would set the order of the texts, representing successive stages in the development of a-ab-ba hu-luh-ha, as follows: B–F–A–Ea–G–Haa–C–D. The chronological order of the copies is disrupted only in the case of Ea since B, A, F, and G are Old Babylonian, Haa is neo-Assyrian, C is neo-Babylonian, and D is Seleucid. Text Ea, although dated in the Seleucid era, seems to share the tradition of text A. In other words, in the continuous process of recopying, the "ancestors" of text Ea do not seem to have been subjected to much re-editing since Old Babylonian times. By setting the texts in the order we did, we do not imply that this order reflects the genealogy of the composition. There is no indication that any given recension here is a direct descendant of its predecessor in our typology. On the contrary, there are some indications of the reverse; for example, neither text C nor text D seems to have inherited the refrain stanzas so prominent in A.

The backbone of the entire framework is text A. Only through this text can the unity of the composition be discerned from B through F (and further into the eršemma). Without it the connection between the earlier parts of the composition (in B and C) and its end (in F) could not possibly be established. It is not only by virtue of the large number of lines from the composition and the catchline which it preserved, but also because it is the one text within which a turning point in the attitude expressed in the composition takes place, and the connection between the lament and the hymn can be established.

In order to show the continuity of the composition and its vicissitudes in the re-editing process, all its recensions have been combined into a composite text whose lines are marked sequentially. In each line the various recensions accounting for it are quoted in full, and where they are accompanied by an Akkadian translation, it too is quoted. "Lower-case" duplicates are quoted only when deemed necessary. It should be emphasized that this is not a "restoration" of the text, as we do not claim that the composition ever existed in such a form. The composite text is merely a matter of expedient methodology.

a-ab-ba hu-luh-ha clearly falls within the domain of congregational prayer. It consists of three major parts: the first is a prayerful lament (*1–*149), the second (*153–*237) is a hymn to Enlil, and the third is the eršemma (*237–*296). The numerous references in the catalogue *IV R* 53 and in the cultic calendars to lines which occur in a-ab-ba hu-luh-ha, and perhaps also the musical notations (?) in text C, also confirm the role of the composition as a text for use in a public service. Syllabic guides for correct pronunciation are found in the form of text B and certain lines in text C (see sections on text B and text C below).

In the following sections we shall discuss the texts individually, in the typological order shown above.

## TEXT B

Text B seems to represent the earliest redaction of the composition. In its present state of preservation it contains six sections (of which only three are complete), separated by division lines. Before the last section there is a line separated from the preceding and following sections by two division lines on either side (iii 4). As we have shown, the original text contained two more sections (stanzas VI and XI) which are entirely lost with the broken part of the tablet. The aforesaid single line and the last section of the text cannot be reconciled with the overall framework of the composition. The last section was left out, whereas the line in col. iii 4 was included because of references to it in the catalogue (*184). Stanza XIII is absent from text B.

The B recension lacks the refrain stanza repeated three times in A (V, VII, IX). Within the thematic sections repetitive elements are kept to a minimum. Enlil's attributes are not quoted in a stylized manner, and in only one place (*99–*102) do they show uniformity of usage of the kind found in A. This phenomenon may be connected with the canonization of Enlil's attributes. This passage in B is the only one suggestive of an early stage in the process of canonization of the selection and order of attributes (see notes to *101). The set of three Enlil attributes used here is not identical with any of the three sets used in text A (see pp. 46f.) but none of those three sets can be considered the precursor of the canonized list of seven epithets.[2]

An important feature which sets text B apart from the other texts is that it is written syllabically, whereas all the other texts are written in the standard Emesal orthography. This means that some key words of the Emesal dialect (some of which are written syllabically), such as $^d$mu-ul-líl, ma-al, gašan, umun, are consistently used in the standard Emesal texts, but the majority of their vocabulary is written in Emegir orthography. This practice is followed to a large extent even in cases where the Emesal Vocabulary provides special forms such as su$_8$-ba(=sipa), du$_5$-mu(=dumu), dìm-me-er (=dingir), etc. Except for a few scattered cases, these forms are generally ignored and only the limited vocabulary of Emesal forms, which are generally employed in other Emesal texts, is employed in a-ab-ba hu-luh-ha. Needless to say, the texts also abound with words for which no special Emesal forms are known.

Text B is entirely syllabic (except the Enlil attribute in lines *31 and *101 which is written in Emegir). By "syllabic" we mean four distinct features: 1. avoidance of CVC signs and the use of CV–VC signs instead; 2. replacement of rare value signs by common value ones (e.g. še for šè) with exceptions in *33 and *41;[3] 3. nonrepetition of consonants (e.g. ú-ra for úr-ra), and 4. avoidance of logograms (e.g. the replacement of EN.LIL$^{ki}$ = nibru by ni-ib-ru). In many cases, indeed in most cases, the reading obtained from the text is quite different from what is known about the pronunciation from the vocabularies and from other syllabic spellings.

In chapter 4 we discuss in more detail the ramifications of the syllabic orthography; at the moment we are interested in its significance. The syllabic text amounts, indeed, to a precise phonetic guide to the pronunciation of the congregational lament. The absence of a divine determinative before Enlil's name lends further support to the theory that divine determinatives were not pronounced before divine (as against royal) names; cf. Hallo, *Royal Titles*, 56 f.

It is our belief that text B is extra-canonical and served as an aid in the

2. To avoid confusion we apply the term "epithets" to those which appear in the lists of seven and twelve heroic names of Enlil (pp. 47 ff.). We apply the term "attributes" to those names which appear in lists of three or less, in texts A, B, Ea, and F (chap. 5).

3. Notice that the Emesal examples quoted above, su$_8$-ba, du$_5$-mu, and dìm-me-er, are written "syllabically" when compared with their logographic Emegir equivalents, but they employ rare-value cuneograms seldom used in Emegir.

teaching of the composition (to the gala priests?) which had to be recited during services. The partly syllabic lines in text C served a similar purpose.

The apparent carelessness with which text B was copied augments the impression that it is indeed extra-canonical. The signs are coarse and of uneven size. The vertical margin line was drawn only to be crossed by some of the verses. The tablet is not divided by horizontal ruled lines as are the other OB texts, A, F, G, and stanza notations are replaced by simple division lines. Still another indication of the extra-canonical character of the text is line iii 4. It is separated from the preceding and succeeding lines by two division lines, indicating that it stands for a whole section to be recited at that point. This section was, no doubt, a refrain, which the (gala?) priests knew and therefore it did not have to be fully written out; see *184 and notes ad loc. In the canonical text A, by contrast, the refrain stanza gud-sún is written in full three times.

Whether a standard Emesal text of the same recension as B ever existed is a moot question. Text A comes close to that if we disregard the absence of the refrain stanza gud-sún in B. One can cite the example of the *Hymn to Šulpae* which is known from four copies of which two are syllabic, yet they do not precisely match the logographic ones.

TEXT F

Text F bears no date or colophon. To judge by the script we would date the copy to the Old Babylonian period. The division into stanzas also points in this direction, since in the various texts of the composition the late copies are divided into sections simply by division lines and not by stanzas.[4] The position of text F within the typology of the texts would also tend to support an early date, but this is in no way a clear indication.

Kramer described this text as part of a " . . . hymn to Enlil glorifying him on the one hand for his enormous size and for the fertility he brings to the earth . . . and on the other hand for the destructive power of his word . . ." (*JCS*, *18* [1964], 47).

The text is divided into four stanzas, marked IX–XII. Following the line marking the twelfth stanza there is an additional line which is the catchline to the next stanza, which is also the concluding eršemma.

We mentioned that by the neo-Assyrian period balag-compositions were regularly concluded by an eršemma. This phenomenon seems to have had its inception in the Old Babylonian period. In the commentary to line *237 we

4. We are unable to establish whether the absence of stanzas is a universal phenomenon in the late texts. Even if they did not totally disappear, they are at least not common in the neo-Assyrian, neo-Babylonian, and Seleucid texts; for further discussion of stanzas see p. 25.

suggest that the eršemma concluding a-ab-ba hu-luh-ha is the Old
Babylonian composition dilmun nigín-ù (text G), which is identified in
its colophon as an eršemma to Enlil. The space on the reverse of text F, left
after the conclusion of the text, would not have accommodated the entire
eršemma (the OB version of dilmun nigin-ù is 34 lines long); the reason
for beginning a new tablet was perhaps the scribe's reluctance to split it.

The structure and contents of the text also suggest an early date. The
seven heroic epithets of Enlil, which are so common in late texts but are also
found in some Old Babylonian texts, are not employed in text F. Nor are
any of the sets of attributes which text A regularly uses employed in a way
which suggests a literary canonization. On the other hand, some of Enlil's
attributes are used haphazardly (e.g., a and m *185, *190, *201; e-lum *198).
The only example that can be viewed as a precursor of a stylized employment
of Enlil's attributes is that of ù-mu-un-e kur-kur-ra in *202 and *213.
These two are the second lines of stanzas X and XI of the text whose structures are identical (see presently). a-a ᵈmu-ul-líl in *193 cannot be
considered an attribute. In text C *3–*8 this expression precedes each one of
the seven canonized epithets of Enlil. It is rather a form of address and can
perhaps be compared with "sipa gù-dé-a" (Hallo, *Royal Titles*, 147).

Of the four stanzas that the tablet originally contained, only three are fully
preserved.[5] Stanzas X and XI (= stanzas *XV and *XVI in the composite
text) show an identity of structure. In the first line a refrain is introduced and
is repeated twice. It is repeated again in the second line of the stanza after
an attribute of Enlil (the same one in both stanzas, see above) and, finally, in
the second half of the last line of the stanza. Similar structure is attested also
in stanza IX (*XIV), but here the last line of the stanza repeats not its first
line but its third (and even there the repetition is not verbatim). But in text A
the parallels of lines 1–2 and lines 3–7 of F, stanza IX, are divided between
two stanzas respectively; see notes to line *185.

Except for this structural pattern, text F lacks the numerous repetitions and
refrains so typical of text A (and also of texts C and D). The style is terse and
the numerous motifs, sometimes treated in poetic doublets, add delightful
freshness to it. In fact, the connection with text A would have been difficult
to recognize if not for the three lines common to both texts (*185, *186,
*192). The mood is totally different, its praise of Enlil sounds sincere and
genuine. Even those passages describing Enlil's destructive powers and the
miseries he is capable of dealing his people are not in the plaintive mood so
dominant in text A, but rather sound like an objective description of his
physical powers, manifest in both benevolent and malevolent activities.

---

5. In stanza IX some of the lines had to be restored but no line is broken beyond
restoration.

In the discussion of text B (above, p. 21) we saw that stanza XIII of text A, which contains allusions to Nippur, is absent from text B (although that text contains stanza XII which also alludes to Nippur). Two lines from stanza XIII of A are included in stanza IX of F (*185 f.) but there are no allusions to Nippur. In the discussion of text A (below), we suggest that Nippur as the subject of a-ab-ba hu-luh-ha was introduced into an already extant composition and this suggestion may be supported by the facts just mentioned. The fact that the F recension is divided into fewer stanzas than the A recension (the lines common to both are in stanzas XIII and XIV of A, but in stanza IX of F) can perhaps be explained by the absence of refrains in the F recension.[6] This, together with the absence of refrains in the thematic stanzas of F might suggest that the text represents the earliest stage in the development of the composition before it was adapted for use in congregational worship. If this is true we would have to place it typologically before B.

TEXT A

Text A is divided into ten stanzas (IV–XIII) averaging seven lines each. According to undocumented statements by Hartmann, "Die Musik," 232 and Langdon, BL, 44 f., stanza divisions were introduced into Sumerian compositions as early as the Ur III period. Possibly they were misled by the fact that compositions such as hymns honoring Ur III kings (but existing in Old Babylonian copies which is of course a different matter) are divided into stanzas. In a-ab-ba hu-luh-ha, stanza rubrics are found in only two of the Old Babylonian texts (A and F), but in the late texts (and also in the Old Babylonian text B) the stanza rubrics are paralleled by simple division lines.

Division into stanzas, found mostly in Old Babylonian copies, cuts across various categories of the Sumerian hymnic literature (Hartmann, "Die Musik," 232 ff.; more recently Hallo, BiOr, 23 [1966], 241).

Text A is the second of a three-tablet recension and it starts with the fourth stanza. This stanza conveys the impression of a lament. With the aid of texts B and C, which contain stanzas II–III of the composition, we can deduce that stanza IV is the concluding section of the first part of the first half of the balag part of the composition. This part (lines *1–*48) alludes to some catastrophe that befell Enlil's people and describes the wailing and mourning which ensued. There are no detailed descriptions of the catastrophe but the "enemy" is mentioned in *16–*17, which indicates that the catastrophe was not caused by natural forces. Otherwise the catastrophe and the mourning are

6. This would not contradict our findings (chap. 2) that both recensions are three tablets long, since the stanzas of text F are 7, 11, 11, and 12 lines long, as against the average seven-line stanzas of A.

referred to in very general terms so that the composition retained its universal appeal and could be used as necessity arose.[7] In other words, this text could be used at any temple demolition and rebuilding ceremony without being adapted anew for each occasion. For a detailed discussion of this aspect of the text see the introduction.

It seems that "my city" in *42 f. has been introduced into the already extant stanza, since the connection to the preceding and succeeding passages is not clear. The parallel section in text B lacks this reference to a city. Stanzas XI and XIII in text A center mainly around the theme of Nippur. This city does get some attention in text B, but it is not as strongly emphasized as in text A. The aforementioned stanza XIII of A, centering around Nippur, is paralleled in text F by two lines, neither of which mentions Nippur.

This evidence, together with the facts mentioned at the end of the previous section (p. 25), would tend to suggest that the lamentation a-ab-ba hu-luh-ha when composed did not have Nippur as its central theme. The composition was adapted for Nippur only at a later stage.

The first part of the first half of the A recension (i.e. stanza IV and what preceded it) paves the way for the second (and last) part of the first half of the balag part of the composition. This part consists of stanzas VI, VIII, and X (and the intervening ones, see presently). These three stanzas address Enlil in an entreating way, with spontaneous cries such as "You are exalted!" "Until when (shall we suffer)?" and "Restore (your) heart!" After each of the thematic stanzas IV, VI, and VIII there comes a refrain stanza which is repeated verbatim as stanzas V, VII, and IX. This 7-line stanza glorifies Enlil by declaring that his name is universally heralded.

With stanza XI there is a definite change in the structure and mood of the composition. The refrain stanza which would have been expected here (after having appeared as stanzas V, VII, and IX) is not repeated, and the address to Enlil changes from the second to the third person.[8] In the thematic stanzas VI, VIII, and X the refrain opens the stanza and is quoted twice. It is repeated in lines 2–4 of the stanzas, after each of the three attributes of the second set of Enlil attributes (see pp. 45 ff.). The main theme of the stanza is introduced in the fifth line and is treated in two or four lines.[9] But in stanzas

7. For the idea of the lament of universal appeal, see Hallo, *JAOS, 88/1 = Essays in Memory of E. A. Speiser*, 1968, 71 ff.

8. In this respect stanza X is already the turning point. The words "'Restore your heart' is said to him" show that here, too, Enlil is spoken of as the subject of the sentence, but he is not directly addressed. The essence of the stanza, however, lies with the plea itself, whereas the words "is said to him" appear only in the fifth line of the stanza.

9. Stanza VI fits this description after the removal of lines 19–20; see notes to lines *104 f.

XI–XIII each stanza is opened not by the refrain but by the third set of Enlil attributes.[10] The attributes are followed by two or four adverbial phrases and the refrain (which is the predicate in each sentence) is repeated in every line of the stanza. The three respective refrains in stanzas XI–XIII are "When will he rise?" "Let him rise!" and "He will look hither." They express the hope that Enlil will rise from his "sleep"—his indifference toward his people which causes them so much agony. This atmosphere of hope is the turning point linking the depressive mood at the beginning of a-ab-ba hu-luh-ha with the hymn at the end of its balag part. Stanza XIII is concluded with a line (*191) which strikes a disharmonious chord with the atmosphere of hope and is perhaps meant to summarize the first half of the composition in one sentence.

TEXT Ea

This text has come down to us in a late copy (245 B.C.E.; see the colophon, above p. 12) but there are some features in it which indicate an ancient tradition, as we shall show. As the reverse shows, text Ea is a part of a larger composition.

All but a few of the lines preserved in the text are accompanied by an Akkadian translation which sometimes comes in the same line with the Sumerian, sometimes in the following line. The few lines not translated are Enlil attributes.

Text Ea relies on an early tradition. In this regard, it does not share with texts C and D their tradition of the twelve heroic epithets of Enlil. This is remarkable if we remember that in the late Enlil texts any excuse seemed valid for the introduction of the seven or twelve epithets. In this respect the text shares with text A the tradition of the early stage of canonization of the Enlil attributes, and in the part that survived it uses the third set (see above, the discussion of A) just as do the parallel sections in text A, lines *152 ff. On the other hand, in the second introduction of Enlil's attributes text Ea has am du$_7$-du$_7$ where text A writes am ná-dè, *172 ff. In the same section the text quotes two more attributes which seem to be out of place (*175 f.).

Yet, despite its seemingly good tradition, the text did not escape the vicissitudes of a late copy. There are cases of misinterpretation and mistranslation, and even of miscopying. In line *160 the scribe states that he skipped 34 lines (a list of structures in Nippur, some lines of which are found in the duplicate Eb).

10. There are two deviations: in stanza XI the third attribute was accidentally omitted and later added on the left edge; in stanza XIII the third attribute is altogether omitted.

## TEXT G

Text G is the Old Babylonian version of the eršemma. In its literary style it resembles text A. The text opens with an appeal to Enlil (here addressed as Dilmun) to turn around and look at his city. The theme is repeated after each of the twelve epithets of Enlil, which are followed by two additional ones. There follows a laconic enumeration of seven cities and their shrines. These too are accompanied by the theme of "Turn around and look at your city!" Finally, there comes a description of a city in agony whose suffering at the hand of an enemy is compounded by famine.

In the late version of this eršemma there is an additional line after the concluding line of the OB version. It seems that this final line (*296) is an integral part of the eršemma and was accidentally omitted from the OB version.

## TEXT Haa/Hab[11]

The neo-Assyrian version of the eršemma is half again as long as the OB version (text G). It is 51 lines long as against the latter's 34; fifteen of these are provided with an Akkadian translation.[12] This inflation of volume is accounted for by several factors. Text Haa employs the twelve heroic epithets of Enlil (augmented by two additional ones [*251 f.] which are not mentioned anywhere else in a-ab-ba hu-luh-ha). In addition to the temples of Nippur, Isin, Ur, and Larsa mentioned in the G recension, the H recension also includes Sippar, Babylon, and Borsippa. Finally, this text adds another line to the thematic part of the eršemma which is not included in the OB version (see *296).

## TEXT C

Text C, over one hundred lines long, of which over ninety are preserved, is divided by heavy ruled lines into four sections. The first two lines of each section were included by the scribe in one case (whereas the rest of the lines in this text are included in one case apiece). The second line in each one of these four cases is an attempt to render the first such line syllabically; see notes to *1, *28, *41, *73.

---

11. This discussion is based on text Haa. Its duplicate, Hab, preserved only the first and last lines of the text, whereas the rest has been skipped by the scribe. See notes to *238 and *296.

12. In the Composite Text we assign a single number to the Sumerian line and its Akkadian translation; cf. Civil, *JNES, 26* (1967), 200.

On the other hand, each line of the text, *except the four double-lines*, is followed by a min(= "ditto") sign at the end of the line.[13] This min sign is missing at the end of line 3 (*2) but it has a small èn written above the line after the first half of the line (a-a ᵈmu-ul-líl), and eš-še nu-si-du-a after the second half of the line. In the next six lines (the epithets of Enlil) these small words are replaced by min signs, both in the middle and at the end of the line.

The double-line phenomenon is closely associated with the distribution of the min signs. These signs stand for a refrain. The refrain is the first line of each section (and the words above the line in lines *2–*8, see notes to line *2). The syllabic line is a stage direction device whose purpose is to provide a correct pronunciation for the otherwise logographically written refrain. In other words, it serves the same purpose as text B. Why it is only the refrain which is provided with a syllabic companion is a different question; perhaps the text and the refrain were chanted by separate choruses.

Another stage direction device is, perhaps, the notations on the left edge of the tablet but they remain, for the most part, unintelligible (as already pointed out by Kramer, *JCS, 18* [1964], 36 n. 5);[14] see the transliteration of text C, pp. 55 ff.

Toward the end of the reverse the text is disrupted. Rev. 39 contains two half-lines which appear elsewhere in the text; the same is true of rev. 41, but its second half continues on the next line, 42, which contains sections from three different lines; see notes to lines *89, *90, *104, and *117. Rev. 43 (*118) seems to be out of place; see notes ad loc. The reason seems to be a broken *Vorlage*. The content of text C "consists largely of hymnal, plaintive and prayerful stereotype passages which were used repeatedly in the lamentations current in Post Sumerian days."[15] There is no better proof for this than the numerous duplicates to the various sections of the text which appear in other compositions. One of these sections proves now to go as far back as the Fara period (see notes to *13). In other words, the creative efforts invested in the composition of this text were directed at arranging existing clichés, rather than writing new ones.

Text C differs substantially from text A in two respects: as its central theme it does not dwell exclusively on Nippur, but it mentions Babylon as

13. For a similar phenomenon see *CT, 42*, no. 12.

14. We included the notations only in the Connected Transliteration, but not in the Composite Text. They are an-na, e, a, ru, ma-a, ru-un, ka-i, ka-a and ú. For an-na see èn-du an-na = *elitum ša zamāri, CAD, E*, s.v. *elitam*. About these and other musical notations see W. G. Lambert in H. Goedicke, ed., *Near Eastern Studies in Honor of William Foxwell Albright* (Baltimore and London: The Johns Hopkins Press, 1971), 337 ff.

15. S. N. Kramer, *JCS, 18* (1964), 36.

well (*23). The reason for this may lie in the political and cultural circumstances under which the text was edited, but in the existing part of the text
there is no more elaboration on this point. In text A, however, elaboration
on the Nippur theme comes only in its second half, which could have been
paralleled in the third and fourth tablets of the C series.

The second striking difference between texts A and C is that C does not
make extensive use of a refrain stanza. The refrain stanza V, VII, and IX of A
is paralleled in C only once (*49 ff.). The reason for this omission may
simply be the fact that in C there is a refrain after every line, as we suggested
above.

TEXT D

Text D was transliterated and translated by Langdon, *SBP*, 89 ff. He
assigns it to a series of the Word of Enlil and assumes that the tablet is the
sixth, and last, of that series. Unfortunately, he does not indicate what
these assumptions are based on.

The Akkadian translation accompanying some lines in the text reveals
some interesting features which show that the meaning of the Sumerian text
was to some extent lost on the scribe. There are cases of misinterpretation of
the Sumerian verbal structure and of "harmonization" of the text; see notes
to *140–*144 and *199.

With text D is seems that our composition reached the final stage in its
history. Although we cannot verify Langdon's statement that this tablet is the
sixth in its series, the possibility cannot be ruled out. After all, many of the
Seleucid texts from Babylon and Uruk pertaining to Enlil and to other gods
do constitute multi-tablet series. From the literary point of view, text D does
not differ greatly from text C, to wit, it is full of numerous repetitions and
lack of literary creativity. Also, they both share the twelve-epithet tradition.
They differ, however, in their tablet arrangement—whereas text C is part of a
four-tablet recension, text D is part of a six(?)-tablet recension.

One major theme—the pacification of the heart (stanza IX in A)—is
treated at great length in the preserved part of text D. But since the reverse
agrees with stanzas XIII and XIV of the A series, it is probable that one or
two of the intervening stanzas had their corresponding parts in the broken
part of the tablet. That all three intervening stanzas were paralleled in that
part is hardly likely, as it would have required enormous space. The introduction of Enlil's "genealogy" (*144 ff.) is curious. The fragmentary shape
of that section does not allow a sound evaluation of its contents.

The connection between the lament and the hymn to Enlil in a-ab-ba
hu-luh-ha, which we have pointed out above in our discussion of F, comes

out even more clearly in text D, where elements of both the lament and the hymn are written on the same tablet, and the connection between A and F is more safely established. The lack of absolute correspondence between the two texts following lines *192 is due to the great typological difference between the two recensions.

CHAPTER 4

# Syllabic Orthography

GENERAL

A basic linguistic fact concerning the texts of a-ab-ba hu-luh-ha is that all of them are written in the Emesal dialect. Some deviations from standard Emesal orthography are displayed by text Fd, which are apparent against the background of the duplicates, but the text is Emesal nonetheless.

The reason for writing this composition in the Emesal dialect is its employment in worship and its recitation by the gala priests. A discussion of the role of the Emesal dialect in the cult and the part played by the gala priests can be found in Krecher, *Kultlyrik* 12 ff., 26 ff., and 35 f., and in Renger, *ZA, 59* (1969), 189 ff.

Even within the alleged dialectal unity of the texts there are two distinct strata. The overwhelming majority of the material is written in the standard Emesal dialect, known from the Emesal Vocabulary and from numerous literary compositions.[1] The common feature of all these texts is a basic stock of dialectal forms which are distinct from their main-dialect counterparts, and are used in place of them. The vocabulary of the Emesal dialect is quite limited and outside it Emesal texts make widespread use of main-dialect forms. Even within the limited availability of Emesal forms, Emesal texts are not consistent in employing them, and in some cases prefer Emegir forms to available Emesal ones (see pp. 42 f.).

The features which distinguish the Emesal forms markedly from their Emegir counterparts fall into four major categories: 1. phonological (dìm-me-er = dingir; mu = giš; e-zé = udu; i-bí = igi; še-er-ma-al = nir-gál etc.); 2. morphological, presumably representing a different stage in the history of the individual form (gašan, ga-ša-an and šen = nin; umun, ù-mu-un and am-an = en (< *emen); mu-lu = lú etc.); 3. lexical (umun = lugal) or apparently lexical (ir, ga = túm), and 4. orthographic (di-èm = dím; me-er = mir etc.).

1. For a comprehensive list of Old Babylonian Emesal texts see Krecher, *Kultlyrik,* 14 ff.

To a certain extent the reading of Emesal forms is known because they are consistently spelled syllabically (as some of the examples quoted above show), but otherwise their reading is known from conventional vocabularies, which sometimes add the note EME.SAL after the respective entries (e.g. *CT*, *12*, 4 ii 11 [*á*-A-*nāqu*]; *ZA*, *9*, 162:18 ["Berlin Vocabulary VAT 244"]).

Most of the texts of a-ab-ba hu-luh-ha are written in standard Emesal orthography, and by and large conform to these standards. Linguistically, then, they do not offer much which was hitherto unknown. Two texts, however, deviate from these standards: text C includes four lines which are written syllabically, and text B is written syllabically throughout (except for two half-lines).

A superficial reading of text B reveals that the reading of Emesal and Emegir forms obtained from the syllabic spelling is different from what is conventionally supposed; the spellings of this text do not conform to the ones recorded in vocabularies which contain a "pronunciation" column. In the following sections we present the linguistic data, classified into phonemic categories and compared with their standard Emesal and Emegir equivalents. (For further comparison we quote cases from other syllabically written texts.[2])

### THE LINGUISTIC DATA: CONSONANTS

In the standard Emesal dialect, consonantal shifts from Emegir involve mainly shifts between points of articulation; e.g. Emegir igi = Emesal i-bí, Emegir dagal = Emesal damal. In text B, however, most of the consonantal shifts (from Emegir and from standard Emesal) involve the distinction "voiced" vs. "voiceless."[3] Other shifts are also attested, as well as consonant elision.

### Voiced and Voiceless

#### *Text B Voiceless = Standard Emesal Voiced*

$$/k/ = /g/$$

du-ka = $du_{11}$-ga (*32, *33); ku-le = gul-e (*41); ki = $gi_4$ (*126, *127; but cf. gi = $gi_4$, *116); du-ku = duggu (>dungu, *29; see notes ad loc.). Cf. ku-ma-al = gú-gál, = *gugallum* "chief of irrigation," Emesal Voc. II 17 with footnote; (cf. however, Jacobsen's remark about the possible

2. The comparandus in this chapter is the Emegir form as employed in standard Emesal texts, unless otherwise indicated. The other syllabically written texts may be either Emegir or Emesal, see below.

3. Cf. Poebel, *GSG*, § 37. The terms "voiced" and "voiceless" are used here conventionally, without preference for any specific pronunciation; for an extensive treatment of the problem see I. J. Gelb, *MAD*, 2 (2d ed.), 28 ff. and especially 33 ff.

etymology of the word, namely $ku_6$-gál, *JNES*, *5*, 130); ka-nu-na = gá-nun-na (*CT*, *44*, 13:22; notice that the syllabic spelling reflects the Emegir form although the text is Emesal); mu-maš-ku-nu-um = giš-maš-gurum (*AfO*, *16*, 63); ka-ša-an = ga-ša-an (*ZA*, *56*, 7, 31; *Sumer*, *13*, 81:3–7); ku-ru-ša = guruš-a (*ZA*, *56*, 26); ku-zi = guškin (? *ZA*, *56*, 21 f.); -ki = -$gin_x$ (= GIM; *ZA*, *57*, 42); e-ni-i[m-q]a?-ra = é-níg-ga-ra (*Sumer*, *11*, pl. XVI, 10; cf. Falkenstein, *ZA*, *55*, 56); ka-la-ak-ka = kala-ga (*Sumer*, *11*, XVI, 3); ki-ì-ki = ki-en-gi (ibid., 4); ku-le = gul-e (BE, 30/1, 5 v 1).

A reverse shift occurs in maš-gi-in = maškim (*Šulpae Hymn*, 50).

$$/p/ = /b/$$

Only one shift is attested: (ša)-pa = (šà)-ba (*108). In all other occurrences of the suffix -bi the shift does not take place and the phoneme /b/ is rendered as voiced; see below. Elsewhere the shift is attested in ni-ip-pi-ig-ru = ní-bí-in-gùr-ru (*Ur-Nammu*, 10/68[4]); pa-ra = bára (ibid. 9/66); pà-an-su-r(a), pa-an-su-úr = banšur (*ZA*, *55*, 61); ap-pa-re = ambar(-e) (*appāru* "swamp," *AfO*, *16*, 62, but cf. ab-ba-re, ibid.); a-áš-pa-la = áš-bal-e (*erretum* "curse," *Sumer*, *11*, XVI 16). The reverse shift is not attested in text B but cf. the Emesal $su_8$-ba = Emegir sipa (e.g. Emesal Voc. II 12; line *37).

$$/t/ = /d/$$

ti- = dè- (*181, *183). Elsewhere this shift is attested in du-tu = $du_{11}$-$du_{11}$ (*ZA*, *55*, 56), ta-al-la = dalla (*Šulpae Hymn*, 66); ú-tu-ug = udúg (*Ur-Nammu*, 1/52); te-li = diri (*Coronation of Ur-Nammu*, 25 f.).

### Text B Voiced = Standard Emesal Voiceless

$$/d/ = /t/$$

(n)a-nu-da = an-úr-ta (*29); du=túg (*103). Elsewhere: ù-du = ù-tu ("may I bring" *AfO*, *16*, 62); nam-da-ad-gu-ud = nam-tag-dugud (*ZA*, *57*, 40), du-da = tu-da ("born," ibid. 42).

### Text B Voiced = Standard Emesal Voiced

$$/b/$$

bi- = bí- (prefix, *32 f., *103); bi- = ba-e- (*103, *104); -bi = -bi (suffix, *44–*48); ni-ib-ru = nibru (*182).

---

4. *Ur-Nammu* refers to the syllabic Ur-Nammu hymn, edited with its parallel logographic portion by A. Sjöberg, *Orientalia Suecana*, *10* (1961), 3 ff.; the numbers refer to the syllabic and logographic lines respectively.

## /d/

e-di-ni = edin-na (*44); bi-du-la = ba-e-dul-la (*103); en-du = èn-du (*45); du-ra-an-ki = dur-an-ki (*182).

## /g/

ge = ge (*45, *47 f.); -gi = -gin$_x$ (*29); si-ge-a = sìg-ge-a (*46 f.); sa-gi-ki-ga = sag-GÍG-ga (*102); gu = gú (*103); ú-ga = uga (*108 f.).

## /z/

-zi, -zu = -zu (*103, *104); zi-zi = zi-zi (*181, *183).

*Text B Voiceless = Standard Emesal Voiceless*

## /k/

mu-na-ka = mu-na-ak-e (*108); ka-na-da = ka-na-ága-da (*116); -(a)k = -(a)k (gen. postposition, *109, *142); tu-ku = tuku (*140); [ši]-iš-ku-ra = siskur-ra (*142).

## /p/

sa-pa = sipa (*102, but cf. su$_8$-ba, Emesal Voc. II 12).

## /s/

sa-an = sag (*103, *115); sa-pa = sipa (*102); su = sù (*108); su-a = sá (*33).

## /t/

ti = ti (*32); tu-ku = tuku (*140).

### Other shifts

*Text B /m/, /n/ = Standard Emesal /g̃/; text B /n/ =*
*Standard Emesal /m/*

sa-an = sag̃ (*103, *115); hu-mu = hug̃-ù (*141). Elsewhere: hu-úr-sá-ne (*ZA*, *57*, 32); hu-sa-m(à) (ibid.) = hur-sag̃-g̃á; pa-bi-il-sa-ám = ᵈpa-bil-sag̃ (*ZA*, *56*, 33); še-en = sag̃ (Emesal Voc. II 181). Cf. also the various syllabic spellings of níg̃ with the last consonant rendered as /m/, /n/ or altogether omitted, Falkenstein, *ZA*, *55*, 56. Other cases in which logographic /g̃/ is rendered either /m/ or /n/ in syllabic spellings are ne-ti-in (*AfO*, *16*, 63), mu-tin/mu-ti-in (Emesal Voc. I 79 f., II 126 f.) = g̃eštin; di-ne-er (*AfO*, *16*, 63; *Šulpae Hymn*, passim), dìm-me-er (e.g., Emesal Voc. I 1) = dig̃ir; ne-pa-ar, mi-ba-r(i) = gi₆-pàr (Bergmann *apud* Sjöberg, *Nanna-Suen*, 103). It seems that within a given text the treatment of individual words is consistent. In the case of text B, /b/ and /m/

occur as the equivalents of /g̃/ in two separate words. (For the rendering of Emesal /g̃/ by /-n-g/ in text C and elsewhere see notes to line *41.). On the other hand it seems that the distinction between /n/ and /m/ is ill defined[5]; cf. Emesal mu-gib$_x$ = Emegir nu-gig (Emesal Voc. II 78 ff.) but nu-gi-an-na in the syllabic Emesal text *Sumer, 13*, 81:3 which reflects the Emegir form nu-gig-an-na (cf. Edzard, *ZA, 55*, 104 f.); ab-si-im-ma = ab-sín-na ("furrow," *ZA, 56*, 42 f.). The occurrence of /n/ in syllabic and Emesal orthographies instead of /m/ in Emegir is attested in nu-nús = munus (Emesal Voc. II 68); gi$_4$-in = gemé (ibid. 87; Gordon, *Sumerian Proverbs*, 143, 225 f., 228). A case of text B /n/ = standard Emesal /m/ is an-da-ma-le = àm-da-ma-al-en (*29, *31, *33) but this shift also occurs in standard Emesal, see *294; an- = àm- is also attested in *Ur-Nammu*, 3/55.

### Text B /š/ = Standard Emesal /s/, /z/

[ši]-iš-ku-ra = siskur$_x$-ra (*142; cf. also šeš-ku-re in *CT, 44*, 14:30. Read with Oberhuber, *OLZ, 59* [1964], 559, sis-ku-re? See also Sollberger, *Or NS, 24* [1955], 18); in text C: iš-še-en-ni = ezin$_x$ (*1); še-gig-ga = sìg-gig-ga (? *46 f.). /š/ in Emesal and syllabic texts = /s/, /z/ in Emegir is attested in še-en = sag̃ (Emesal Voc. II 181); ši = zi (= *napištum* e.g., *87 ff., *157 f.); še = izi (Emesal Voc. III 99); še-eb = sig$_4$ (e.g. *AS, 12*, 76); šu = sum (*Ur-Nammu* 3/54); šu-ud = sù-ud (*AfO, 16*, 63); ša = sa$_4$ (*Sumer, 11*, XVI 20); mušen = mu-sa$_4$-a, mu-sig$_5$ (? see notes to *87). The reverse shift is attested in text C, si-du-a = šed-dè (*1 f.) and elsewhere in: pà-an-su-úr = banšur (*Šulpae Hymn*, 61); su-úr = šúr (ibid. 50); sa-ga = ša$_6$-ga (*ZA, 56*, 19); zi-ig, sig = šeg$_9$ (ibid. 41); a-ma-sá = amaš-a (? *CT, 44*, 13:7). Alternation between /z/ and /š/ independent of dialectal differences is attested in še-er-tab-ba = zar/zàr-tab-ba ("cornstack," Civil, *JCS, 20* [1966], 124 n. 17); cf. also Gelb's suggested readings išin, izin, and isin for EZEN, *MAD, 2²*, 210.

### Flapped /r/

In text B: su-ta (*108), in text C: sù-ta (*13), sù-rá (*15), all = sù-rá; cf. notes to *13. Perhaps also (n)a-nu-da = an-úr-ta (*29).

### Loss[6] and non-gemination of consonants

#### In final position

Four cases attested in text B: du = túg (*103); ša = šà-ab (= Emegir šà[-g], *108, *126, *127, *141); tu-ku-a = tuku-àm (*140); an-da-ma-le = àm-da-ma-al-en (*29, *31, *33). Elsewhere the loss of a final

---

5. Cf. Poebel, *GSG*, § 60 ff.
6. Cf. Poebel, *GSG*, § 39 ff.

consonant is attested in hu-ša = huš-àm (*Ur-Nammu*, 7/62, 8/64). In the first two instances, du and ša, the loss of the consonant, although at the end of a lexical unit, occurs in the middle of an utterance. In the other two instances from B the loss occurs at the end of an utterance, whereas in *Ur-Nammu* it occurs before a vowel.

### In middle position

Loss of a consonant occurs in two cases: /g̃/ is lost in ka-na-da = ka-na-ág̃a-da (*116); /r/ is lost in (n)a-nu-da = an-úr-ta (*29); cf. hu-sa-mà = hur-sag̃-g̃á (*ZA*, *57*, 32). For the loss of intervocalic consonants (as in the first example, above) cf. súr < sumur$_x$ (*ezzu* "fierce," Bergmann, *ZA*, *57*, 36); e-šen = ešemen (*JNES*, *23*, 9); ha-za-he-e = hi-is$^{sar}$ zà-hi-li (*AfO*, *16*, 63) and see Poebel, *GSG* §§ 25, 43 f. The only certain case of non-gemination occurs in mu-le-el = $^d$mu-ul-líl (where the gemination is the result of assimilation of /n/–/l/ in the original form *umun-líl; *28, *100, *109, *116). In the following cases non-gemination can better be described as a deviation from the general practice of repeating the last consonant of a lexical element before a vocalic grammatical element: e-di-ni = edin-na (*44); ira = ér-ra (*44, *46, *47); ma-nu-na = mà-nun-na (= Emegir gá-nun-na; *45); du-la = dul-la (*103); ma-ra = mar-ra, ú-ra = úr-ra (*104).

### THE LINGUISTIC DATA: VOWELS

In general, vowel shifts between Emegir and Emesal affect mainly two categories: the front vowels /e/ and /i/ on the one hand, and the back vowel /u/ on the other. Both categories of shifts are represented in text B, although not equally.

### The Front Vowels

#### Text B /i/ = Standard Emesal /e/

e-di-ni = edin-e (text A: edin-na; *44); i-ni-im, i-ni-m(a) = e-ne-èm (= Emegir inim; *109, *184); i-ni-ra = e-ne-ra ("to him;" *140, similarly i-ni-ir, *Ur-Nammu*, 3/54); mi-na-ši = me-na-šè (*28; but cf. mi-na-še below). The same shift in the directional postposition is attested in ga-ne-ši = gána-šè (*AfO*, *16*, 62) and in me-pa-ar-ši = gi$_6$-pàr-šè (Sjöberg, *Nanna-Suen*, 103); more cases are quoted by Falkenstein, *ZA*, *55*, 51, with n. 153; ir, i-ra = ér(-ra) (*44, *46, *47).[7]

---

7. The reading ér (not ír) for A.IGI is assured by Diri III (Meissner, *BAW*, *2*, 83 ff.), 149 ff. where the first column indicates the reading by e-er; Deimel's indicator i-ir quoted from this source in *ŠL*, 579:382k should be corrected accordingly. Cf. now also Kagal A i 1 ff., (= *MSL*, *13*, 232).

i-ši-še = i-še₈-še₈ (*44, *45, *48). The apparent inconsistency in the syllabic treatment of še₈ is perhaps due to contraction of the second še₈ with the verbal suffix -e, namely, *i-ši-ši-e; see notes to *44. Some other examples of syllabic /i/ = logographic /e/: i-ri-im-gá-al/la = erím-gál-la, i-ri-gá-al/la = erím-gál(-la) (*Ur-Nammu*, 2/53, 7/63); but cf. lú-e-ri-im (*ZA*, *57*, 38); mi-ri = giri (*Ur-Nammu*, 3/55) but me-ri (Emesal Voc. II 197);[8] ki-i-ki = ki-en-gi (*Sumer*, *11*, XVI 4); in = en (ibid. 18), ì-in-si = ensí (ibid.),[9] sa-gi-iš = sag-e-eš (*Ur-Nammu*, rev. 1/69; in this text there is no case of syllabic /e/ = logographic /i/); zi-di-iš = zi-dè-eš (*Šulpae Hymn*, 17); hi-bu-ur = ᵍⁱhenbur (*AfO*, *16*, 62); ši = še (ibid.); ši-bar = šeg₉-bar (ibid. 63; that text contains examples of reverse shift as well, see below); ši-in, sig, zi-ig all = šeg₉ (*ZA*, *56*, 41); a-ši = anše (*Šulpae Hymn*, 36); zi-di = zi-dè (*ZA*, *57*, 37; read simply zi-de?) and, finally, gi₄-in-e/gi₄-in-na = gemé (Gordon, *Sumerian Proverbs*, 143).

## Text B /i/ = Standard Emesal /i/

bi- = bí- (prefix; *32, *33); ti = ti(l) (*32); ì-lu = i-lu (*41, *184); e-di-ni = edin-e (*44); a-ši-ir = a-še-er (= Emegir a-nir,[10] *41; the same form is attested in *CT*, *44*, 13:13, 15, 26, 27, and in *CT*, *44*, 14:11); -bi = -bi (suffix, *44–*48); i- = ì- (prefix, *44–*48); si-ge = sìg-ge (*46, *47); gi-ki-ga = ɢíɢ-ga (*102); -ni- = -ni- (infix, *104); ki-gi₄ (*126, *127); gi = gi₄ (*116); ši-iš-ku-ra = siskur-ra (*15); zi = zi (*181, *183); ni-ib-ru = nibru^{ki} (*182); ki = ki (*182); a-li-ma-ha = alim-maha (*183); -ni = -ni (suffix, *182).

## Text B /e/ = Standard Emesal /i/

In text B only one word contains the vowel /e/ where its standard Emesal equivalent has an /i/: le-el = líl. In all but one of the six occurrences this spelling is employed in the name Enlil. The non-Enlil case is in line *183 where the interpretation is uncertain. The Enlil occurrences are *28, *100, *109 (mu-le-la-ke), *116, and *127. Elsewhere /e/ is attested in Emesal and syllabic Emegir where /i/ occurs in standard Emegir in the following cases: dìm-me-er (e.g. Emesal Voc. I 1), di-ne-er (e.g. in the syllabic versions of *Šulpae Hymn*, passim) = dingir;[11] ha-za-he-e = hi-is^{sar} zà-

8. The data on gíri in the Emesal Voc. (mi-ri in II 97, but me-ra in II 127 and me-ri in II 180) cannot be established as contradictory; the two former examples are restored; me-ri in III 91 comes from a different manuscript.

9. The pure syllabic nature of *Sumer*, *11*, XVI is somewhat marred by the use of the ambivalent ɴɪ in ki-i-ki and ì-in-si, when the common ɪ sign was at the disposal of the scribe (e.g. in the Akkadian line 8). Was ɴɪ used for /iğ/?

10. For the reading of ɴɪʀ as nir (with /i/) cf. Sᵃ 392 (*MSL*, *3*, 41) and 139:128.

11. This example is uncertain; according to *CAD*, I/J, s.v. *ilu* lexical section, the syllabic indicators for the reading dingir do not contain an unequivocal /i/ vowel in

hi-li ("cress," *AfO*, *16*, 63); me-ri = gíri (Emesal Voc. II 180), gìri
(ibid. 197, but mi-ri also occurs as the equivalent of both forms, see
above); ne, ne-en₆, ne(m) = níg (Falkenstein, *ZA*, *55*, 56; forms with
/i/ also occur in syllabic texts, such as ni, ni-im, ibid.); èm = níg (passim);
še-em = nin (Emesal Voc. II 70). In text C: še = ši (= Emegir zi, *89).

## Text B /e/ = Standard Emesal /e/

a-e = a-e (*41); -e = -e (verbal suffix) in: ku-le = gul-e (*41),
i-si-ge-a = ì-sìg-ge-a (*46, *47), i-ši-še = ì-še₈-/še₈ (*44, *45, *48;
uncertain, see above); e-di-ni = edin-na (*44); en-du = èn-du (*45);
ge = ge (= Emegir gemé; *45, *47, *48); mi-na-še = me-na-šè
(*99–*102; but see above: mi-na-ši); -e = -e (postposition) in: u-ga-e =
uga-e (*108, *109), mu-le-la-ke = ᵈmu-lìl-la-ke₄; el-lu-um = e-
lum (= Emegir alim, *114, but cf. the syllabically written Emegir form
a-li-ma-ha = alim-mah(a), *183); e = è (*115). In the syllabic-com-
panion-lines of text C: -še-e = -šè (postposition, *28).

## The Back Vowel /u/

The second group of vocalic shifts in text B involves the vowel /u/. This
vowel is affected in three cases, but remains intact in some twenty others. In
order to demonstrate the shifts affecting this vowel we depart from the former
pattern of discussion to approach the problem apart from text B. In two of the
three cases /u/ is replaced by /i/, and in one case it seems to have undergone a
vocalic metathesis. The two former cases are: ni-iš- = nu-uš- (*41, a
preformative written syllabically, with the retention of the /u/, even in Emegir
[see notes to *41] and also in the syllabic text *CT*, *44*, 13:11); -zi = -zu
(second person suffix, *104). The change may be due to regressive dissimila-
tion, as the next syllable begins with /u/; text B retains this suffix intact in
*103. A vocalic metathesis seems to have taken place in su-a ì-im-du =
sá um-mi-du₁₁ (*33).

The "weakening" of the vowel /u/ into a front vowel in text B is by no means
a unique feature; some of the characteristic features of the Emesal dialect
involve this shift. The most notable examples are e-zé = udu (e.g. Emesal

---

the second syllable. On the other hand, those entries which do show an /i/ vowel in the
second syllable, render the second consonant in the form as /m/, not /g̃/. In other
words, there is no clearcut evidence for a second /i/ in the form dingir. The syllabic
renderings of this word are: di-in-gír, di-gi-ir (in both of which the second vowel
can be read /e/), di-mi-ir (in lexical lists) and the two Emesal forms listed above. The
regular transliteration of the form as dingir is, then, a mere convention and the
Emegir and Emesal forms may not differ in the second vowel.

Voc. II 89); zé-eb = duh (same word? ibid. III 111); zé-em = sum (176); notice that even in Emegir the logogram appears with /i/ and /e/ vowels, e.g. sì, sè); zib, zé-eb = dùg (ibid. I 96, III 16 respectively); zé-eb = tùm (I 96); zé-zé = dun-dun (III 115); $^d$zé-er-tur = $^d$tur$_x$-du (I 78; cf. Jacobsen, *JNES*, *12* [1953], 164 n. 14); me-zé-er = mu-dur$_x$ (BU) (Emesal Voc. III 92 and Jacobsen); zé-bi-da = dugud (Emesal Voc. II 22). A few more cases are ambiguous, as the vowel involved can be either /e/ or /i/: di = du (*alāku*, Emesal Voc. III 2 f.); me-er-si = gír-su (ibid. I 95, *ZA*, *56*, 36 f.); di-tu = du$_{11}$-du$_{11}$ (*AfO*, *16*, 61); si-is-he = sùh-sùh-e (ibid. 62 n. 11); li-li = lú-ulù (Falkenstein, *ZA*, *55*, 57 n. 170; Emesal?).

The material collected above, and especially that from the Emesal Vocabulary, seems to suggest that in those cases where Emegir /u/ appears in Emesal as a front vowel, the Emesal Vocabulary prefers /e/ almost exclusively; but the evidence does not stand on a solid basis. Equally inconclusive is the evidence for defining the limit between /e/ and /i/ in Emesal and in syllabic texts.

The shift between /u/ and the front vowels is not unidirectional. Some Emesal words do contain an /u/ vowel where the Emegir equivalents contain a front vowel: mu(š) = ğiš (passim); u$_5$ = ì (Emesal Voc. II 75); mu-un-ga(r) = níğ-ga (ibid. III 34 f., but èm = níg, 36); e-lum = alim (I 5); su$_8$-ba = sipa (II 12) and, finally, the Emesal equivalents of en (< *emen, Poebel, *GSG*, §§ 25, 43):ù-mu-un (passim), [mu-u]n-ga-ar, and m[u-u]n-ku$_5$ (in the Emesal column of engar and enku [wr. ZAG.HA], Emesal Voc. II 15 and 26 respectively, where the en- element is not necessarily identical with en "lord, priest"), and, perhaps, ù-un (unless it is a mistake for ù-mu-un, *ZA*, *57*, 36). In text B mu-le-el (*28, *100, *109, *116, *127) conforms to the practice in standard Emesal as does e-lu-um, while a-li-ma-ha (*183) conforms to Emegir usage.

As against the two cases in which Emegir /u/ appears as /i/ in text B, there are numerous cases where the original vowel remains intact. These are: du-ku = dungu (< duggu, *30); du-ka = du$_{11}$-ga (*32, *33); ì-lu = i-lu (*41, *184); ku-le = gul-e (*41); en-du = èn-du (*45); gu = gú (*103, *104); -zu = -zu (second person suffix, *103); du = túg (*103); du-la = dúl-la (*103); ú-ra = úr-ra (*104); (n)a-nu-da = an-úr-ta (*29); su = sù (*108); mu- = mu- (prefix, *108, *142); ú-ga = uga (*108, *109); du = du (*115); ú = ù (preformative, *116, *126, *127); hu-mu = huğ-ù (*141); ši-iš-ku-ra = siskur-ra (*142); ni-ib-ru = nibru$^{ki}$ (*182); du-ra-an-ki = dur-an-ki (*182). Text B nu (*183) is syllabic spelling for nú (= NÁ). On the readings nú, ná for NÁ see *MSL*, *3*, 152 no. 374; *8/1*, 55 n. 1, 56 n. 1; *13*, 176 ii 7' and Jacobsen, *Tammuz*, 348 n. 65.

## Changes Involving Other Vowels

In this category only a few cases are observed, and most of them can be ascribed to causes that are not phonological.

### Text B /a/ = Standard Emesal /i/

One case involving a gross deviation from usage either in Emegir or standard Emesal is sa-pa = sipa (*102). This form stands in contrast not only to the Emegir form widely used in Emesal, but also to the proper Emesal form su₈-ba recorded in the Emesal Vocabulary and in some Emesal texts. The shift may be due to assimilation, as may be the case in la-la mi-du = líl àm-mi-in-su-ub (*Ur-Nammu*, 5/59, 6/61; meaning uncertain).

### Text B /a/ = Standard Emesal /e/

i-ra = ér-re (*46, *47) may simply be a case of a difference in the choice of a postposition, cf. *Lamentation over Ur* 125 with n. 129; a-li-m(a) = Emesal e-lum (*183) is a syllabic rendering of the Emegir form, and is contrasted with el-lu-um (*115). The shift mu-na-ka = mu-un-ak-e (*108) may be governed by non-phonological factors.

### Text B /i/ = Standard Emesal /a/

Two uncertain examples are attested. e-di-ni = edin-na (*44) is more likely to be another case of paradigmatic postposition preference, and seems to stand for edin-e with an /i/ = /e/ shift, cf. above. The interpretation of line *183 where -di = -da (postposition) occurs is uncertain.

## Contractions

### Text B /i/ = Standard Emesal /a-e/

bi- = ba-e (prefix + second person infix, *103, *104); cf. zi-me-en = za-e-me-en (*Šulpae Hymn*, 14).[12]

## Syncopation[13]

el-lu-um-lu = e-lum mu-lu (*115); cf. ki-ib-la = ki-bala (*Ur-Nammu*, 8/64).

---

12. We choose to transliterate zi, in preference to Falkenstein's ze- because Emesal normally uses zé for /ze/ and zı for /zi/.
13. See Poebel *GSG*, § 21.

## Sandhi[14]

Three cases are attested: du-ku-ge-en-na-nu-da = duggu-gin$_x$
an-ur-ta (*29); a-li-ma-ha = alim maha (*183); i-ni-ma-ni-lu
i-lu = inim-a-ni i-lu i-lu (*184). See sandhi form quoted by Jacobsen,
AS, 16, 78 n. 9.

### CONCLUDING REMARKS[15]

Text B is too short to allow a conclusive phonological statement. But some
tentative observations can be made from the scant data that could be gathered.

In the consonantal structure of the text the feature which emerges most
prominently in our survey is the one suggesting that the main difference
between the syllabically written Emesal text B and the logographically
written ones concerns the "voiced" vs. "voiceless" consonants. In six
(perhaps even eight) cases text B displays a voiceless consonant where the
standard Emesal equivalent is voiced. The reverse is true in only one case.
These shifts take place only among the velar, dental, and bilabial stops. The
one shift attested in text B within the sibilants is limited to /š/:/s/. In the
liquids text B has, as could be expected, /m/ and /n/ for /g̃/. Loss of consonants also occurs in middle and final positions.

As to the vowels, the main changes take place within the front vowels
(/e/ and /i/) on the one hand, and between these and the back vowel /u/ on
the other. Of the first type, there are six, or possibly seven forms in which
text B contains an /i/ where standard Emesal contains an /e/. The reverse
situation occurs in only one form. Two particular cases in B contain an /i/
where the standard Emesal equivalents have /u/, and no occurrence of the
reverse is attested. Only one significant shift involving /a/ can be discerned
in text B.

It should be emphasized that in many cases, both consonantal and vocalic,
the deviations from standard Emesal are, in fact, deviations from Emegir
usages found in Emesal contexts. This does not mean, however, that text B
is a true manifestation of the Emesal dialect. A good number of features in
this text stand in contrast with what is known about Emesal phonology,
whether through the Emesal Vocabulary or through syllabic spellings in
standard Emesal texts. These are ka-na(-da) = ES ka-na-ág̃a(-da) =
EG kalama(-da);[16] sa-pa = ES su$_8$-ba = EG sipa; ša = ES šà-ab =
EG šà(-g); mu-le-el = ES $^d$mu-ul-líl = EG $^d$en-líl; ma-nu-na =
ES ma-nun-na = EG g̃á-nun-na; a-ši-r = ES a-še-er = EG a-nir;

14. On sandhi in general see L. Bloomfield, *Language* (2d ed. 1935), 186 ff.

15. For the syllabic spellings in text C see notes to *1, *28, *38, *41, and *73.

16. This form poses a problem as it seems that the Emesal and Emegir versions
changed roles; cf. Hallo, *Royal Titles*, 86.

i-ni-im = ES e-ne-èm = EG inim; ni-iš- = ES nu-uš- = EG nu-uš-; du-ku = ES zé-[be]-ed = EG dungu (<duggu). Apparently, some of the syllabic spellings of text B look more like syllabic renderings of the Emegir forms, and less like their Emesal equivalents.

The picture emerging from our findings in text B ought to raise some questions concerning syllabic vis-à-vis logographic spellings in both Emegir and Emesal. Text B and other syllabic Emesal texts, like syllabically written Emegir texts, show deviations from what is conventionally accepted as their logographic equivalents. On the other hand, there are many similarities between the syllabic versions of the two dialects. What is, then, the true relationship between syllabic Emegir and its logographic parallel? And what is the relationship between the two Emesal versions? If the conventional, logographic Emesal—which does use syllabic spellings occasionally—is the reflection of a pronunciation different from that of the main dialect, why does it not reflect *all* the differences? And if the syllabic spellings of Emegir texts reveal some features in common with Emesal, where does the border between the two dialects lie?

A first step towards answering these questions must be a close analysis of all the syllabic texts available, both Emesal and Emegir; such an investigation is far beyond the scope of this study and should be made the subject of a separate study.[17]

What is also needed are examinations of the Sumerian syllabaries used for the different periods and (as far as possible) for the different geographical regions—perhaps on the model of Sollberger's syllabary of the pre-Sargonic "royal" inscriptions from Lagaš.[18] These should then be compared with the Akkadian syllabaries of the respective periods and regions.

Only after the steps recommended here are taken, can an effective investigation be conducted into the nature of the relationships between Emegir and Emesal on the one hand, and between these and their respective syllabic versions on the other.

17. See the contributions of J. Krecher in *ZA*, *58* (1967), 16 ff., *WO, 4/2* (1968), 252 ff. and *Heidelberger Studien zum alten Orient* (1967), 87 ff.

18. *ZA*, *54* (1961), 1 ff.

# CHAPTER 5

# The Epithets of Enlil

## DIVINE EPITHETS

The problem of divine epithets is among the most intriguing in Sumerian literature and in the domain of royal and votive inscriptions. It has never been given the attention it deserves as an important facet of Sumerian literary style on the one hand, and as a means of gauging the development of Mesopotamian religion and thought on the other. The only comprehensive treatment this problem has received was Tallqvist's *Akkadische Götterepitheta* (= Studia Orientalia, 7, 1938). This book, much as it is an indispensable tool for the study of divine epithets, is little more than a classified list of deities and their respective epithets. This list includes hundreds of titles, some of which are attributed to certain gods exclusively and some shared by several deities. Naturally some of the epithets are "official" titles assigned to the deities in accordance with their function and rank in the pantheon. This is the case, for example, with the title di-ku$_5$-mah, "The August Judge," assigned to Uta, who is traditionally considered the divine judge. The majority of the divine epithets, however, do not seem to be connected with any such divine function in the organized pantheon or in the organized world. Their origin must be sought in the mythological background of Mesopotamia, although the existing body of Mesopotamian mythological literature may not solve all problems. Some epithets seem to originate in the Mesopotamian concepts which attribute supernatural powers to deities.

In a-ab-ba hu-luh-ha three stages in the development of the epithets of Enlil can be distinguished: (1) a haphazard use of epithets in texts B and F; (2) regular, stylized use of three sets of epithets in texts A, B, and E, and (3) regular, stylized use of a string of seven epithets in some Old Babylonian texts (e.g. G, Cj) and in late texts, and strings of twelve epithets in most of the neo-Babylonian and Seleucid texts (C, D, and others), and even fourteen epithets in text Haa. In the late periods the seven Old Babylonian epithets were augmented by five (or seven, in Haa) more epithets which are the proper epithets of other gods. For the sake of clarity we use the term "epithets" only for those appearing in the third stage of development. For the names occurring in the first two stages we use the term "attributes."

### CASUAL USAGE AND EARLY STAGES OF CANONIZATION

Text F uses some attributes of Enlil in a haphazard way which shows no regularity. am "Wild Ox" occurs in lines *185, *192, and *194. This attribute was eventually included both in the sets of three attributes of text A and in the seven heroic names (see below); in both cases it is qualified by an adjective. It seems that in the early periods it is predominantly Enlil who is honored with this title, although in the late periods it is shared by other deities (*Götterepitheta*, 165 f. s.v. *rimu*). Tallqvist cites an Old Babylonian passage in which Ninurta is called am sag "Prime Wild Ox," but the interpretation of the passage is uncertain. It occurs in the date formula Ammi-ditana 31: mu *am-mi-di-ta-na* lugal-e ᵈnin-urta am sag á-dah-a-ni-šè ᵍⁱˢgu-za mah-a sag-[íl]-la é nam-til-la-šè ì-ni-in-ku₄-ra (see *RLA*, 2, 189). There are some difficulties in this passage and am sag may not be the attribute of Ninurta. e-lum "Dignitary" as an attribute of Enlil occurs only once in text F, but appears regularly in texts A and E. It is the Emesal form of alim, and is so closely associated with Enlil that in the Emesal Vocabulary I 5 it is, in fact, equated with Enlil. The only attribute which is quoted in text F in any regular manner is ù-mu-un-e kur-kur-ra (which also appears as the first of the seven heroic epithets; see below). In text F it occurs in the second lines of identically construed stanzas (*202, *213). Enlil's name is sometimes preceded by the term a-a "Father." It occurs in text F *193 as a form of address.

dilmun as an attribute of Enlil occurs in texts F and G, and the H texts. In the latter (from the neo-Assyrian and Seleucid periods) the postdeterminative ki is added, which indicates that only in the late periods was this attribute identified with the land Dilmun. The origin of this attribute is not clear, but see notes to *237.

Text A uses three sets of attributes of Enlil, comprised of three attributes apiece. The pattern is not found in text B, but in one instance, in stanza VIII, one such set occurs with a slight change. The passage in question is *99 f.; in *100 ᵈmu-ul-líl is paralleled in B by the logographic kur-gal a-a ᵈen-líl-lá (similarly B i 3 = *31) and in *102 sipa sag-gíg-ga is paralleled in B by sa-pa sa-gi-ki-ga. (For the last attribute see below.)

The attribute kur-gal occurs twice in text B (*31, *101). It is one of the oldest attributes of Enlil, and is attested already in the Fara period in a text from Abū Salābīkh (AbS T, 44a, iii 5; see R. Biggs, *JCS*, *20* [1966], 79). About the possible origin of this attribute see Falkenstein, *SGL*, *1*, 26, 42. a-a occurs in *101 and *116. e-lum appears in *114 and alim in *183, both written syllabically. These two are respectively the Emesal and Emegir forms of the same word, meaning "dignitary" (*kabtum*; Emesal Vocabulary II 23) and both appear among the three sets of attributes in text A (see below).

A cumbersome attribute which occurs only in texts B and C is dungu-gin$_x$ an-úr-ta "like a cloud, (rising) over the horizon." It appears in this form in text C and is written syllabically in the parallel line in text B (*29 and see notes ad loc.). It occurs again in C 40 = *40.

In text A, a full-fledged stylized use of attributes of Enlil is brought to the fore. It falls short of the Old Babylonian canonized list of the seven heroic names, as the latter survived intact into the late periods and in certain cases was expanded to include twelve and even fourteen epithets. Yet, the regularity shown in the use of the attributes in text A does indicate that they have undergone some degree of canonization. There are three-line sets, each quoted three times in text A.

The first set is quoted in the first three lines of the refrain stanza V (= VII = IX; *47 ff., *92 ff., *119 ff.). The first attribute is gud-sún "Wild Bull" (cf. (ù-)sún "Wild Cow," Römer, *Königshymnen*, 152) and e-lum "Dignitary" (see above). The second attribute of the first set is kur-gal a-a ᵈmu-ul-líl "the Great Mountain, Father Enlil" which is discussed above.

The third attribute is sipa sag-gíg-ga "Shepherd of the Black-headed." This attribute, which is the only one also included in its present form in the seven heroic epithets, is accompanied by an Akkadian translation in *IV R*, 18, 3:4 f.: sipa sag-gíg-ga = *šá re-é-i ṣal-mat qaq-q[a-di]*. The earliest attestation of this phrase is not as a divine attribute but as a royal epithet—and in Akkadian. It was assumed by Ipiq-Adad II of Ešnunna (Edzard, *ZwZw*, 162). It is then used as an attribute of Šamaš in the Yahdunlim inscription (*Syria, 32*, 12 ff.) i 7—again in Akkadian. Its earliest Sumerian attestation is as an epithet of Rim-Sin of Larsa (UET, 8, 86:28).[1] Cf. also notes to *21.

These data reflect, perhaps, a transference of a royal epithet to the divine order.

sipa sag-gíg-ga is only one of several combinations which is formed with each of its immediate constituents. For royal epithets compounded with sipa in the early periods see Hallo, *Royal Titles*, 141, 147 ff. For compounds with "Black-headed" in bilingual and Akkadian contexts see *CAD, Ṣ*, 75 f. s.v. *ṣalmat qaqqadi*; on the structure of the idiom see von Soden, *JNES, 19* (1960), 163 f.

The second set of Enlil's attributes appears in the second to fourth lines

---

1. sipa sag-gíg-ga occurs as Šulgi's title in Šulgi Hymn A line 5 in copies from the Old Babylonian period, but not in contemporary records. The title lugal sipa sag-gíg-ga occurs as a title of Šu-Suen in an Old Babylonian Sammeltafel copy of several of his inscriptions; see Edzard, *AfO, 19* (1959–1960), 7 col. iii 12; and Seux, *Épithètes royales akkadiennes et sumériennes* (1967), 444.

of each of the stanzas VI, VIII, and X (*74 ff., *100 ff., and *127 ff.). In each case the attribute is followed by the thematic refrain of the stanza. The first line in this set is not an attribute but simply the name of Enlil. The second attribute of this set is ᵈmu-ul-líl kur-kur-ra "Enlil of the Foreign Lands." We prefer to translate kur-kur "foreign lands" and not "mountains" because of the apparent connection between this attribute and the first of the seven heroic epithets, "King of the Foreign Lands," in which kur-kur obviously cannot be translated "mountains" (see immediately below). The third attribute is the same as the third attribute of the first set, namely, "Shepherd of the Black-headed."

The third set of attributes is attested both in text A and in text Ea. Its first member is am "Wild Ox," its second member is, again, Enlil's name and its third member is alim "Dignitary," whose Emesal equivalent e-lum occurs in the first set.[2] The third set is quoted in the last three stanzas of text A, namely XI, XII, and XIII. In the first of these (*152 ff.), the third attribute was mistakenly omitted from the text but was added on the left edge of the tablet (*154). In the third occurrence of the third set (*185 ff.) the third attribute is altogether omitted from text A, but is duly present in the parallel section in text Ea (*187). Text Ea, which follows the pattern of text A in quoting the attributes of Enlil, supplies an Akkadian translation for some of them. The only unusual phenomenon in this translation is that it consistently renders am by *bēlum* even in am du₇-du₇ which it translates *be-lum mut-tak-bu* (*172). Text Ea also adds some attributes to the three that it shares with text A; *155, *161, and *175 f.

The regular use and fixed order of Enlil's attributes as shown in texts A and Ea may lead one to suppose a well-established tradition for such use. But it seems to be a phenomenon with limited distribution; so far as I know this usage is not found in any other texts. This fact is understandable when we consider that already in the Old Babylonian period there existed a list of seven heroic epithets which are discussed below.

### THE HEROIC EPITHETS[3]

The seven heroic epithets of Enlil appear only in Emesal texts (and only in balag and eršemma compositions?). They appear in several Old Babylonian

2. The Akkadian loan word *alimu* occurs only once, in a synonym list, where it is equated with *kabtum*, which is the common Akkadian translation of alim; see *CAD*, *A/1*, s.v. *alimu*.

3. In *SBH*, pp. xv f. Reisner lists all the occurrences in that volume of the scribal note x MU.MEŠ GU₄.UD.MEŠ, which he interprets as x *šumē qardūti* ("x heroic names"), meaning that x heroic names have been omitted by the scribe. While this interpretation is plausible in some cases (see, for example, n. 4), it cannot be so in others, where the

texts but are more common in late ones. In the latter group, five (and even seven) additional epithets are sometimes added. The seven original epithets proclaim Enlil's sovereignty over Sumer and the rest of the world on the one hand, and praise his superior qualities on the other. The five additional epithets are borrowed from other deities. A partial list of the occurrences of the heroic epithets can be found in Falkenstein, *SGL*, *1*, 27. To this list add: *BA*, *5*, 683:1–7; *IV R*, 28* no. 4, obv. 21–32[4] and rev. 8–19; *BL*, 93:3–13; *SBH*, 21 rev. 44–54; *SBH*, 26 obv. 15–21; *CT*, *42*, 1 obv. 3–12, rev. 1–7, 20–31. In Falkenstein's list the first three references are Old Babylonian texts; add: *CT*, *15*, 13:3–9. In *KAR*, 9 and *BA*, *5*, 666 there are some irregularities in the list of the epithets. From this list the occurrences in a-ab-ba hu-luh-ha are *2 ff. (in text C), *50 ff. (C and duplicates), *75 ff. (C), *128 ff. (D), and *237 ff. (G, Haa). In text G only the original seven epithets are quoted; in C, D, and Haa the twelve, but in the latter two more are added.

Following is a brief survey of the heroic epithets. The first epithet is umun kur-kur-ra "King of the Foreign Lands." We prefer to translate umun "king" and not "lord" (see Emesal Vocabulary II 9: u-mu-un = lugal = *šarru*) as this epithet occurs in the form lugal kur-kur-ra already in Old Sumerian (Sollberger, *Corpus*, Entemena 28/29 i ff.). The Akkadian equivalent of the first epithet is attested in *SBH*, 4, 94 f. e-lum-e umun kur-kur-ra-ke₄ = *kab-tu be-el ma-ta-a-tu*. Although this source interprets umun as "lord," we feel that the evidence of the Old Sumerian source is weightier. About a possible connection between this epithet and an epithet of the é-kur see notes to lines *157 f.

The second epithet umun du₁₁-ga zi-da "Master of the Fulfilled Speech" is applied to other gods besides Enlil (van Dijk, *SGL*, *2*, 32, 154). An Akkadian translation of this epithet occurs in the fragment K. 4659 (*BA*, *5*, 666) 5 f. *be-lum šá qi[bissu kinat]*. Another allusion to Enlil's fulfilled speech is, for example, *ša amātsu kīnat* (quoted without reference, *Götterepitheta*, 301); cf. also Goetze, *Crozer Quarterly*, *23* [1946], 70:45 and *Hymn to Enlil* 1.[5]

---

obvious meaning of the note is "x lines skipped" (see *158). This objection notwithstanding, the term "heroic epithets" is quite appropriate for designating the seven and twelve epithets.

4. In the duplicate text *SBH*, 46 the parallel passage quotes only the first and last of the twelve epithets (rev. 15–17); in the intervening line there is the note 10 MU.MEŠ GU₄.UD.MEŠ. Although Reisner's interpretation fits here (above, n. 3) there is no proof that this is what the Seleucid scribes had in mind.

5. The personal names du₁₁-ga(-ni)-zi(-da) etc. (e.g. UET, 3, 9, *NG*, *3*, 43, TMH, *1/2*, 19) are probably to be connected with the lexical entry du₁₁-ga-zi ⟨sanāqu⟩ *šá qibitim* in K. 73 (Nabnitu N) 24 (*V R* 41); cf. the Old Babylonian names *Sāniq-pišu* and the like. Stamm, *Namengebung*, 233.

The third epithet is $^d$mu-ul-líl a-a ka-na-ága "Enlil, Father of the Nation." It is not clear why Enlil's name is included in the epithet.[6]

It is interesting to note the contrast between the second epithet "King of the Foreign Lands" and the present one which has "warmer" connotations, as does the fourth epithet, sipa sag-gíg-ga, which is discussed above; cf. also Hallo, *Royal Titles*, 147.

The fifth epithet, i-bí-du$_8$ ní-te-na is problematic. Falkenstein translates "weitsichtiger durch dich selbst" (translation of *CT*, *15*, *SAHG*, 76 f.). Van Dijk translates "qui est voyant par lui même" (*AcOr*, *28*, 29 n. 75). Jacobsen suggests "his own scout (or lookout)." Of the Akkadian translation, only [. . . *ra*]-*ma-ni-šú* is left (*BL*, 208:15 f.). For further comment on this epithet see notes to *6.

The sixth epithet, am erín(-na) di-di is translated *ri-i-mu mu-di-il um-ma-ni-šú* "Wild Ox Who Lets His People Wander" in K. 599:11 f. (OECT, 6, plate III). Ignoring this translation and interpreting am = *qarrādu* "warrior," Jacobsen suggests "The Warrior Who Gives the Marching Orders to the Army," namely, who leads his troops to battle; for different interpretations see Falkenstein, *SGL*, *1*, 27, von Soden, *OrNS*, *24* (1955), 382, and *CAD D* and *AHw* s.v. *dâlu*.

The seventh epithet, ù-lul-la ku-ku "Who Feigns Sleep" (lit. "Who Sleeps a False Sleep") is translated *šá ṣa!-lal sar-ra-a-ti ṣal-lu* (*BL*, 208:17 f.). The origin of the concept may be such allusions to Enlil's "sleep" as expressed in a-ab-ba hu-luh-ha *153 ff. His eventual rise to save his people renders such sleep "false."

In the Old Babylonian period the list ends here. In the late periods five (or seven) more epithets are sometimes added, which are, in fact, the proper epithets of other gods. The eighth epithet is umun $^d$am-an-ki(-ga) "The Lord Enki." (On am-an = en and about the complementary -ga see notes to line *57.) In two cases it is omitted from the list of heroic epithets (*2 ff. and *SBH*, 21 rev. 44 ff.). In a third case it is omitted from its place as the eighth in the list and is added to the tenth epithet with a significant change (text Cb, line *59) thus: $^d$en-bi-lu-lu dumu-sag $^d$en-ki-ke$_4$ "Enbilulu, the First Born Son of Enki." These irregularities reflect, perhaps, the rivalry between Enlil and Enki over the hegemony of the pantheon.[7] The two omissions of statements making Enlil an equal of Enki, and especially the identification of the former with Enbilulu, the son of Enki, suggests that the Babylonian scribes of our texts favored Enki. Clearer still is line *146

6. For further discussion of this epithet see notes to *4.

7. See J. J. A. van Dijk, in P. Asmussen et al., eds., *Handbuch der Religionsgeschichte*, *1* (Göttingen, 1971), 465; S. N. Kramer, "Enki and His Inferiority Complex," *OrNS*, *39* (1970), 103 ff.

where Enki and Ninki are explicitly referred to as Enlil's parents, and there is no reason to believe that his cosmic ancestors[8] are meant.

The ninth epithet is ur-sag ᵈasal-lú-hi (formerly read ᵈasar-lú-dùg etc.) "The Warrior Asalluhi." On the reading see W. G. Lambert, *JCS, 11* (1957), 13. About the identity of this god with Marduk in his role of a rain god, and the interpretation "Asal, the Drenching One," see Jacobsen, *JAOS, 88* (1968), 106 f., n. 10. For further references see Deimel, *Pantheon,* 271; Tallqvist, *Götterepitheta,* 264 f.; and Böhl, *Opera Minora,* (1953), 292, 310.

The tenth epithet is umun ᵈen-bi-lu-lu "The Lord Enbilulu." Since in four of the five additional epithets Enlil is equated with Enki, Marduk, Nabû, and Šamaš, it is hardly likely that in this epithet he is equated with the obscure god Enbilulu. This god is equated with Marduk and with Adad of Babylon and it is probable that here again Enlil is, in fact, equated with Marduk. For references see Deimel, *Pantheon,* 904, Tallqvist, *Götterepitheta,* 292, Emesal Vocabulary I43, Böhl, *Opera Minora,* 297, and especially Jacobsen and Kramer, *JNES, 12* (1953), 167 with n. 24.

The eleventh epithet is ur-sag mu-zé-eb-ba-sa₄-a "The Warrior Mudugasa'a." This is an epithet of Nabû, in the Emesal form whose Emegir equivalent is mu-dùg-ga-sa₄-a (Emesal Vocabulary I 52). Its literal sense, "the one named with a 'good' name," is reflected by the Babylonian name, which in itself may be abbreviated from a longer form; cf. *šu-mu ṭa-bu* ᵈAG; King, *Babylonian Magic and Sorcery* (1896), no. 11:32. For further references see *Pantheon,* 2163, 2179; *Götterepitheta* 376 f., 380 ff. When a ruler is named with a (good) name by a god it implies that he has been given a (royal) title (or throne name); see Hallo, *Royal Titles,* 133 f. Compare also Eannatum's name-giving by Inanna, Stele of the Vultures obv. v. 23–30 (restore line 30 from iv 23).

The twelfth epithet is umun ᵈdi-ku₅-mah "The Lord Dikumah." In this epithet Enlil's name is associated with that of the "August Judge," i.e. Šamaš. For references to the Akkadian equivalent *dajānu ṣīru* see *Götterepitheta,* 81.

In some cases each of the epithets is preceded by umun and ur-sag(-gal) alternately. This is the case, e.g. in text C *9 ff. and Haa *246 ff. (but beginning only with the ninth epithet in each text), and in text D *132 ff. (where the practice begins with the fifth epithet). In other cases, each epithet is preceded by a-a ᵈmu-ul-líl (*2 ff.; *CT, 15,* 10:3 ff. and *SK,* 101:1–2).

In text Haa two more epithets are added (*251 f.). ur-sag ᵈuta-uₓ(GIŠGAL)-lu "the Warrior Uta-ulu." ᵈuta-uₓ-lu "the Divine Cloudy Day" or "South Storm" is an epithet of Ninurta, Enlil's son (!); see notes to *251. The other epithet is umun an-uraš the Lord (of) Heaven and Earth, *252.

8. Van Dijk, *AcOr, 28* (1964), 12.

The last seven epithets are late additions to the original list of seven epithets which appear already in the Old Babylonian period (see above). Of the four gods whose titles are mentioned here, two (Marduk and Nabû) rose to prominence only in the late periods. It is difficult to determine what prompted these additions and what are the reasons for equating these gods or their epithets with Enlil. The possibility cannot be excluded that the priests and scribes tended to establish Enlil's supremacy by implying that the four other gods were, in fact, manifestations of Enlil, while the three cases mentioned above would still place Enki in a higher rank. This tendency, however, can hardly be termed "monotheistic"; cf. W. G. Lambert, *RLA, 3,* 478, § 12.

CHAPTER 6

# The Texts

THE MAJOR TEXTS IN TRANSLITERATION

The numbers on the left follow, with few exceptions, the line numbers of the copyist. The numbers in parentheses indicate location in the Composite Text.

Text A

Obverse
1. (*41) i-lu a-e i-lu a-e a-še-er [nu]-uš-gul-e
2. (*42) ù-mun-un urú-mà kur-gal $^d$mu-ul-líl i-[lu a]-e
3. (*43) ù-mu-un urú-mà kur-gal ù-m[u-un xx i-lu a]-e
4. (*44) edin-na [é]r mu-bi i-[še$_8$-še$_8$]
5. (*45) èn-du ma-nun-na ge-bi i-[še$_8$-še$_8$]
6. (*46) mu-bi ér-re i-sìg-ge-a
7. (*47) ge-bi ér-re i-sìg-⌈ge-a⌉
                ki-ru-gú IV-kam-[ma]
8. (*49) gud-sún e-lum gud-sún mu-zu kur-kur-[šè]
9. (*52) [kur-gal a]-a $^d$mu-ul-líl gud-sún mu-zu kur-kur-[šè]
10. (*53) si[pa] sag-gíg-ga gud-sún mu-zu kur-kur-šè
11. (*62) mu-zu kur-ra mu-un-ma-al-la-[šè]
12. (*64) kur elam$^{ki}$-ma mu-un-ma-al-⌈la⌉-[šè]
13. (*65) an-na úr-ba mu-un-ma-al-la-šè
14. (*67) ki-a zà-ba mu-un-ma-al-la-šè
                ki-ru-gú V-kam-ma
15. (*73) [ši]-mah-en ši-mah-en
16. (*74) $^d$mu-ul-líl ši-mah-en
17. (*75) $^d$[mu]-⌈ul⌉-líl kur-kur-ra ši-mah-en
18. (*78) sipa sag-gíg-ga ši-mah-en
19. (*104) gú-zu úr-ra ba-e-ni-mar-ra ši-mah-en

20. (\*105) šà-za èn-tar-bi ši-mah-en
21. (\*87) mušen ši-bi-ta a-e àm-šú-šú
22. (\*88) mušen gì[r-g]i-lu ši-bi-ta a-e àm-šú-šú
23. (\*90) mu-lu ka-na-ága-da ba-da-gur-ra-na
24. (\*91) sag-gí[g-g]a-na gú-z[à-g]a bí-íb-lá-a-ta
ki-ru-gú VI-kam-ma
25. (\*92) gud-sún [e-l]um gud-sún mu-zu kur-kur-šè
26. (\*93) kur-gal a-a $^{d}$mu-u[l-lí]l gud-sún mu-zu kur-kur-šè
27. (\*94) sipa sag-gíg-ga gud-sún mu-zu kur-kur-šè
28. (\*95) mu-zu kur-ra mu-un-ma-al-la-šè
29. (\*96) kur elam$^{ki}$-ma m[u-u]n-ma-al-la-šè
30. (\*97) an-na úr-ba mu-un-ma-a[l-l]a-šè
31. (\*98) ki-a zà-ba mu-ma-al-la-šè
ki-ru-gú VII-kam-ma
32. (\*99) me-na-šè me-na-šè
33. (\*100) $^{d}$mu-ul-líl me-na-šè
34. (\*101) $^{d}$mu-ul-líl kur-kur-ra me-na-šè
35. (\*102) sipa sag-gíg-ga me-na-šè
36. (\*108) š[à-b]a $^{ú}$NAGA$^{ga.mušen}$-˹e˺ šà-ab su$_{x}$-ud mu-un-ak-e
37. (\*109) $^{ú}$NAGA$^{ga.mušen}$-e [inim] $^{d}$mu-ul-líl-lá-šè šà su$_{x}$-ud mu-un-ak-e
38. (\*110) e-lum mu-lu ka-na-ága-da ba-da-sal-la-[x]
39. (\*111) e-lum $^{d}$mu-ul-líl sag-gíg-ga-ni ba-da-lá-e-en-na
˹ki˺-ru-gú VIII-˹kam˺-ma
Reverse 40. (\*119) gud-sún e-lum gud-sún mu-zu kur-kur-šè
41. (\*120) kur-gal a-a $^{d}$mu-ul-líl gud-sún [mu-zu] kur-kur-šè
42. (\*121) sipa sag-gíg-ga [gu]d-sún mu-zu kur-kur-šè
43. (\*122) mu-zu kur-ra mu-ma-al-[la-š]è
44. (\*123) kur elam$^{ki}$-ma mu-un-ma-al-la-šè
45. (\*124) an-na úr-b[a] mu-ma-[al]-la-šè
46. (\*125) ki-a zà-[ba m]u-ma-al-la-šè
ki-˹ru˺-gú IX-kam-ma
47. (\*126) šà-ab gi$_{4}$-ù [šà-ab] gi$_{4}$-ù
48. (\*127) $^{d}$mu-ul-líl šà-ab gi$_{4}$-ù
49. (\*128) $^{d}$mu-ul-líl kur-kur-ra šà-ab gi$_{4}$-ù
50. (\*131) sipa sag-gíg-ga šà-ab gi$_{4}$-ù
51. (\*140) šà-ab gi$_{4}$-ù gi$_{4}$-ù e-ne-ra tuku-àm
52. (\*141) šà-ab hun-ù hun-ù e-ne-ra tuku-àm

ki-ru-gú X-kam-ma
53. (*153) am al-ná te mu-un-zi-zi
54. (*154) $^d$mu-ul-líl al-ná te mu-un-zi-zi
54a. (*155) alim-ma al-ná te mu-un-zi-zi
55. (*156) nibru$^{ki}$-a dur-an-ki-ri te mu-un-zi-zi
56. (*157) nibru$^{ki}$ ki nam-tar-tar-ri te mu-un-zi-zi
57. (*158) é ši ka-na-ág-gá mu-ma-al-la-ri te mu-un-zi-zi
58. (*159) ši kur-kur-ra mu-ma-al-la-ri te mu-un-zi-zi
ki-ru-gú XI-kam-ma
59. (*172) am ná-dè dè-en-zi-zi
60. (*173) $^d$mu-ul-líl ná-dè dè-en-zi-zi
61. (*174) alim-ma ná-dè dè-en-zi-zi
62. (*177) gud-niga á-gur-gur-ra dè-en-zi-zi
63. (*178) udu en-zi šà-gada-lá-a-da dè-en-zi-zi
64. (*179) ud$_x$ ne-èm-àr-ra-kú-a-da dè-en-zi-zi
65. (*180) gukkal-guru$_x$(E.IB)-lá-lá-da dè-en-zi-zi
ki-ru-gú XII-kam-ma
66. (*185) am zi-ga u$_6$-di àm-du$_{11}$ .
67. (*186) $^d$mu-ul-líl z[i-g]a u$_6$-di àm-du$_{11}$
68. (*188) nibru$^{ki}$ dur-an-ki-ri u$_6$-di àm-du$_{11}$
69. (*189) nibru$^{ki}$-a ki nam-tar-tar-ri u$_6$-di àm-du$_{11}$
70. (*191) mu-e-tu$_x$-tu$_x$-bé-en-dè-en mu-e-g[i$_{16}$-i]l-gi$_{16}$-il-dè-en
ki-ru-gú XIII-kam-ma
Catchline
(*192) am zi-ga-ni an-né [nam]-ús
Colophon  70 mu-bi-im
iti zíz-a u$_4$ mina-kam
mu *sa-am-su-[i-lu-na]* lugal


## Text B

Col. i    1. (*28) [mi-na-š]i mu-le-el mi-na-ši
2. (*29) [du]-ku-ge-en-na-nu-da-an me-a an-da-ma-le
3. (*31) kur-gal $^d$en-líl-lá me-a an-da-ma-le
4. (*32) an-bi-du-ka me-en-ti
5. (*33) ki bi-du-ka su-aì-im-du me-a an-da-ma-le
6. (*41) ì-lu a-e ì-lu a-e a-ši-ir ni-iš-ku-le
7. (*44) e-di-ni ir mu-bi i-ši-še
8. (*45) en-du ma-nu-na ge-bi i-ši-še

9. (*46) mu-bi i-ra i-si-ge-a
10. (*47) [ge]-bi i-ra i-si-ge-a
11. (*48) ge-bi ì-ši-še

Col. ii  1. (*99) mi-na-še mi-na-še
2. (*100) mu-le-el mi-na-še
3. (*101) kur-gal a-a ᵈen-líl-lá mi-na-še
4. (*102) sa-pa sa-gi-ki-ga mi-na-še
5. (*103) gu sa-an-zu-a du bi-du-la
6. (*104) gu-zi ú-ra bi-ni-ma-ra
7. (*108) ša [su]-ta mu-na-ka ša-pa ú-ga-e
8. (*109) ú-ga-e i-ni-im mu-le-la-ke < ?>
9. (*115) el-lu-um-lu sa-an-du na-am-ta-ba-ra-e
10. (*116) a-a mu-le-el ka-na-da gi-ú

11. (*126) ša ki-ú ša ki-ú
12. (*127, *140) mu-le-el ša ki-ú
13. (*140) i-ni-ra tu-ku-a
14. (*141) [ša h]u-mu hu-mu
15. (*142) [mu-lu ši]-iš-ku-ra-ka
16. (*142) [......] mu-na-bé

Col. iii  1. (*181) [......ti]-in-zi-zi
2. (*182) [...n]i-ib-ru du-ra-an-ki-ra-ka
3. (*183) a-li-ma-ha nu le-el-di ti-in-zi-zi

4. (*184) i-ni-ma-ni-lu-i-lu

## Text C

1. (*1) [ez]inₓ hu-luh-ha-zu a šà-ìb-baⁱ-zu èn-šè
   nu-šed₇-dè
2. (*1) ⌜a⌝-a ezinₓ nu-si²-TAB-du-a iš-še-en-ni: e-
   zinₓⁱ hu-luh-ha-zu-ú
3. (*2) a-a ᵈmu-ul-líl ᵉⁿ umun kur-kur-ra ᵉˢ⁻ˢᵉ ⁿᵘ⁻
   ˢⁱ⁻ᵈᵘ⁻ᵃ
4. (*3) a-a ᵈmu-ul-lílᴵᴵ umun [d]u₁₁-ga zi-daᴵᴵ
5. (*4) a-a ᵈmu-ul-lílᴵᴵ ᵈmu-ul-líl a-a ka-nag-gá
6. (*5) a-a ᵈmu-ul-lílᴵᴵ sipa sag-gíg-gaᴵᴵ
6a. (*6) a-a ᵈmu-ul-lílᴵᴵ: i-bí-du₈ ní-te-naᴵᴵ
7. (*7) a-a ᵈmu-ul-lílᴵᴵ am erín di-diᴵᴵ
8. (*8) a-a ᵈmu-ul-lílᴵᴵ ù-lul-la ku-kuᴵᴵ
9. (*9) an-na:alim-maᵃ ur-sag ᵈasal-lú-hiᴵᴵ
10. (*10) e:ur-sag-galˡᵃ umun ᵈen-bi-lu-luᴵᴵ
11. (*11) an-na:alim-maᵃ ur-sag mu-zé-eb-ba-sa₄-aᴵᴵ
12. (*12) e:ur-sag-galˡᵃ umun ᵈdi-ku₅-mah-aᴵᴵ

13.  (\*13) e:u$_4$$^!$-ri-da$_4$$^a$ u$_4$-sú-ta-ri-ta$^{II}$
14.  (\*14) e:gi$_6$-ri-da$_4$$^a$ gi$_6$-bad-ta-ri-ta$^{II}$
15.  (\*15) e:mu-ri-da$_4$$^a$ mu-sù-rá-ri-ta$^{II}$
16.  (\*16) e:u$_4$ dam kúr-re ba-ab-zé-èm-mà-ta$^{II}$
17.  (\*17) e:u$_4$ dumu kúr-ra ba-ab-zé-èm-mà-ta$^{II}$
18.  (\*18) ma-la TÚG LUL-na dam ì-ug$_5$-a-ta$^{II}$
19.  (\*19) e:damì-ug$_5$ dam ì-<ug$_5$-a-ta>$^{II}$
20.  (\*20) a:dumu ì-ug$_5$ dumu ì-<ug$_5$-a-ta>$^{II}$
21.  (\*21) urú-zu hul-hul-lu-dè itima am-gin$_x$ sipa
         im-gi-ra-a$^{II}$
22.  (\*22) nibru$^{ki}$ hul-hul-lu-dè itima <am-gin$_x$ sipa
         im-gi-ra-a>$^{II}$
23.  (\*23) TIN.TIR.KI hul-hul-lu-dè itima <am-gin$_x$ sipa
         im-gi-ra-a>$^{II}$
24.  (\*24) a:gi-gun$_4$-na $^{gi}$KID$^!$.MAH-a $^{a-mu-ru^!-gin_x}$ šu
         im-gur$^!$-ra-ta$^{II}$
25.  (\*25) ru:igi-du$_8$ a é-mu e-ne àm-me urú-mu e-ne
         ma àm-me$^{II}$
26.  (\*26) igi-du$_8$ a gina-mu e-ne àm-me gal-mu e-ne
         ma àm-me$^{II}$
27.  (\*27) e:nam-kúr$^?$ gig u$_8$-a u$_8$-a u$_4$ me-na bí-ni-íb-
         zal$^{II}$

28.  (\*28) ma-a:me-na-šè $^d$mu-ul-líl me-na-šè siskur
         me-na-šè èn-šè nu-šed$_7$-dè
29.  (\*28) mu-ul-líl me-na-še e-ú-nu-UK me-na-še-e
30.  (\*29) dungu-gin$_x$ an-úr-ta me-na-šè$^{II}$
31.  (\*30) e:dungu-gin$_x$ an-úr-ta kur-gal $^d$mu-ul-líl
         me-na-šè$^{II}$
32.  (\*32) e:èm-bí-du$_{11}$-ga-zu im-ta-e-ug$_5$$^{II}$
33.  (\*33) ki bí-du$_{11}$-ga-zu sá-um-mi-du$_{11}$$^{II}$
34.  (\*34) èm bí-du$_{11}$-ga-zu ba-e-diri-diri$^{II}$
35.  (\*35) ki na-ám-ku$_5$-da-zu ba-e-dè-til$^{II}$
36.  (\*36) sipa nu-gam-ma e-zé ì-ni-gub$^{II}$
37.  (\*37) su$_8$-ba$^a$ ù-nu-ku en-nu-un-gá bi-tuš$^{II}$
38.  (\*38) ru-un:ú nu-ma$_4$-a edina-na bí-in-ma$^{II}$
39.  (\*39) a-a $^d$mu-ul-líl gi-di-nu en-edin-na ba-ni-in-
         su$^{II}$
40.  (\*40) dungu-gin$_x$ an-úr-ta kur-gal $^d$mu-ul-líl e-ne
         im-ta-gá-gá

41.  (\*41) ka-i:i-lu-gá-e$^!$ i-lu-àm a-še-er nu-gá-gá
42.  (\*41) a-še-ru nu-ú-gá-a-a-gu-ú a-še-er nu-ga-an-
         $^⌜$gu$^⌝$-ú

43. (*42) e:umun urú-mù ì-lu-àm a-še-er [nu-gá-gá<sup>II</sup>]

44. (*43) e:umun urú-mu giri$_x$-zal-zu-šè i-lu-àm a-še-er [nu-gá-gá<sup>II</sup>]

45. (*44) a:edin-na ér-gig mu-un-še$_8$-še$_8$[<sup>II</sup>]

46. (*45) en-dìm(RAB + GAN)-ma-èš isíš[<sup>II</sup>]

47. (*46) e:mu-bi ér-ra al-še-gig-ga

48. (*47) e:ge-bi ér-ra al-še-gig -ga[<sup>II</sup>]

49. (*46) [m]u-bi ér-ra al-sìg-gi-g[a<sup>II</sup>]

50. (*47) [.....] ⌜ér-ra⌝ [.............]

Reverse  2. (*56) ù-lul-[la ku-ku gud < sun >]

3. (*57) umun$^e$ $^d$am-an-[ki-ga gud- < sún > <sup>II</sup>]

4. (*58) ur-sag $^d$asal-lú-h[i gud- < sún > <sup>II</sup>]

5. (*59) umun $^d$en-bi-lu-lu gud[-< sún > <sup>II</sup>]

6. (*60) ur-sag $^d$mu-zé-eb-ba-sa$_4$-a gud[-< sún<sup>II</sup>]

7. (*61) umun $^d$di-ku$_5$-mah-a$^a$ gud[-< sún > <sup>II</sup>]

8. (*62) e:mu-zu kur-ra mu-un-ma-al-la-šè an ní-bi nam-dúb-[ba<sup>II</sup>]

9. (*63) an ní-bi nam-dúb ki ní-bi nam-[sìg<sup>II</sup>]

10. (*65) e:an-na úr-bi-a mu-un-ma-al-la[-šè<sup>II</sup>]

11. (*66) e:ki-a úr-bi-a mu-un-< ma-al-la-šè > [<sup>II</sup>]

12. (*67) ru:ki-a zà-bi-a mu-un-< ma-al-la-[šè > <sup>II</sup>]

13. (*68) ki-a gaba-ba mu-un-< ma-al-la-[šè > <sup>II</sup>]

14. (*69) kur ní-ri-a mu-un-< ma-al-la-[šè<sup>II</sup>]

15. (*70) ru:kur an$_x$⌐-na mu-un-< ma-al-la-[šè > <sup>II</sup>]

16. (*71) kur á$^?$-diri mu-un-< ma-al-la-[šè > <sup>II</sup>]

17. (*72) kur-ra an da-ma-al-la-šè mu-un-ma-al-la-šè an ní-b[i nam-dúb<sup>II</sup>]

18. (*73) ka-a:za-e mah-me-en za-e mah-me-en

19. (*73) [za-e e]-lum-ma-e-me-en ⌜a⌝<sup>me-en</sup> za-e mah-me-en e-lum-ma za-e mah-me-en

20. (*75) ú:umun kur-kur-ra za-e <mah-me-en> <sup>II</sup>

21. (*76) umun du$_{11}$-ga-zi-dè za-e <mah-me-en> <sup>II</sup>

22. (*77) $^d$mu-ul-líl a-a ka-nag-gá za-e <mah-me-en> <sup>II</sup>

23. (*78) sipa sag-gíg-ga za-e <mah-me-en> <sup>II</sup>

24. (*79) i-bí-du$_8$ ní-te-na za-e <mah-me-en> <sup>II</sup>

25. (*80) am erín di-di za-e <mah-me-en> <sup>II</sup>

26. (*81) ù-lul-la ku-ku za-e <mah-me-en> <sup>II</sup>

27. (*82) umun$^e$ $^d$am-an-ki-ga za-e <mah-me-en> <sup>II</sup>

28. (*83) ur-sag $^d$asal-lú-hi za-e <mah-me-en> <sup>II</sup>

29. (*84) umun $^d$en-bi-lu-lu za-e <mah-me-en> <sup>II</sup>

30. (*85) ur-sag $^d$mu-zé-eb-ba-sa$_4$-a za-e <mah-me-en> <sup>II</sup>

31. (*86) umun ᵈdi-ku₅-mah-aᵃ za-e <mah-me-en>ᴵᴵ
32. (*103) ɢɪš:mu-lu sag-zu-a túg ba-e-dul'-laᴵᴵ
33. (*104) e:gú-zu úr-ra ba-e-ne-mar-raᴵᴵ
34. (*106) šà-zu ᵍⁱpisan-ginₓ èm-ba-e-šú-a
35. (*107) elum mu-uš-túgᵍᵉštᵘᵍ-zu úr-ra mi-ni-íb-ús-
       siᵃᴵᴵ
36. (*112) ᵈmu-ul-líl šu-zu-ta šu sá-a nu-ma-alᴵᴵ
37. (*113) ᵈmu-ul-líl me-ri-zu-ta me-ri sá-a nu-ma-alᴵᴵ
38. (*114) e:za-ra dìm-me-er sá-a nu-è-aᴵᴵ
39. (*105) e:šà-zu èn-tar-bi mušen ši-bi-taᴵᴵ
40. (*87) e:mušen ši-bi-ta i-lu ši-bi-ta é-a-na šú-šúᴵᴵ
41. (*89) ru-un:še-še gig ér gig i-lu še-bi-taᴵᴵ
42. (*117) e:um-ma-šú-šú ka-nagaₓ-da gú-zu úr-ra ba-
       e-ne-mar-raᴵᴵ
43. (*118) sag-gíg-ga-na gú-e ge₄-bi de₅-de₅-gaᴵᴵ

Catchline (*99) me-na-šè me-na-šè
Colophon dub-mina-kam a-ab-ba hu-luh-ha nu-al-til
       ᴵTIL.NU.GAR

## Text D

Obverse 1. (*128) e-lum-e umun kur-kur-ra šà-ab gi₄-ù gi₄-ù
       2. (*129) umun du₁₁-ga zi-da šà-<ab gi₄-ù gi₄-ù>
       3. (*130) ᵈmu-ul-líl a-a ka-nag-gá šà-<ab gi₄-ù gi₄-ù>
       4. (*131) sipa sag-gíg-ga šà-<ab gi₄-ù gi₄-ù>
       5. (*132) ur-sag i-bí-du₈ ní-te-en šà-<ab gi₄-ù gi₄-ù>
       6. (*133) umun am erín-na di-di šà-<ab gi₄-ù gi₄-ù>
       7. (*134) ur-sag ù-lul-la ku-ku šà-<ab gi₄-ù gi₄-ù>
       8. (*135) umun ᵈam-an-ki šà-<ab-gi₄-ù gi₄-ù>
       9. (*136) ur-sag ᵈasal-lú-hi šà-<ab gi₄-ù gi₄-ù>
10a. (*137) umun ᵈen-bi-lu-lu šà-<ab gi₄-ù gi₄-ù>:
10b. (*138) ur-sag ᵈmu-zé-eb-sa₄-a šà!-<ab gi₄-ù gi₄-ù>
11. (*139) umun ᵈdi-ku₅-mah-àm šà-<ab gi₄-ù gi₄-ù>
12. (*140) šà-ab gi₄-ù gi₄-ù dè-ra-an-tuku-a
13. (*140) *lib-bu tu-ra-am* ɪɪ *liq-qa-bi-ka*

14. (*141) šà hun-gá-ù hun-gá dè-ra-an-tuku-a
15. (*141) *lib-bu nu-ha-am* ɪɪ *liq-qa-bi-ka*
16. (*142) mu-lu siskurₓ-ra-ke₄ siskurₓ-ra dè-ra-ab-bé
17. (*142) *šá ik-ri-bi ik-ri-bi liq-qa-bi-ka*
18. (*143) mu-lu a-ra-zu-ke₄ a-ra-zu dè-ra-ab-bé
19. (*143) *šá tés-li-ti tés-li-ti liq-bi-ka*
20. (*144) an-uraš-a ki-še!-gu-nu-ra
21. (*145) [x]-lumʔ-maʔ-zu ᵈen-ki ᵈnin-ki

22. (*146) [mud]na ki-ága-zu ama-gal $^d$nin-líl
23. (*147) [egí ni]n$_9$!-gal-zu ga-šà-an-kè[š$^{ki}$-ke$_4$]
24. (*148) [inim?]-ma-dé-dé ga-ša-an[nibru$^{ki}$]
25. (*149) [uku]-uš kala-ga-zu umun $^d$[nin-urta]
26. (*150) [sukk]al-mah-zu [kingal $^d$nusku]
27. (*151) [dumu]-ki-ága-zu [gašan-an-na-ke$_4$]
28. (*152) [umun]-si-[gal umun-guruš-a-ke$_4$]

Reverse
1.      [                                          ]
2. (*188) [nibru]$^{ki}$-a[.......]-ta
3. (*187) [nibru]$^{ki}$-a [ki nam-tar-t]ar-ra-ta
4. (*187) [........] *a-[šar ši-m]a-a-tú i-šim-mu*
5. (*190) [.. še]-eb-ba ki
6. (*190) [...]á(?)-mar ri-ri: *ana i-ga-re-tu*
7. (*191) ba-e-tu$_{10}$-tu$_{10}$-ba-en-dè ba-e-gi$_{16}$-li-ìm-mà-e-dè

8. (*192) am zi-g[a-n]i an-ná nam-[ús]
9. (*192) [....] *ti-bu-ut-su šá-mu-ú en-de-et*
10. (*193) [$^d$mu-u]l-líl am!-zi-ga-àm an-<na nam-ús>
11. (*194) [alim-ma] am zi-ga-àm an-<na nam-ús>
12. (*195) a-a $^d$mu-ul-líl umun kur-kur-ra
13. (*196) alim-ma umun nibru$^{ki}$-a

15. (*197) umun e-ne-èm-mà-ni an-e nu-íl-e
16. (*197) *šá be-lu a-mat-su šá-mu-ú ul ina-aš-šu-ú*
17. (*198) $^d$mu-ul-líl e-ne-èm-mà-ni ki nu-íl-e
18. (*198) *šá $^d$II a-mat-su* KI-*tim ul ina-aš-ši*
19. (*199) umun šu aša$_x$-ni an-e nu-íl-e
20. (*199) *šá be-lu ti-ri-iṣ qa-ti-šú šá-mu-ú ul ina-aš-šu-ú*
21. (*200) $^d$mu-ul-líl me-ri aša$_x$-ni ki nu-íl-e
22. (*200) <              > me-ri ús-sa-na<      >
23. (*200) <              > *ši-ki-in še-pe-⌜e⌝* <      >
24. (*200) [$^d$II] *ti-ri-iṣ še-pe-šú* KI-[*tim ul ina-aš*]-*ši*


Text Ea

1. (*153) [am al-n]à te nu-un-zi-zi
2. (*153) [*be-lum*] *šá ṣal-lu mi-nam la i-te-e*[*b-bi*]
3. (*154) [$^d$mu]-ul-líl-lá am al-ná[....]
4. (*154) $^d$NINNU *be-lum šá ṣal-lu mi-nam la i-te-eb-*[*bi*]
5. (*155) alim-ma am al-ná te <nu-un-zi-zi>: *kab-tu*
     *be-lum šá ṣal-lu mi-na*[*m ....*]
6. (*156) a-a $^d$mu-ul-líl-la urú-na nibru$^{ki}$ te <nu-un-zi-zi>: *a-bi* $^d$NINNU *a-lu ni-ip-pu-*[*ru*]

7. (*160) é-kur-ra é šà-ge-pà-da [ᵈmu-ul-líl-lá(?)]
8. (*160) *šá* É II *bi-it i-tu-ut kun-nu lìb-ba-[šú]*
8a (*160a) 34 MU.MEŠ GUD.MEŠ
9. (*171) umun ka-nag-gá é-darà-an-na
10. (*171) *be-lum ma-a-tú ana* É II
11. (*172) am du₇-du₇ te nu-um-zi-zi
12. (*172) *be-lum mut-tak-bu mi-na la i-te-eb-ba*
13a. (*173) ᵈmu-ul-líl-lá am du₇-du₇ te <nu-um-zi-zi>:
13b. (*174) alim-ma am du₇-du₇ te <nu-um-zi-zi>
14a. (*175) a-a ᵈmu-ul-líl-lá umun kur-kur-ra:
14b. (*176) alim-ma umun nibruᵏⁱ
15. (*178) e-zé èm-kú-e šà-gada!-lá-a-ta
16. (*178) *ṣe-e-nu ina a-kal-lu lìb-bi a-di la i-ni-[x]*
17. (*179) e-zé èm-kú-e kú-a-t[a]
18. (*179) *ṣe-e-nu a-kal-lu ina a-kal-lu*
19. (*180) gukkal-íB-lá-a-ta te nu-um-zi-zi
20. (*180) *gu-uk-kal-lum ina* UK-*ba-ti-šú a-*NI-*lum mi-nam la i-te-eb-ba*
21. (*185) [. . . .] u₆ˡ-di-ga àm-zé-[x]
22. (*185) [. . . .] ì-x-du₁₁(?)
23a. (*186) [. . . . . . .] ˹zi-ga˺(?)
23b. (*187) ˹:alim-ma am zi-ga-àm u₆-˺[x]

## Text F

Obverse   1. (*185) am zi-g[a u₆-di à]m-du₁₁
2. (*186) a-a ᵈmu-[ul-líl z]i-ga u₆-di [àm-du₁₁]
3. (*192) am zi-g[a-n]i an-né nam-[ús]
4. (*193) ᵈmu-ul-[líl] zi-ga-ni an-né na[m-ú]s
5. (*199) e-lum-e šu-ni tab-ba-bi an-né na[m-ú]s
6. (*200) ᵈmu-ul-líl-le me-ri gub-ba-bi ki-[e] n[am-ú]s
7. (*201) am zi-ga-ni an-né ba-ab-ús
8.        ki-ru-gú IX-kam-ma
9. (*202) za-e bí-du₁₁ za-e bí-du₁₁
10. (*203) ù-mu-un-e kur-kur-ra za-e bí-du₁₁
11. (*204) èm-e a-ba mu-un-gul za-e-mèn mu-e-gul-gul
12. (*205) èm-e a-ba mu-un-sì za-e-mèn mu-e-sì-sì
13. (*206) ᵈmu-ul-líl é zi-da gi-sig mi-ni-ku₄-ku₄
14. (*207) du₅-mu mu-lu zi-da-ke₄ kimu-ni-ri-ri
15. (*208) ᵈmu-ul-líl túg-gal-gal šedₓ-dè ba-e-gam
16. (*209) gána-ni gána da-ma-al-la šà-mar-re ba-e-gam

17. (*210) ki ri-ri-ra ki mu-ni-tar
18. (*211) pú-sag-bala-e-ra pú-sag mu-ni-tar
19. (*212) za-e bí-du₁₁ ši-im-diri-ge-en
20.         ki-ru-gú X-kam-ma
21. (*213) za-e mah-mèn za-e mah-mèn
22. (*214) umun-e kur-kur-ra za-e mah-mèn
23. (*215) an-e a-ba mah-mèn za-e-mèn mah-mèn
24. (*216) ki-e a-ba mah-mèn za-e-mèn mah-mèn
25. (*217) ù-mu-un zà-an-na ù-mu-un zà-ki- ⌜ke₄⌝
26. (*218) kur ᵈutu-è-a-ta kur ᵈutu-šú-a-šè
27. (*219) kur-ra ù-mu-un nu-mu-un-ti za-e ù-mu-un
           ab-ak
28–29. (*220) ᵈmu-ul-líl kur-kur-ra ga-ša-an nu-mu-un-ti
           dam-zu ga-ša-an ab-ak
30–31. (*221) im an-na a ki-a ᵈmu-ul-líl eškiri dìm-mi-ir-
           r[e-ne] za-e-da ša-mu-e-da-ma-al
32. (*222) mu-lu gu mú-mú-mèn mu-lu še [mú-mú-mèn]
33. (*223) [ᵈ]mu-ul-líl me-lám-zu engur-ra kua mu-
           [ni-íb-šèg-šèg]
34. (*224) za-e ma[h-mèn]
35.         ki-ru-gú [XI-kam-ma]
Reverse 1–4.     (broken)
5. (*232) [......]mu-bi [še-àm-š]a₄
6. (*233) [......]ge-bi še-à[m-š]a₄
7. (*234) [n]iʾ u₈ al-lu u₈ al-tuš
8. (*235) [gu]dʾ àm-me u₈ al-lù u₈ al-gi₆
9. (*236) [.....a]ma-a a-di-di-in
10.         ki-ru-gú XII-kam-ma
11. (*237) ⌜dil⌝-[mu]-un nigín-ù uru!-zu u₆ ga-e-du₁₁
12. (*237) [(erasure)] IGI.DU ga-e-du₁₁

Text G

Obverse 1. (*237) dilmun nigín-ù urú-zu u₆ ⌜di⌝-[du₁₁]
2. (*238) alim-ma dilmun nigín-ù urú-zu u₆ [dè-du₁₁]
3. (*239) ù-mu-un kur-kur-ra-ke₄ nigín-ù urú-z[u u₆
        dè-du₁₁]
4. (*240) ù-mu-un du₁₁-ga zi-da nigín-ù urú-[zu u₆
        dè-du₁₁]
5. (*241) ᵈmu-ul-líl a-a ka-na-ág-gá [nigín-ù urú-zu
        u₆] dè-[du₁₁]
6. (*242) sipa sag-gíg-ga nigín-ù urú-[zu u₆ dè-du₁₁]

7. (*243) i-bí-du$_8$ ní-te-na nigín-ù urú-[zu u$_6$ dè-du$_{11}$]
8. (*244) am erín-na di-di nigín-ù urú-[zu u$_6$ dè-du$_{11}$]
9. (*245) ù-lul-la ku-ku nigín-ù urú-[zu u$_6$ dè-du$_{11}$]
10. (*253) urú-zu nibru$^{ki}$-zu nigín-ù [urú-zu u$_6$ dè-du$_{11}$]
11. (*254) še-eb é-kur-ra-ta nigín-ù [urú-zu u$_6$ dè-du$_{11}$]
12. (*264) ki-ùr ki-gal-ta nigín-ù [urú-zu u$_6$ dè-du$_{11}$]
13. (*265) du$_6$-kù ki-kù-ta nigín-ù [urú-zu u$_6$ dè-du$_{11}$]
14. (*266) šà é-dim$_x$-ma-ta nigín-ù [urú-zu u$_6$ dè-du$_{11}$]
15. (*267) é-ká-mah-ta nigín-ù [urú-zu u$_6$ dè-du$_{11}$]
16. (*268) é-gá-nun-mah-ta nigín-ù [urú-zu u$_6$ dè-du$_{11}$]
17. (*269) ma-mu-šú-a-ta nigín-ù u[rú-zu u$_6$ dè-du$_{11}$]
18. (*270) ma é-gal-mah-ta nigín-ù u[rú-zu u$_6$ dè-du$_{11}$]
19. (*271) še-eb uri$^{ki}$-ma-ta nigín-ù urú-z[u u$_6$] dè-du$_{11}$
20. (*272) še-eb larsam$^{ki}$-ma-ta nigín-ù urú-zu [u$_6$] dè-du$_{11}$
21. (*273) urú a-du$_{11}$-ga a-gi$_4$-a-zu!
22. (*274) a-du$_{11}$-ga a-ta-gar-ra-zu
23. (*281) urú še kuru$_5$-da ki-lá-a-zu
Reverse 24. (*282) [èm]-kú nu-kú-a u$_4$-zal-zal-la-ri
25. (*283) dam tur-ra-ke$_4$ dam-mu mu-ni-ib-bé
26. (*284) dumu tur-ra-ke$_4$ dumu-mu mu-ni-ib-bé
27. (*285) ki-sikil-e šeš-mu mu-ni-ib-bé
28. (*286) urú-ta ama-gan-e dumu-mu mu-ni-ib-bé
29. (*287) dumu bàn-da a-a-mu mu-ni-ib-bé
30. (*288) tur-e al-è mah-e al-è
31. (*292) e-sír-e gub-ba mu-un-sar-re-da$_4$
32. (*293) gal$_4$-la-bi ur-e àm-da-ab-sur$_5$
33. (*294) ság-bi mu-bar-re àm-da-ab-lá
34. (*295) ešemen-ba líl ba-e-sù
Colophon: 34 ér-šèm-ma $^d$en-líl-a-kam


Text Haa

Reverse 5. (*237) dilmun$^{ki}$ nigin-na urú-zu u$_6$ gá-e-dè
6. (*237) *kab-tum*: $^d$*en-líl na-ás-hi-ram-ma ana* URU-*ka tu-ur*: URU-*ka hi-iṭ-ṭi*
7. (*238) alim-ma dilmun$^{ki}$ nigin-na <urú-zu u$_6$ gá-e-dè>
8. (*239) umun kur-kur-ra nigin-na <urú-zu u$_6$ gá-e-dè>
9. (*240) umun du$_{11}$-ga zi-da nigin-na <urú-zu u$_6$ gá-e-dè>

10. (*241) ᵈmu-ul-líl a-a ka-nag-gá nigin-na <urú-zu
    $u_6$ gá-e-dè>
11. (*242) sipa sag-gíg-ga nigin-na <urú-zu $u_6$ gá-e-
    dè>
12. (*243) i-bí-$du_8$ ní-te-en-na nigin-na <urú-zu $u_6$
    gá-e-dè>
13. (*244) am erín-na di-di nigin-na <urú-zu $u_6$ gá-
    e-dè>
14. (*245) ù-lul-la ku-ku nigin-na <urú-zu $u_6$ gá-e-
    dè>
15. (*246) ᵈam-an-ki nigin-na <urú-zu $u_6$ gá-e-dè>
16. (*247) ur-sag ᵈasal-lú-hi nigin-na <urú-zu $u_6$ gá-
    e-dè>
17. (*248) umun ᵈen-bi-lu-lu nigin-na <urú-zu $u_6$ gá-
    dè>
18. (*249) ur-sag ᵈmu-zé-eb-ba-$sa_4$-a nigin-na <urú-zu
    $u_6$ gá-e-dè>
19. (*250) umun ᵈdi-$ku_5$-mah-a nigin-na <urú-zu $u_6$
    gá-e-dè>
20. (*251) ur-sag ᵈuta-$u_x$-lu nigin-na <urú-zu $u_6$ gá-
    e-dè>
21. (*252) umun an-uraš-a-ra nigin-na <urú-zu $u_6$
    gá-e-dè>
22. (*253) ⌈urú⌉-zú nibruᵏⁱ-ta nigin-na <urú-zu $u_6$
    gá-e-dè>
23. (*254) še-eb é-kur!-ra-ta ki-ùr é-nam-ti-la
24. (*255) še-eb sipparᵏⁱ-ta nigin-na <urú-zu $u_6$ gá-e-
    dè>
25. (*256) èš é-babbar-ra! é-di-$ku_5$-kalam-ma
26. (*257) še-eb TIN.TIR.KI-ta nigin-na <urú-zu $u_6$ gá-
    e-dè>
27. (*258) še-eb é-sag-íl-la é-tùr-kalam-ma
28. (*259) še-eb bàd-SI.AB.BAᵏⁱ-ta nigin-na <urú-zu $u_6$
    gá-e-dè>
29. (*260) še-eb é-zi-da-ta é-mah-ti-la
30. (*261) še-eb é-te-mén an-ki é-darà-an-na
31. (*262) [še-eb] ì-si-inᵏⁱ-na-$ke_4$ nigin-na <urú-zu $u_6$
    gá-e-dè>
32. (*263) [še-eb] é-gal-mah é-raba-ri-ri
33. (*273) [urú] a-$du_{11}$-ga a-$gi_4$-a-za
34. (*273) [ālu] *ša naq-rú ú šá-nu-u: a-hu-lap tur-šú*
35. (*274) nibruᵏⁱ a-$du_{11}$-ga a-ta-mar-ra-za

36. (*274) <            > šá naq-ru-u ana me-e sa-lu-u
37. (*275) urú a-du$_{11}$-ga a-gi$_4$-a-za
38. (*276) sippar a-du$_{11}$-ga a-ta <mar-ra-za>
39. (*277) urú a-du$_{11}$-ga a-gi$_4$-<a-za>
40. (*278) TIN.TIR.KI a-du$_{11}$-ga a-ta <mar-ra-za>
41. (*279) urú a-du$_{11}$-ga a-gi$_4$-<a-za>
42. (*280) ì-si-in$^{ki}$-na a-du$_{11}$-ga a-ta <mar-ra-za>
43. (*281) urú še kuru$_5$-da ki-lá-lá-a-zu
44. (*281) a-lum šá še-um ip-par-su-šú uṭ-ṭi-tum iš-šaq-lu-šu
45. (*282) èm-kú nu-kú-e u$_4$-zal-zal-la-ri
46. (*282) ak-ki-lu ina la a-ka-li uš-tab-ru-u
47. (*283) dam tur-ra-ke$_4$ dam-mu mu-ni-íb-bé
48. (*283) šá mu-us-sà ṣi-ih-ru mu-ti-ma i-qab-bi
49. (*284) dumu tur-ra-ke$_4$ dumu-mu mu-<ni-íb-bé>
50. (*285) ki-sikil-mu šeš-mu mu-<ni-íb-bé>
51. (*285) ar-da-tum a-hi-mi <i-qab-bi>
52. (*286) urú ama-gan-mu dumu-mu mu-<ni-ib-bé>
53. (*286) ina a-li um-mi a-lit-tu ma-ri-mi <i-qab-bi>
54. (*287) dumu bàn-da a-a-mu mu-<ni-íb-bé>
55. (*287) mar-tum ṣi-hir-tum a-bi-mi <i-qab-bi>
56. (*292) e-sír-ra gub-ba mu-un-sar-re-e-dè
57. (*292) šá ina su-qi iz-za-az-zu uš-tah-mi-ṭu
58. (*288) tur-e al-è mah-e≪e≫al-è
59. (*288) ṣi-ih-ru i-mah-hi ra-bu-ú i-mah-hi
60. (*289) nibru$^{ki}$ tur-e al-è mah-<e al-è>
61. (*290) TIN.TIR.KI tur-e al-è mah-<e al-è>
62. (*291) ì-si-in$^{ki}$-na tur-e al-è mah-<e al-è>
63. (*293) gal$_4$-la-bi ur-re an-da-ab-sur$_5$
64. (*293) qal-la-šu kal-bu uš-qa-lil: na-ak-ru it-ta-ši
65. (*294) ság-bi mu-bar-ra an-da-ab-lá
66. (*294) [sap]-hu$^!$-us-su bar-bar-ru ú-šaq-lil
67. (*295) ešemen líl-lá-àm e-si
68. (*295) me-lul-ta-šu zi-qi-qam im-ta-la
69. (*296) e-sír la-la-bi nu-gi$_4$-gi$_4$
70. (*296) su-ú-qu šá la-la-a la áš-bu-ú

## Text Ia

Although this text could not be incorporated into our Composite Text,
(see above, p. 14) the parallel lines are indicated in parentheses. Our numbering
counts a Sumerian line and its Akkadian translation as one.

1. (broken)
2. (*253) [x-ur]ú nibru$^{ki}$-ta nigín [                    ]
        ana āli-ka ni-ip-pu-ru na-[ashiramma]
3. (*254) še-eb é-kur-ra-ta ki-ùr [            ]

4. (*257) še-eb TIN.TIR.KI-ta nigín [                    ]
5. (*258) še-eb é-sag-íl-la èš-é-[tùr-kalam-ma]
6. (*273) urú a-du$_{11}$-ga a-gi$_4$-a[                    ]
   *a-lum šá na-ak-ru ú-šá-an-[nu-ú]*
7. (*278) TIN.TIR.KI a-du$_{11}$-ga a-ta-mar-ra
   <                    > *šá ana me-e sa-lu-[ú*          ]

### THE COMPOSITE TEXT WITH COMMENTARY

## Stanza II

(The composite text places these strophic inserts at the beginning of the stanzas, following English usage, instead of at their end, as in Sumerian usage.)

| Lines | Texts | |
|-------|-------|----|
|       | C | Cg |
| 1 | | |
| 2 | | |
| 3 | | |
| 4 | | |
| 5 | | |
| 6 | | |
| 7 | | |
| 8 | | |
| 9 | | |
| 10 | | |
| 11 | | |
| 12 | | |
| 13 | | |
| 14 | | |
| 15 | | |
| 16 | | |
| 17 | | |
| 18 | | |
| 19 | | |
| 20 | | |
| 21 | | |
| 22 | | |
| 23 | | |
| 24 | | |
| 25 | | |
| 26 | | |
| 27 | | |

**\*1** C obv. 1. [ez]in$_x$ hu-luh-ha-zu a šà-íb-ba$^!$-zu èn-šè nu-šed$_7$-
dè

         2. ⸢a⸣-a ezin$_x$ nu-si$^?$-TAB-du-a iš-še-en-ni: e-zin$_x$
hu-luh-ha-zu-ú

         1. Oh, your angry dwelling(?), father(?), your angry heart, until
when will it not be pacified?

         2. (Largely unintelligible)

The restoration of the first sign in the first line is suggested on the basis
of the second line (and cf. Hallo, *JCS*, *17* [1963], 52 f.). Kramer's restoration
am (*JCS*, *18* [1964], 36) is not likely. The role of TAB in line 2 is unclear,
but the reading si-du-a occurs as the refrain in lines \*2 ff. The Glossenkeil
seems to introduce a variant (iš-še-en-ni = e-zin$_x$). The sign which we
read zin$_x$ is unidentifiable—it may be ŠEN. The reading is based on circum-
stantial evidence.

Line 2 seems to be a phonetic rendering of line 1, although it is very
difficult and may be corrupt. Syllabic versions of logographically written lines
appear in text C after the first line of each of the four stanzas respectively,
and this is also the reason why the scribe included the two first lines of each
section in one box (obv. 1/2, 28/29, 41/42 rev. 18/19); see pp. 28 f.

For the reading ezin$_x$ (ŠE.TIR) see *ŠL*, 367:186. The meaning is hard to
determine in our context: it could be a variant of TIR = *atmanu* "shrine" or
the like, *šubtum* "dwelling," for which see *CT*, *18*, 34 a 9 f. (= Antagal, III,
253 f.)[1] and S$^a$ Voc. Fragm. AG 3′ (*MSL*, *3*, 87) and cf. *CAD A/2* s.v.
*atmanu* and Hallo, *JCS*, *23* (1970), 58 n. 10. It is not likely that we are
dealing here with the goddess Ezinu; on that goddess, see Krecher, *Kultlyrik*,
132 f.

A passage' similar in contents is *SBH* I (p. 130 ff.) obv. 46 f.: umun
ka-nag-gá $^d$mu-ul-líl šà-sù-rá šà-zu èn-šè nu-hun-gá = *be-lum
ma-a-tú* $^d$II *lìb-bi ru-ú-qa lìb-ba-ka a-di ma-ti la i-nu-hu* "Master of the
country, Enlil, fathomless heart, until when will your heart not relax?" A
similar theme in a shorter form can be found in lines \*141 f.; cf. also lines
\*108 f.

On the addition of an /u/ vowel after certain words in the syllabic-companion lines (nu-si-du-a = nu-šed$_7$-dè?) see notes to \*41. On ezin$_x$ =
iš-še-en-ni see p. 36.

**\*2** C obv. 3. a-a $^d$mu-ul-líl $^{èn}$ umun kur-kur-ra $^{eš-še \ nu-si-du-a}$
Father Enlil until (when will he not calm down?) King of the
Foreign Lands, until when will he not calm down?

---

1. The text in *CT*, *18* reads GIŠ-*ma-nu*; its first publication in *II R* 34 (1866) reads
AB-*ma-nu*. The word was correctly read *at-ma-nu* by J. N. Strassmaier, *Alphabetisches
Verzeichniss der assyrischen und akkadischen Wörter* . . . (1886), no. 186.

That the small èn written above the line represents a refrain seems clear from the fact that in the next six lines containing the epithets of Enlil (*3–*8) a "ditto" sign (min) appears in the only occurrences in text C where a refrain is introduced in the middle of the line. It can be readily understood: of the three strings of twelve Enlil epithets[2] in text C (the others: *50 ff. and *75 ff.), ours is the only one in which each of the "original" seven epithets (but not the additional five) is preceded by the address form a-a ᵈmu-ul-líl, after which a refrain can be as easily introduced as after the epithets itself.

The refrain at the end of the line (which is repeated after each line in the first section of text C, through line *27) is similar to, but not identical with, the second half of line 1. There Enlil is addressed in the second person and it is his heart which is to calm down. Here he is referred to in the third person. The fact that no min sign but the refrain itself follows this line indicates that, in contrast with the other three stanzas of text C, it is not the second line of stanza II which contains the refrain, but rather the third. This can also be the reason for the lack of a ruled line between lines 2 and 3 so that the first three lines of stanza II of text C are included in one box.

The Emesal umun (also ù-mu-un) is an example of an Emesal form representing a different stage in the development of a word from its Emegir equivalent (see chap. 4). According to Poebel, *GSG* paragraphs 25 and 43, the Emegir en stems from *emen, with the elimination of the intervocalic /m/. An Emesal form with the /m/ eliminated, ù-un, is also attested; cf. Bergmann, *ZA*, 57 (1965), 36. In Emesal ge = Emegir gemé it is the Emegir form which retained the intervocalic /m/; see notes to line *45.

*3 C obv. 4. a-a ᵈmu-ul-líl$^{II}$ umun [d]u$_{11}$-ga zi-da$^{II}$
      Father Enlil, ᵈᵗᵒ· Master of the Fulfilled Speech, ᵈᵗᵒ·
*4 C obv. 5. a-a ᵈmu-ul-líl$^{II}$ ᵈmu-ul-líl a-a ka-nag-gá
      Father Enlil, ᵈᵗᵒ· Enlil, Father of the Nation, ᵈᵗᵒ·

ka-nag-gá, written ka-na-ága, ka-na-ág-gá in early texts, is the form which appears in Emesal texts. In Emegir texts the form is kalam (also written ka-la-ma, ka-nam, ka-na-ma [*ŠL*, 312, 2]). The distribution of the word between Emegir and Emesal is diametrically opposed to what would be expected; the Emegir forms would be expected to have /g̃/ as the second consonant, which would appear as /m/ in Emesal contexts. The Emegir form can be explained as a loan from Emesal, but it is more difficult to explain the Emesal form: it seems that the two forms exchanged roles (cf. notes to *87).

2. On the epithets of Enlil see chapter 5.

Although the literal meaning of k a l a m is "country" (*mātum*), it narrowed its scope to "The Country" par excellence, namely, Sumer and, eventually, to "the nation," i.e. the Sumerians. We prefer to translate "nation" here because of the connection to "father." On the philological and linguistic aspects of the word see Hallo, *Royal Titles*, 86 f.; Jacobsen, *JAOS, 59* (1939), 487 n. 11; Krecher, *Kultlyrik*, 108 n. 309, cf. also notes to line *90.

*5 C obv. 6.   a-a ᵈmu-ul-líl$^{\mathrm{II}}$ sipa sag-gíg-ga$^{\mathrm{II}}$
             Father Enlil, ᵈᵗᵒ· Shepherd of the Black-headed, ᵈᵗᵒ·
*6 C obv. 6a.  a-a ᵈmu-ul-líl$^{\mathrm{II}}$: i-bí-du₈ ní-te-na$^{\mathrm{II}}$
             Father Enlil, ᵈᵗᵒ· the One Inspecting for Himself, ᵈᵗᵒ·

As was already observed by Kramer (*JCS, 18* [1964], 36 n. 1) the fifth epithet of Enlil was accidentally omitted by the scribe and then added on the right edge; cf. a similar insertion in text A, *155. Note the inconsistency in Emesal usage in this line: while i-bí is the Emesal form of igi, du₈ is an Emegir form; its Emesal equivalent is zé(-b); Emesal Voc. III 110 ff. The two wedges divide the line into two halves: on the obverse and reverse the copy has a vertical line running throughout the text, but Kramer's collation shows no such line *JCS 23*, 10. For ní-te see van Dijk, *AcOr, 28*, 28 f. n. 75.

*7 C obv. 7.   a-a ᵈmu-ul-líl$^{\mathrm{II}}$ am erín di-di$^{\mathrm{II}}$
             Father Enlil, ᵈᵗᵒ· the Warrior Who Leads the Troops, ᵈᵗᵒ·
*8 C obv. 8.   a-a ᵈmu-ul-líl$^{\mathrm{II}}$ ù-lul-la ku-ku$^{\mathrm{II}}$
             Father Enlil, ᵈᵗᵒ· Who Feigns Sleep (lit. Who Sleeps a False Sleep), ᵈᵗᵒ·
*9 C obv. 9.   alim-maᵃ ur-sag ᵈasal-lú-hi$^{\mathrm{II}}$
             Dignitary, the Warrior Asalluhi, ᵈᵗᵒ·

This is the ninth epithet of Enlil; the eighth has been omitted. The latter can be found in C rev. 3 (*57) and 27 (*82). alim is an example of an Emegir usage quite commonly found in Emesal texts. The Emegir form is also used in line *11 and elsewhere. The Emesal equivalent is e-lum. The small a inscribed above the line seems to be a repetition of the preceding vowel, just as do the similar a signs in lines *11 and *13–*15. The small la signs which follow gal in lines *10 and *12 repeat the preceding consonants. They do not seem to fulfil any grammatical function, and may be stage direction devices.
*10 C obv. 10.  ur-sag-gal$^{\mathrm{la}}$ umun ᵈen-bi-lu-lu$^{\mathrm{II}}$
             The Great Warrior, the Lord Enbilulu, ᵈᵗᵒ·

About the small l a inscribed above the line cf. notes to line *9.
*11 C obv. 11.  alim-maᵃ ur-sag mu-zé-eb-ba-sa₄-a$^{\mathrm{II}}$
             The Dignitary, the Warrior Mudugasa'a, ᵈᵗᵒ·

*12 C obv. 12. ur-sag-gal$^{la}$ umun $^d$di-ku$_5$-mah-a$^{II}$
   The Great Warrior, the Lord Dikumah, $^{dto.}$
*13 C obv. 13. u$_4^1$-ri-da$_4^a$ u$_4$-sù-ta-ri-ta$^{II}$
   Since that day, since that day long ago, $^{dto.}$

The reading u$_4^1$ (copy has NA; cf. also line *16) is justified not only by the context (see following lines) but also by the duplicates; see presently.

We read -da$_4$ rather than -dam, as this reading is favored by the complement -a. If the reading -dam was meant, we would have expected a complement -ma, as is the case with gal-la in lines *10 and *12; cf. notes to line *9. The duplicate in Cg reads -ta and so do some of the other duplicates (see below), but none reads -dam. -da$_4$ is, then, a variant of the postposition -ta.

The -ri- in both parts of the line is an affix indicating remoteness, in our case temporal but elsewhere also spatial (e.g. in lines *153 ff.) "yonder (there and then)." Cf. the Akkadian translation of u$_4$-ri-a (below) and also OBGT Ia 5′–7′, where the affix stands in minimal contrast with -ne- and -še-: lú-ne-na-àm = *an-na-šu* "he is here," lú-še-na-àm = *a-na-ma-šu* "he is at the place concerned," lú-ri-na-àm = *ul-la-šu* "he is there."

Remoteness is also expressed in a phrase closely linked with our line, u$_4$-ri-a-ta = *ina ūmi ullûti* (cf. van Dijk, *AcOr, 28*, 24). Jacobsen mentions the affix -ri- briefly in AS, 16, 89 n. 13; the cases discussed by Krecher, *ZA, 57* (1965), 12 ff. do not bear upon our instance.

The occurrence in the present line of sù-ta brings a third element into the Sumerian consonant /d-r/. In Old Babylonian texts the tendency is to complement sù either by -ud (e.g. in the Warad Sin inscription *CT, 1*, 46:21$^3$) or by -rá (= DU; e.g. in *Hymn to Enlil*, 1). su$_x$-DU(su$_x$[= BU] has the same meaning as sù) is glossed -ra in the Old Babylonian text *CT, 42*, 4 ii 3$^4$. In later texts the complement -da is favored. The complement -ta is rare; it is attested in the present line (neo-Babylonian copy) and in two Old Babylonian texts: in the syllabic text B of a-ab-ba hu-luh-ha (su-ta, *108) and in a literary catalogue from Ur (Kramer, *RA, 55* [1961], 171:29), u$_4$-su$_x$-ta-ri-a. The instability is well demonstrated in our text C which writes sù-ta in the present line, but sù-rá two lines later (*15). This fluctuation in /d/r/t/ may indicate a Sumerian consonant similar to the flapped /r/ in the pronunciation of certain words in British English.[5] The form *porridge* ( < *poddidge* < *pottage*),

3. Warad Sin no. 7 in Hallo's bibliography of Early Old Babylonian royal inscriptions, *BiOr, 18* (1961), 9. For an additional copy of this inscription see now D. Owen, *JCS, 23*, 72 f., photo p. 74.

4. The reference is quoted by van Dijk, *AcOr, 28*, (1964) 17 n. 35; the text was edited by Kramer, *PAPS, 107* (1963), 501 ff.

5. See D. Jones, *An Outline of English Phonetics*, 9th ed. (1962) § 753: "Flapped *r* is formed like rolled *r* but consists of only one single tap of the tip of the tongue against the teeth ridge." Cf. also § 750.

for example, is the result of the neutralization of /t/ and flapped /r/.[6] Another case of flapped /r/ in Sumerian is gú-ru = gud; see notes to *49. A similar Sumerian phenomenon is the exchange of /r/ and /l/; cf. te-li = diri as a variant form in *The Coronation of Ur-Nammu*, 25 f., and ki-ib-bar-la = ki-bala, Sjöberg, *Orientalia Suecana*, *10*, 3, Corrected *AFO*, *24*, 41.

The idea of "from the days of yore" is well known in Sumerian literature. According to van Dijk (*AcOr*, *28*, 16 f.), a good number of literary texts with a mythologic introduction begin with $u_4$-ri-a etc. *Gilgameš, Enkidu and the Nether World*, and *The Instructions of Šuruppak* are entered in literary catalogues by $u_4$-ri-a $u_4$-sù-rá/ta-ri-ta.[7] The three line cliché $u_4$-ri-a etc. /$gi_6$-ri-a etc. /mu-ri-a etc. (as it appears in *13–*15, for example) has now turned out to be as old as the Fara period (Biggs, *JCS*, *20* [1966], 81, with some variations). For further references see Sjöberg, *OrNS*, *33* (1964), 108. A detailed discussion, with many quotations, of the historiosophic background of these phrases is offered by van Dijk, in *AcOr*, *28*. As to the parallel passage in text Cg (*13–*15) he remarks (33) that in that text the phrases are used simply as clichés, and this seems to be the case in text C.

*14 C obv. 14. $gi_6$-ri-da$_4$$^a$ $gi_6$-bad-ta-ri-ta$^{II}$
      Since that night, since that night long ago, $^{dto.}$

For the a inscribed above the line cf. notes to *9; for the postposition -da$_4$ cf. notes to *13. In many duplicates of this line, $gi_6$ in the second half of the line is qualified by sù, with bad occurring in the example quoted by van Dijk, *AcOr*, *28*, 17. It must denote, therefore, the same idea as sù and I interpret it with the meaning *nesû* "to become far away, remote".[8] $gi_6$-ri-a-ta ... is translated =*ina mūši ullûti* (ibid. 24).

*15 C obv. 15. mu-ri-da$_4$$^a$ mu-sù-rá-ri-ta$^{II}$
      Since that year, since that year long ago, $^{dto.}$

This line is omitted in the parallel passage of Cg. Note the difference between sù-rá in the present line and sù-ta in line *13, and cf. notes ad loc.

---

6. C. T. Onions, *The Oxford Dictionary of English Etymology* (1966), s.v. *porridge*.
The name zi-$u_4$-sud-rá survived in Hellenistic sources in forms which reflect the pronunciation of two consonants /d-r/ (Xisouthros etc., Jacobsen, AS, 11, 76 n. 34). This situation may indicate the mechanical transliteration of the signs SUD.RA which had been conservatively preserved as part of the name without being subjected to the change sù-rá > sù-da.

7. See Hallo, *JCS*, *20* (1966), 90 f. nos. 8 and 89.

8. A reading sumun for BAD, with the meaning *labiru* "old, ancient," cannot be excluded; cf. Sollberger, TCS, 1, Glossary 642.

**\*16** C obv. 16. $u_4$ dam kúr-re ba-ab-zé-èm-mà-ta$^{II}$
　　　　　Since the day the wives were delivered unto the enemy, $^{dto.}$

The translation of dam in the plural is accounted for by the infix -b-denoting collective plural, which is grammatically "inanimate." kúr "enemy" is also treated as collective plural as indicated by the postposition -e; ordinarily -ra would have been used (Jacobsen's remark). The treatment of collective plural as "inanimate" is best demonstrated in the *Sumerian King List*, where the formula for the reign of a single king is RN mu x ì-a$_5$ "RN reigned x years," but summing up the total of a dynasty (even if it consists of one king only), the formula is x lugal mu-bi y íb-a$_5$ "x kings reigned y years" (Jacobsen, AS, 11, 62, 129 f.). Similarly see the contrast ì-dib (sg.) vs. íb-dib (pl.) in economic texts (e.g., Hallo, *JCS*, *14* [1960], 106).

**\*17** C obv. 17. $u_4$ dumu kúr-re ba-ab-zé-èm-mà-ta$^{II}$
　　　　　Since the day the sons were delivered unto the enemy, $^{dto.}$

In the duplicate line Cg 28, $u_4$ is replaced by gi$_6$. Notice the non-Emesal usage of dumu here and in \*20, in preference to the Emesal form du$_5$-mu (\*207).

**\*18** C obv. 18. ma-la TÚG LUL-na dam ì-ug$_5$-a-ta$^{II}$
　　　　. . . . . since the wife died, $^{dto.}$

The first half of the line is unclear. The duplicate Cg 29 is broken, and what is left is ma-la [x-ú]s luḷ?-la dam ì-ug$_5$[x$\dot{x}$]. The first half can be interpreted, perhaps, as "friends (wearing) 'false' garments," i.e. acting in a treacherous way. For ma-la(-ag) = "friend" see Falkenstein, *Indogermanische Forschungen*, *60* (1950), 116; Gordon, *Sumerian Proverbs*, 89 f., and Wilcke, *ZA*, *59* (1969), 75, 88, 94.

**\*19** C obv. 19. dam ì-ug$_5$ dam ì<-ug$_5$-a-ta>$^{II}$
　　　　　The wife died, since the wife died, $^{dto.}$

**\*20** C obv. 20. dumu ì-ug$_5$ dumu ì<-ug$_5$-a-ta>$^{II}$
　　　　　The son died, since the son died, $^{dto.}$

Cf. notes to \*17.

**\*21** C obv. 21. urú-zu hul-hul-lu-dè itima am-gin$_x$ sipa im-gi-ra-a$^{II}$
　　　　　To devastate your city the shepherd rampaged in the Holy of Holies like a wild ox, $^{dto.}$

For urú as a variant of uru "city" in Emesal texts see Falkenstein's note in *MSL*, *4*, 12 n. 1b. The shepherd is probably an allusion to Enlil who is

the "Shepherd of the Black-headed." Cf. also *SBH*, 37 rev. 11 f.: mu-lu
èm-gi-ra-na = *da-i-ki-šú*. On itima see Falkenstein, *ZA*, *57* (1965), 100.

*22 C obv. 22. nibru^(ki) hul-hul-lu-dè itima <am-gin_x sipa im-
gi-ra-a>^(II)
  To devastate Nippur, the shepherd rampaged in the Holy
  of Holies like a wild ox, ^(dto.)

The literary pattern used in the couplet *21/*22 is well known in Sumerian
literature: the central theme of the couplet is introduced in general terms in
the first stich ("your city") and in specific terms in the second ("Nippur");
cf. also *87/*88 and, similarly, *108/*109, *273/*274, *275/*276, *277/*278,
and *279/*280.

*23 C obv. 23. TIN.TIR.KI hul-hul-lu-dè itima <am-gin_x sipa
im-gi-ra-a>^(II)
  To devastate Babylon, the shepherd rampaged in the Holy
  of Holies like a wild ox, ^(dto.)

The mention of Babylon here is the deed of a late scribe (or redactor). The
text was originally devoted to Nippur; in order to enhance its appeal to
contemporaries it had to be "updated," and this was done by inserting
Babylon. This adaption to historical and cultural conditions was done quite
superficially as there is no further elaboration on the Babylonian theme.

*24 C obv. 24. gi-gun₄-na ^(gi)KID!.MAH-a ^(a-mu-ruᵗ-gin_x) šu im-gur!-
ra-ta^(II)
  Since he (Enlil) swept away the temple tower like a big reed
  mat, ^(dto.)

The translation šu--gur = "to sweep away" is suggested by Jacobsen,
see *ŠL*, 354:171b. The superscribed a-mu-ru(-gin_x) is a phonetic indicator
of ^(gi)KID.MAH, offering a variant of muru; cf. *CAD B* s.v. *burû*. A passage
similar to our line is *SBH* 4:24 f.: e-ne-èm-mà-ni ^(gi)muru-àm ama
dumu-bi šu-ba ì-íb-gur-re = *a-mat-su um-ma mar-tam ki-ma bu-re-e*
[*ú-kap*]-*pár* "His (Enlil's) word sweeps away mother and daughter like a
reed mat" (restored from *BA*, *5*, 617:6). See, however, Landsberger's
different interpretation, "*The Date Palm and its By-products*," AfO Beiheft,
17 (1967), p. 33. On reed mats see A. Goetze, *JCS*, *2* (1948), 165 ff.

*25 C obv. 25. igi-du₈ a é-mu e-ne àm-me urú-mu e-ne ma
àm-me^(II)
  The onlooker is saying "Woe, my house! Where is it?
  (Woe,) my city! Where, oh where is it?" ^(dto.)

ma seems to be a contracted form of ma-a *ajiš* "where?"

*26 C obv. 26. igi-du$_8$ a ⌜gina⌝-mu e-ne àm-me gal-mu e-ne
ma àm-me$^{II}$
The onlooker is saying "Woe, my baby! Where is it? Woe,
my big son! Where, oh where is he?" $^{dto.}$

For gina (TUR + DIŠ) = "baby, infant child" see *CAD G* s.v. *ginû* C and
Goetze, *JCS, 13* (1959), 124.

*27 C obv. 27. nam-kúr? gig u$_8$-a u$_8$-a-e u$_4$ me-na bí-ni-ìb-zal$^{II}$
Oh, bitter hostility and crying, how long will it go on like
this? $^{dto.}$

For u$_8$-a as the sound of crying and moaning cf. notes to *234. For
u$_4$-zal see line *282, *AHw* s.b. *berû* Št, and cf. van Dijk, *AcOr, 28*, 39 n.
109. For the second half of the line cf. u$_4$ na-me-šè = *ana ki ma-ṣi* [$u_4$-$m$]$i$
"until how many days?" Berlin Vocabulary VAT 244′ (Reisner, *ZA, 9*
[1894], 149 ff.) iii 10, and *AHw*, 622 s.v. *ki maṣi*.

Stanza III

|  | Lines | B | C | Ca | Cf | Ch | Ck |
|--|-------|---|---|----|----|----|----|

*28 B i 1.      [mi-na-š]i mu-le-el mi-na-ši
How long, Enlil, how long?

C obv. 28. me-na-šè $^d$mu-ul-líl me-na-šè siskur me-na-šè
èn-šè nu-šed$_7$-dè

29. mu-ul-líl me-na-šè e-ú-nu-UK me-na-še-e

28. How long, O Enlil, how long, until when prayers, until
when will he not be pacified?

29. Enlil, how long, . . . how long?

As observed in notes to *1 and in p. 28, line 29 is a syllabic variant of line 28, and possibly in itself the result of more than one version. As in the present line B, it does not have the determinative before the divine name but, unlike the latter, it writes líl and not le-el. Notice also the two different spellings of -šè in C 29 as against the spelling of the B line. Text B is consistent with its spelling mi-na-ši only in col. i, whereas in col. ii it always spells mi-na-še (*99 ff.). The only consistent difference between B and the other texts is the former's spelling mi- in the first syllable, against the others' me-. What e-ú-nu-UK stands for is unclear.

Both me-na-šè and èn-šè are translated *adi mati* (OBGT I 734 and 738 respectively). From their distribution in a-ab-ba hu-luh-ha it seems that me-na-šè is used as a spontaneous cry (which we translate "how long?") and èn-šè is used as an adverbial expression (which we translate "until when?").

The difference between the early (Old Babylonian) B recension and the late (neo-Babylonian) C recension in this line is typical of the difference between the two texts: the former is spontaneous and brief, the latter is inflated, repetitive and contains one full, syntactically construed sentence.

*29 B i 2.     [du]-ku-ge-en-na-nu-da-an me-a an-da-ma-le
              (Enlil,) like a cloud over the horizon, where will you alight
              from there?
   C obv. 30. dungu-gin$_x$ an-úr-ta me-na-šè[II]
              (Enlil,) like a cloud over the horizon, how long? [dto.]

For the reading dungu (IM.DIRI) see Emesal Voc. III 119 with footnote ad loc. and, for further references, Landsberger, *WZKM*, *57* (1961), 7. The form dungu is Emegir, and it appears four times in the middle column (= Emegir) of the Emesal Vocabulary, equated with Akk. *erpu* (III 119–122); the only changes occur in the left column (= Emesal). This column shows four variants, all broken. From the first two (119 f.) one can reconstruct a form like *zé-be-ed (see footnotes ad loc.); since dungu is a variant form of dugud (Landsberger, *WZKM*) = Emesal zé-bi-da (Emesal Voc. II 22), this reconstruction is very plausible. In *CT*, *42*, 4 i 6 IM.DIRI-gi is glossed du-gu-gi. These data and the spelling du-ku in the present B line indicate that the /ng/ consonant in dungu is not a genuine /ğ/, for that consonant would appear invariably as /m/ both in the Emesal Vocabulary and in text B. To be sure, the former does offer two forms with /m/ immediately following the two forms with /b/. Furthermore, in the footnote to the relevant section in Emesal Voc. the indicator for the reading dungu (from Diri) is given as du-un-gu, but UN can stand also for uğ (see notes to line *38).

The solution to the conflicting evidence may be that originally the form contained a long unnasalized consonant /g/ *duggu which developed a

secondary nasalization > dungu; the unnasalized form accounts for the
entries with /b/ in the Emesal vocabulary and for the syllabic spellings with
a palatal (/g/ or /k/); the nasalized version accounts for the (artificial?)
entries with /m/ in the Vocabulary. Cf. also nigir > nimgir = Emesal libir
(e.g. Emesal Voc. I 77) but also ni-mi-ir (Poebel, *ZA*, *39* [1927], 145).

We analyze the B line as follows: dungu-gin$_x$ an-úr-ta-àm me-a
àm-da-gál-en (translation above and cf. p. 42). an- is probably a partially
assimilated form of àm-, due to the proximity of the infix -da-; cf. also *294.
For ma-al = gál "to alight," see Jacobsen *apud* Gordon, *Sumerian Proverbs*,
472 f. For the postposition -gin$_x$ written syllabically -ge-en see Sjöberg,
*Nanna-Suen*, 9.

The most revealing fact about this line is the Enlil attribute "like a cloud,
over the horizon." In our line the attribute appears before the "inner"
refrain (i.e. the one fully written in the line, in contrast with the "ditto."
refrain) me-na-šè, much like the Enlil attributes in the same position in
text A stanza VIII (*99 ff.); in the next line (*30) it serves as an apposition
to kur-gal $^d$mu-ul-líl. In both lines, the expression would not make
much sense within its context if we simply interpreted it literally; even less
so in line *40 where the expression can only be interpreted as an apposition
to the other attribute in the line.

an-úr: *išid šamē* "horizon" (lit. "sky, bottom part") appears as poetic
couplet with an-pa: *elat šamē* "zenith" (lit. "sky, top part") and the two
expressions are also used in hendiadys; see Sjöberg, *Nanna-Suen*, 175, and
*CAD* s.v. *elâtu* A 5c and *išdu* (bilingual section).

*30 C obv. 31. dungu-gin$_x$ an-ùr-ta kur-gal $^d$mu-ul-líl me-na-
šè[II]
Like a cloud over the horizon, Great Mountain Enlil, how
long? [dto.]

See notes to line *29.

*31 B i 3. kur-gal $^d$en-líl-lá me-a an-da-ma-le
Great Mountain Enlil, where will you alight from there?

Even in the syllabic text B, conventional spellings occur, namely, in our
line and in ii 3 (*101), both being the name of Enlil accompanied by an attribute. This inconsistency with the general character of the text is due to the
great frequency of allusions to Enlil in literary texts, and we must assume, of
course, that scribes did not "specialize" only in syllabic or logographic texts.
Writing habits from the logographic texts (with which scribes were more
familiar) could sometimes slip into syllabic texts.

For the second half of the line see notes to line *29.

*32 B i 4.    an-bi-du-ka me-en-ti
              That which you have promised you have fulfilled,
    C obv. 32. èm-bí-du$_{11}$-ga-zu im-ta-e-ug$_5$ $^{II}$
              As much as you have promised, you killed, $^{dto.}$

Only the first part of respective lines are duplicates. The B line stands for what would be in standard Emesal èm-bí-du$_{11}$-ga mu-e-ne-til. To be sure, this sentence never occurs in our texts as a whole, but its two parts do appear separately in different combinations: the first part is duplicated in the C line, above, and the second part is duplicated by the second part of line C 35 (*35).

Line C 32 lends further support to Jacobsen's assigning of the second person -e- infix of the transitive active preterite verb to a rank following the a-series dimensional infixes, but preceding the i/e-series infixes (*AS*, *16*, 93 n. 15). Line *35 is another case in point.

*33 B i 5.    ki bi-du-ka su-a ì-im-du me-a an-da-ma-le
              Wherever you promised, you have reached, where will you
              alight from there?
    C obv. 33. ki bí-du$_{11}$-ga-zu sá um-mi-du$_{11}$ $^{II}$
              That which you promised, you have accomplished, $^{dto.}$

Cf. text Ca 23 f.: ki bí-du$_{11}$-ga-[x] sá um-mi-[x] = *e-ma táq-bu-u tak-ta-šad*-[x(?)].

In both B and C the verb is construed differently from the verb in the preceding line. The most significant fact revealed by text B in this line is the phonetic rendering of sá by su-a. Nowhere in the available syllabaries is the vowel /u/ attested with any of the values of this sign (DI). One might compare, however, the cuneogram HA which has the syllabic value kua, S$^a$ 38 (*MSL*, *3*, 17). It is possible, however, that sá-u > su-a is a case of vocalic metathesis. For the refrain in the B line see notes to *29.

*34 C obv. 34.  èm bí-du$_{11}$-ga-zu ba-e-diri-diri$^{II}$
                Whatever you promised you have exceeded, $^{dto.}$
    Cf. Ca 25 f.:  èm bí-du$_{11}$-ga-zu ba-e-diri-diri = *el šá táq-bu-u tu-ta-te-er*.

The passage beginning in this line and continuing through line *37 is duplicated by Cf (with interlinear translation), Ch, and Ck, and is discussed by Krecher, *Kultlyrik*, 209 f.

*35 C obv. 35. ki na-ám-ku$_5$-da-zu ba-e-dè-til$^{II}$
              You have finished with your cursed place, $^{dto.}$

Ca 27 is an accurate duplicate of this line; its translation reads: *e-ma ta-at-mu-u tag-ta-mar*. Cf. also Cf 41 f., Ch 20, and Ck 20.

Reading tar for $ku_5$ (TAR) is excluded by the complement -da. On the other hand, $ku_5$, like sù, is complemented by a flapped *r* (= /r-d/; see notes to line *13 and the material concerning TAR in Römer, *Königshymnen*, 125, n. 13). The reading $ku_5$ is also supported lexically: in their respective translations, the scribes of Ca and Cfa employ the verb *tamū* which is attested for $ku_5$ (-d) but not for tar, in *CT*, *12*, 14 ii 39 (á = A = *nāqu* III): <ku-ud> = <TAR> = *ta-mu-u*.

Notice that the Assyrian line Ca ("Whatever you swore you have accomplished") is not an accurate translation of the Sumerian. Other inaccuracies in the Akkadian translation of Ca (*KAR*, 375, ii) are not hard to discern: in col. ii 9 f. sa is written above the line, as a phonetic indicator for sá, whereas the situation should be reversed, as is clear from the context. The Akkadian line correctly translates *šētu* which is the translation of sa ("net"). The same type of mistake appears in lines 11 f.

*36 C obv. 36. sipa nu-gam-ma e-zé i-ni-gub[II]
     A shepherd who would not lie down he installed over the sheep, [dto.]

This line is left untranslated in Ca 39, and all that is left of the translation in Cf 44 is [...]-*šá ina ṣe-e-ni tuš-ziz* where [...]-*šá* must be restored as a form of the verb *kanāšu*; cf. also Ch 21 and Ck 21. For the possibility of reading GAM as gurum or girum$_x$ see *Kultlyrik*, 197.

Notice the change from second to third person in this and the following lines. The Akkadian translation of Cf 44 does not reflect the change, but in the next line (*37) it contains two versions; cf. notes ad loc.

*37 C obv. 37. su$_8$-ba[a] ù nu-ku en-nu-un-gá bi-tuš[II]
     A shepherd who does not fall asleep he placed on guard, [dto.]

Two of the duplicates of this line have interesting variants; Ca 31 f.: su$_8$-ba ù nu-ku en-nu-un-na bí-tuš = *ra-di-a la ṣa-li-il* [*ana ma*]-*ṣar-tim tu-še-ši-*[*ib*]. (The Akkadian translation has apparently replaced *rē'u* "shepherd" by *rēdû* "soldier"; for the sibilant in *naṣāru* see A. Goetze, "The Sibilant in Old Babylonian '*naẕārum*'," *OrNS*, *6* [1937], 12 ff.) The surviving sections of Cf 45 f. read: [.....] en-nu-ga(!) bí-tuš = [....]-*li-la ana ma-ṣar-tim tu-še-šib: ú-šib*. (In this text the change to third person is reflected; see above, notes to *36.) Three more duplicates are Ch 22, Ck 22, and *SBH*, I (p. 130), obv. 14 f.; all read en-nu-un-gá; cf. also *CAD*, Ṣ, 72 s.v. *ṣālilu*.

The three different spellings of en-nu-un-gá etc. can be augmented by en-NUN-mu hé-a, *CT*, *16*, 46:178 (translated *lu-ú na-ṣir-šú*, ibid. 180).

They reflect a nasalized $/\tilde{g}/$, namely ennuǧa. About the neo-Assyrian analysis of this consonant as $/n$-$g/$ (as reflected in line Cf 45; see above) see notes to line *41. Cf. also p. 80. According to Falkenstein, GSGL, 1, 26 n. 4, the word appears as en-nu in the Old Sumerian and neo-Sumerian periods. For further references to ennuǧa see Krecher, Kultlyrik, 201; Sollberger, TCS, 1, Glossary 199; and especially van Dijk, ZA, 55 (1963), 88 f.

su₈-ba is the Emesal form of sipa (Emesal Voc. II 12) but it is seldom used. The role of the following -a is unclear. Jacobsen suggests that the superscribed small -a perhaps marks the hiatus between su₈-ba and ù nu-ku.

*38 C obv. 38. ú nu-ma₄-a edin-na bí-in-ma$^{\text{II}}$
    Grass which is not grown (i.e. weeds) he grew in the steppe, $^{\text{dto.}}$

The interpretation of this line is partly suggested by Jacobsen, who also suggests that ma = ma₄; the latter can also be read mú; it occurs in both readings with the meaning waṣû "to sprout" when referring to plants. Cf. also ma-a = ma₄-a, Bergmann, ZA, 56 (1964), 43. A similar passage is ú-téš nu-tuk edin-na bí-in-ma₄ = šammu la bušti ina ṣēri ušteṣâ "'shameless' grass he grew in the steppe" (restored from two copies; Kultlyrik, 206).

*39 C obv. 39. a-a $^{\text{d}}$mu-ul-líl gi-di-nu en-edin-na ba-ni-in-su$^{\text{II}}$
    Father Enlil, reeds (for lamentation flutes), which had not been there (?), proliferate in the high steppe, $^{\text{dto.}}$

gi-di = šulpu apparently designates both "reed" and the type of flute made of that reed; see CAD, E, 138 s.v. ša embūbi where lú-gi-di = ša šulpim "reed-flute player." Cf. also Hartmann, "Die Musik," 108 f.; Landsberger, JNES, 8 (1949), 280 n. 106. WZKM, 26 (1912), 127 ff. For a postpositioned -nu see GSGL, 1, 150. The verb su is used here as the intransitive of su-su = ruddû (Ai I iv 68; MSL, 1, 13). One can also understand the verb with the meaning šapāku "to heap up." Since the verb is rendered in the passive voice, a translation "are made to proliferate" is more appropriate.

en-edin-na for an-edin-na may be a case of regressive vowel assimilation; for recent references see Römer, Königshymnen, 201.

*40 C obv. 40. dungu-gin$_{\text{x}}$ an-úr-ta kur-gal $^{\text{d}}$mu-ul-líl e-ne im-ta-gá-gá
    The Great Mountain, Enlil, like a cloud over the horizon, where will he settle down from there?

For e-ne = e-ki-a-am "where?" see Langdon, OECT, 6, 23:15 f.

Stanza IV

(A: ki-ru-gú IV-kam-[ma])

| | Lines | | Texts | |
|---|---|---|---|---|
| | | A | B | C |
| | 41 | | | |
| | 42 | | | |
| | 43 | | | |
| | 44 | | | |
| | 45 | | | |
| | 46 | | | |
| | 47 | | | |
| | 48 | | | |

*41 A 1.    i-lu a-e i-lu a-e a-še-er [nu]-uš-gul-e
    B i 6.    ì-lu a-e ì-lu a-e a-ši-ir ni-iš-ku-le
          A wailing, oh, a wailing, oh, could he only hold back the
          lament!
  C obv. 41. i-lu-gáˡ-e! i-lu-àm a-še-er nu-gá-gá
          A wailing, it is a wailing, a lament is not set up,
      42. a-še-ru nu-ú-gá-a-a-gu-ú a-še-er nu-ga-an-ˊguˊ-
          ú
          A lament is not set up, a lament is not set up.

a-e is the sound of wailing.[9] This and other vowel sequences simulate sounds
of wailing in some of the texts of Reisner, *Sumerisch-babylonische Hymnen*.
They are conveniently arranged in the introduction to that volume, p. xvi. a
and u serving the same purpose are also found in *CT*, *42*, 12. For i-lu
"wailing" see the references in *Kultlyrik*, 148 f. and 208. The spelling ì-lu
in text B is surprising since that text normally uses unambiguous cuneograms
(see p. 22), but compare its use of ì- as a prefix in i 5 (*33). Or can we suppose
an early form *nilu of this word? Text B, however, spells i-lu in iii 4 (*184).
(About the disappearance of /n/ in initial position see Falkenstein, *Das
Sumerische*, 28.)

nu-uš- is explained by Jacobsen, AS, 16, 74, as a verbal profix expressing
an unrealizable wish. Further references for nu-uš-gul-e can be found in
*Kultlyrik*, 78, and *CAD*, *D*, s.v. *damāmu*. The preformative nu-uš- is spelled
syllabically even in Emegir, for lack of an appropriate CVC sign. The
conflicting evidence concerning the vowel of this preformative between the
A and C versions on the one hand, and B on the other, raises some questions.
Allegedly all the texts of a-ab-ba hu-luh-ha are in Emesal, and if the

9. It is not very likely that i-lu a-e is a form of the compound verb i-lu--du₁₁/e;
cf. YNER, *3*, 78.

form in question does not differ from its Emegir correspondent (as A and
C suggest) why is the form attested in B different? And if the Emesal form
is different from its Emegir correspondent, why is the difference not reflected in the spellings of A and C? One possibility is that these two texts
merely follow conventional Emegir orthography in this case even as they do in
logographic spellings; another might be that even within Emesal itself there
are some variations.

As observed above (pp. 28 f.), line C 42 is a syllabic version of C 41, but
unlike the other three syllabic-companion lines in text C, this one repeats
(twice) only the second stich of line 41. This seems to indicate that only this
stich is to be repeated as a refrain after each line of stanza IV; cf. notes to *1.

It seems that in line C 42 the scribe tried to convey an accurate phonetic
version of the second stich of line 41. Presumably he interpreted the nasalized
/g̃/ as the sequence /n-g/, and perhaps it was articulated this way in the neo-
Babylonian period when text C was copied; cf. also the spelling en-nun-ga
for ennuga̧ in the neo-Assyrian text Cf in notes to *37.

Th. Jacobsen suggests that i-lu-gá-e might reflect a glide between i-lu
and a-e. In CT, 42, 12:29 f., i-lu gá is glossed i-lu-ú-ú-ak-ke-e and, in
the left hand margin, opposite line 33, the gloss i-lu-u-ak-ke-e is found.
a-še-er is the Emesal form of a-nir "lamentation," showing the /n/ > /š/
shift; see GSG, § 83 and cf. še-er = nir in various combinations in Emesal
Vocabulary II 20 f., 88, 160. Cf. also Kultlyrik, 91 f.

A curious feature, common to at least three of these syllabic-companion
lines in text C, is the addition of a vowel /u/ at the end of certain words.
Thus in line 2 (*1) nu-si-du-a (= nu-šed₇-dè); in line 42 (*41) a-še-ru
(= a-še-er), gá-a-a-gu-ú (= gá-gá), ga-an-ᵍu¹-ú (= gá-gá);[10]
and in rev. 19 (*73). Line 29 (*28) may also contain one such case; see notes
ad loc.

nu-gá-gá in text C, replacing nu-uš-gul-e of text A, may be the result
of a broken Vorlage; cf. also notes to *89.

Some other expressions for "setting up a lament" or "shedding tears"
employing the verb gá-gá (as in a-še-er nu-gá-gá, C 41) are ér--gá-gá
(e.g. Two Elegies 52), i-si-iš--gá-gá (Lamentation over Ur, 422), and cf.
also The Curse of Agade, 204 ff. What may be meant in the C lines by "a
lament is not set" is that as differentiated from spontaneous wailing, no formal
lament is set.

*42 A 2.           ù-mu-un urú-mà kur-gal ᵈmu-ul-líl i-[lu a]-e
                   Lord of my city, Great Mountain Enlil, a wailing oh!
C obv. 43.  umun urú-mu i-lu-àm a-še-er [nu-gá-gáᴵᴵ]
                   Lord of my city, there is wailing, a lament [is not set up, ᵈᵗᵒ·]

10. Commenting on this phenomenon in line 42 Kramer observes that "The first half
seems to be Akkadianized Sumerian," JCS, 18, 35 n. 5.

The differences between the two versions in the first part of the line are not very significant; since this line is a spontaneous cry, addressed to the god ("lord of my city") in the second person, deviations from the recorded tradition could be expected. For urú as a variant of uru see notes to *21.

This line is significantly absent from text B, but that text does share the Nippur theme with the other texts (*179 ff.).

*43 A 3.      ù-mu-un urú-mà kur-gal ù-m[u-un x x i-lu(?) a]-e
              Lord of my city, Great Mountain, lord . . . . a wailing oh,
    C obv. 44. umun urú-mu giri$_x$-zal-zu-šè i-lu-àm a-še-er [nu-gá-gá$^{II}$]
              Lord of my city, there is wailing over your Splendor, a lament [is not set up, $^{dto.}$]

giri$_x$-zal is used here as an epithet of Nippur (or of the Ekur?). Its occurrence in close association with cities and temples is well attested; see Sjöberg, *ZA*, *55* (1963), 4 f. and 10. Cf. however, TCS, 1, Glossary 410.

*44 A 4.      edin-na [é]r mu-bi ì-[še$_8$-še$_8$]
    B i 7.    e-di-ni ir mu-bi i-ši-še
              Over the shack this young man is shedding tears,
    C obv. 45. edin-na ér-gig mu-un-še$_8$-še$_8$[$^{II}$]
              Over the shack, he is shedding bitter tears [$^{dto.}$]

For the vocalic aspects of the B line see pp. 37 f. The seemingly inconsistent treatment of še$_8$ in the B line may be due to the contraction of the suffix -e of the present-future into the second ši. e-di-ni perhaps = edin-e. mu is the Emesal form of giš = *eṭlu* "young man" (any connection to gìš = *zikaru*?).

The unpublished fragment K. 5007 (ref. courtesy M. Civil) is a duplicate of text C obv. 41, 43–48 (*41–*47), with an Akkadian translation. W. W. Hallo has kindly transliterated the text at the British Museum for us. For the present line it has edin-na ér-[xx] = *ina$^?$ bi-tum* [xx] (lines 7 f.). For edin = *bītum* see *SBH*, 54:51 f.: áb-e edin-na-na ér-gig mu-un-ma-[al] = *lit-tum ana* É-*šú mar-ṣi-iš i-bak-ki*. Following a suggestion by Th. Jacobsen that edin = "ruins," we would translate edin = *bītum* as "shack."

*45 A 5.      èn-du ma-nun-na ge-bi ì-[še$_8$-še$_8$]
    B i 8.    en-du ma-nu-na ge-bi i-ši-še
              A dirge over the storehouse, this girl is mourning.
    C obv. 46. en-dìm(RAB + GAN)-ma-eš isíš[$^{II}$]

The reading of the C line is tentative, and the meaning is obscure.

On èn-du (and other spellings) "song" (Akk. *zamāru*), see Hallo, *JAOS*, *83* (1963), 174, and more recently J. Krecher, *Kultlyrik*, 223. A recent variant is en$_x$(ŠA)-du (Civil, at the American Oriental Society meeting 1966; Hallo, *JCS*, *20* [1966], 91 n. 19, [where SA is a misprint for ŠA]). A. Deimel's translation "singen" (*ŠL*, 59:30) is incorrect since both references feature a noun, not a verb.

ma-nun (Emegir gá-nun, Akk. *ganūnu*) is a storage house or the living quarters of a temple or a palace, (*CAD*, *G*, 42 f.; E. Sollberger, TCS, 1, Glossary 278). In our context it must refer to some part of the Ekur; cf. also ma-nun-mah-àm $^d$mu-ul-líl-lá in *165. For further references see *Kultlyrik*, 82 and M. Lambert, *RLA*, *3*, 143 ff.

For the Emesal form ge see the glossary s.v. Morphologically, ge represents Emegir gemé; the elimination of /m/ in intervocalic and other positions is not common, but is by no means unique in either Emegir or Emesal; see A. Poebel, *GSG*, §§ 25, 43, and above, p. 37. A reverse situation, in which an Emesal form retains an intervocalic /m/ where its Emegir equivalent does not, is found in umun = en(<*emen); see notes to *2.

*46 A 6.          mu-bi ér-re ì-sìg-ge-a
     B i 9.        mu-bi i-ra i-si-ge-a
                   This young man is shaking in tears,
     C obv. 47.    mu-bi ér-ra al-še gig-ga
                   This young man is bitterly crying,
            49.    [m]u-bi ér-ra al-sìg gi-g[a$^{II}$]
                   This young man is bitterly shaking in tears, [dto.]

The duplicate line in K. 5007 (cf. notes to *44) has mu-bi ér-ra al-še [xx] = *ina bi-ki-ti mar-ṣi-iš i-dam-[mu-um]*. še here and in C 47, 48 is syllabic spelling for še$_8$; cf. above *44.

Lines *46–*50 are partly paralleled by UET, 6/2, 203 obv. 1–6. We have changed the order of the C lines, namely, C 47, 49 are presented here, C 48, 50 in *47 according to their respective subjects. Text A has ér-re (= ér-e), the other three *ér-a; the latter seems more appropriate as ér is used adverbially here. For the interchange /s/ - /š/ see p. 36; for ér-ra > i-ra, see p. 37.

*47 A 7.          ge-bi ér-re ì-sìg-⌈ge-a⌉
     B i 10.       [ge]-bi i-ra i-si-ge-a
     C obv. 48.    ge-bi ér-ra al-še gig-ga[$^{II}$]
            50.    [.....] ⌈ér-ra⌉ [.............]
                   This girl, shaking in tears, (C.: [dto.])

The lines in C show precisely the same variations as in the preceding one. From the traces of C 50 it does not seem that it corresponds to any of the three preceding lines in text C.

*48 B i 11. ge-bi ì-ši-še.
          This girl is crying.

The reason for repeating the second half of B i 8 (*45) is unclear. Perhaps the next line in B (which is broken away) repeats the second half of B i 7 (*44), thus forming the mu:bi couplet in an inverted order.

## Stanza V

### (A: ki-ru-gú V-kam-ma)

| Lines | A | C | Cb | Cc | Cj |
|---|---|---|---|---|---|
| 49 | ⌐ | Broken | ⌐ | ⌐ | ⌐ |
| 50 |  | Broken |  |  |  |
| 51 | ⌐ | Broken |  |  |  |
| 52 | ⌐ | Broken |  |  |  |
| 53 | ⌐ | Broken |  |  |  |
| 54 | ⌐ | Broken |  |  |  |
| 55 |  | ⌐ |  |  |  |
| 56 |  |  | ⌐ |  | ⌐ |
| 57 |  |  |  |  |  |
| 58 |  |  | ⌐ |  |  |
| 59 |  |  |  |  |  |
| 60 |  |  |  |  |  |
| 61 |  |  |  |  |  |
| 62 |  |  |  | ⌐ | ⌐ |
| 63 |  | ⌐ | ⌐ |  | ⌐ |
| 64 | ⌐ |  |  |  |  |
| 65 | ⌐ | ⌐ | ⌐ |  |  |
| 66 |  |  |  |  |  |
| 67 | ⌐ |  |  |  |  |
| 68 |  |  |  |  |  |
| 69 |  |  |  |  |  |
| 70 |  |  |  |  |  |
| 71 |  |  |  |  |  |
| 72 |  | ⌐ | ⌐ |  |  |

*49 A 8.  gud-sún e-lum gud-sún mu-zu kur-kur-[šè]
    Cb. 1.  gud-sún-na e-lum gud-sún-e mu-zu kur-kur-ra
        Wild Bull, Dignitary, Wild Bull, when your name is over the foreign lands,

As already recognized by Kramer (JCS, 18 [1964], 36 n. 4), text C rev. 1–17 is duplicated with minor changes by SBH, 22 rev. 1–22 (= text Cb in the Composite Text). Since six lines are missing at the beginning of the rev. of

C we substitute in the Composite Text the duplicate lines from Cb. Text Cb is one line shorter than the restored length of the duplicate section in C, since C rev. 3 and 5 are inscribed in one line in Cb 10 (see notes to *57). Notice the orthography in the parallel line UET, 6/2,203 obv. 5: gú-ru su-nu e-lum gú-ru su-nu mu-zu kur-kur-a;[11] it indicates that the /d/ of gud is, in fact, a flapped /r/, see notes to *13.

The present line appears also as the incipit line of a balag composition dedicated to Enlil, NBC 1315 (*RA*, *16* [1919], 208; the first ten lines of this composition are incorporated in the Composite Text as text Cj.). The first half of the line is entered several times in the neo-Assyrian catalogue *IV R*², 53; cf. pp. 17 f. In a-ab-ba hu-luh-ha this line is the first of the refrain stanza V = VII = IX, cf. p. 26.

Line *49 occurs with Akkadian translation in text Cc 1 f.: [. . . .] mu-zu kur-kur-šè = [. . . . *be*]-*lum* MU-*ka ana ma-ta-a-tum*. The translation is incorrect in that it translates the Sumerian postposition -šè by Akkadian *ana*. It implies that the postposition is affixed only to kur-kur ("your name is over the foreign lands"). Lines 11–14 in stanza V of A (*64–*67), each of which ends with -šè suffixed to a nominalized sentence, indicate that -šè in each of the lines 8–10 (*49–*53) functions as a subjunctive element "when," and not as a postposition. By the same token, the postposition -(r)a in the Cb line is wrong. The main sentence on which the adverbial clauses *49–*61 depend is line *62 (cf. notes ad loc.) which, in turn, is coupled with *63. Only in text A is the subjunctive element -šè repeated after each line, whereas in Cj it is repeated only before the main sentence, and similarly in C and Cb.

The terms e-lum and gud-sún are two of the attributes of Enlil which are not included in the seven heroic epithets. They belong to the first of the three sets of attributes of Enlil used in text A; cf. p. 46.

*50 Cb 2. umun kur-kur-ra gud-sún-na
        King of the Foreign Lands, Wild Bull,

The fact that the -na is written at the end of the line (with a wide space separating it from the preceding sún) indicates that the second part of the preceding line is not to be repeated. In the following lines of Cb only gud is inscribed in the second half of the line, with the rest of the line left blank and to be completed sún-na, as in the present line. Cf. also the duplicate lines Cc 4, Cj 2 and UET, 6/2, 203 obv. 6, which reads gú-ru-su-nu for gud-sún; cf. notes to *49.

*51 Cb 3. umun du₁₁-ga-zi-da gud- <sún-na>
        Master of the Fulfilled Speech, Wild Bull,

11. I wish to thank Th. Jacobsen for this reference.

Cf. the duplicate lines Cc 5 and Cj 3.

*52 A 9.  [kur-gal a]-a ᵈmu-ul-líl gud-sún mu-zu kur-kur-[šè]
            Great Mountain, Father Enlil, Wild Bull, when your name is over
            the foreign lands,
     Cb 4. ᵈmu-ul-líl a-a ka-nag-gá gud-<sún-na>
            Enlil, Father of the Nation, Wild Bull,

In the A-line, it is the second attribute of the first set of attributes which is
quoted (see p. 46); in the C-lines (Cb 4, Cc 6, Cj 4), it is the third of the
seven heroic epithets (see pp. 47 ff.).

*53 A 10. si[pa] sag-gíg-ga gud-sún mu-zu kur-kur-šè
            Shepherd of the Black-headed, Wild Bull, when your name is
            over the foreign lands,
     Cb 5. sipa sag-gíg-ga gud-<sún-na>
            Shepherd of the Black-headed, Wild Bull,

For this attribute see p. 46. Cf. the duplicate lines Cc 7 and Cj 5.

*54 Cb 6. i-bí-du₈ ní-te-na gud-<sún-na>
            The One Inspecting for Himself, Wild Bull,

Cf. the duplicate Cj 6; Cc 8 has ní-te-en; cf. also *132.

*55 Cb 7. am erín-na di-di gud-<sún-na>
            The Warrior Who Leads the Troops, Wild Bull.

The duplicates of this line are Cc 9 and Cj 7. Text C starts again in this
line but only traces of the AM are preserved.

*56 Cb 8. ù-lul-la ku-ku gud-<sún-na>
            The One Who Feigns Sleep, Wild Bull,

Only the first two signs are preserved in C rev. 2; the other duplicates of
this line are Cc 10 and Cj 8.

*57 C rev. 3. umunᵉ ᵈam-an-[ki-ga gud-<sún>ᴵᴵ]
            The Lord Enki, Wild Bull, ᵈᵗᵒ·

The line is restored after C rev. 27 (*82) and cf. also Cc 11 (where Enki's
name is not complemented by -ga) and Cj 11. Kramer's observation (AS, 12,
73) that ᵈam-an-ki is not "Wildstier (?) Himmels und der Erde" (e.g.
in RLA, 2, 376) but an Emesal form of the name Enki is now borne out by
Emesal Voc. I 38. Another form is ᵈam-ma-an-ki (Götterepitheta, 287).
aman is a reflection of the "original" form of en(< *emen); see J. J.
Finkelstein, JCS, 17 (1963), 42 and van Dijk, UVB, 18 (1962), 46. The entry
ᵈumun-ki = ᵈen-ki in Emesal Voc. I 2 may be artificial (contrary to the

view of Landsberger, *MSL*, *4*, 4 ad loc.) About the prolongation -ga in
Enki's name see Sollberger's suggestion, TCS, 1, Glossary 393. C rev. 6
(*60) shows that, unlike text Cb, sún in text C is not followed by -na.
About the absence of this line from Cb see notes to *59.

*58 C rev. 4. ur-sag ᵈasal-lú-h[i gud-<sún>ᴵᴵ]
            The Warrior Asalluhi, Wild Bull, ᵈᵗᵒ·

Cf. the duplicate lines Cb 9 and Cc 12.

*59 C rev. 5. umun ᵈen-bi-lu-lu gud-[<sún>ᴵᴵ]
            The Lord Enbilulu, Wild Bull, ᵈᵗᵒ·

Cf. the duplicate line Cb 10: umun ᵈen-bi-lu-lu dumu-sag ᵈen-ki-
ke₄; and see the discussion on p. 49. Of the duplicate Cc 13 only gud is
preserved.

*60 C rev. 6. ur-sag ᵈmu-zé-eb-ba-sa₄-a gud-[<súnᴵᴵ]
            The Warrior Mudugasa'a, Wild Bull ᵈᵗᵒ·

Cf. the duplicate lines Cb 11, Cc 14 (three signs preserved).

*61 C rev. 7. umun ᵈdi-ku₅-mah-aᵃ gud-[<sún>ᴵᴵ]
            The Lord Dikumah, Wild Bull, ᵈᵗᵒ·

Cf. the duplicate line Cb 12; in Cc 15 only one sign is partly preserved.

*62 A 11.    mu-zu kur-ra mu-un-ma-al-la-[šè]
             When your name rests over the mountains,
    C rev. 8. mu-zu kur-ra mu-un-ma-al-la-šè an ní-bi nam-
             dúb-[baᴵᴵ]
             When your name rests over the mountains, the sky itself
             trembles; ᵈᵗᵒ·

The C line is accurately duplicated by Cb 13, whereas Cj 9 shows two
slight variations. The syntactical function of this line underwent a good deal
of transformation between its A and C versions. In text A the entire stanza V
is a refrain; it dwells on Enlil's worldwide power which is heralded by his
"name" (mu). Although each of the seven lines of the stanza is construed as
a dependent clause (suffixed by -šè = "when" as a subjunctive element)
this stanza V does not anticipate a main clause but it comes as an after-
thought following stanza IV in which the suffering of Enlil's people is
described. In text C the segment corresponding to lines 8–10 of stanza V
(namely *49–*61) is construed the same way, but it anticipates the main
clause which finally appears in the present line. Cf. also the discussion of this
line by Poebel, *ZA*, *37* (1927), 248 f.

On the assertative preformative nam- see Falkenstein, *ZA*, *47* (1942), 181
ff. and Jacobsen, AS, 16, 73 n. 4; cf. also *192 ff. For dúb occurring with the
meaning "to tremble, shake" with reference to the sky see van Dijk, *SGL*, *2*,
45. With the meaning "to relax" the word occurs in the name of the temple
é-ní-dúb-bu in Isin; Hallo, *JNES*, *18* (1959), 54 (but see Falkenstein, *ZA*,
*56* [1964], 87 n. 61) and Krecher, *Kultlyrik*, 139 f.

*63 C rev. 9. an ní-bi nam-dúb ki ní-bi nam-[sìg$^{II}$]
          The sky itself trembles, the earth itself shivers, $^{dto.}$

Can this phrase be the origin of Enlil's attribute *rimu munarriṭ šamê u erṣeti*
(see *Götterepitheta*, 299)? The duplicates of this line are Cb 14 and Cj 10.

*64 A 12. kur elam$^{ki}$-ma mu-un-ma-al-⌈la⌉-[šè]
          When it rests over the mountains of Elam,

The absence of this line from the late versions of this section is noteworthy.
In the Old Babylonian period the mountains of Elam symbolized the foreign
world par excellence; their inhabitants were usually hostile. Elam signified
that quarter from which an attack by a foreign nation was most likely to
come and on which a constantly wary eye must be kept. The assertion that
Enlil's power is exercised over Elam reflects, perhaps, pride and security
after Elam's defeat at the hands of Hammurapi in his 29th year, a mere
thirteen years before text A was copied or edited (see C. J. Gadd, *CAH*², *2*,
chap. V, "Hammurabi and the End of his Dynasty," p. 10). By the time
text C was copied the situation could have been different in two ways: either
Elam was independent and it could not be claimed that Enlil's name "rests"
there, or it was long pacified and this fact did not carry enough import to
merit any special attention in a literary text of this type.

*65 A 13.      an-na úr-ba mu-un-ma-al-la-šè
    C rev. 10. an-na úr-bi-a mu-un-ma-al-la-[šè$^{II}$]
          When it rests over the horizon, (C: $^{dto.}$)

See notes to line *66 and cf. the duplicate Cb 15.

*66 C rev. 11. ki-a úr-bi-a mu-un-<ma-al-la-šè> [$^{II}$]
          When it rests over the "foundation of the earth," $^{dto.}$

This line is an artificial parallel to the preceding one, unsuccessfully coined
after its pattern and apparently meant to inflate the volume of the text.
an-úr *išid šamê* of the previous line is a well known expression, sometimes
paired with an-pa *elât šamê* "zenith" in literary compositions.[12] On the

12. Kramer's suggested reading an-sàg for an-PA (*Sumer*, *4*, 21) is disproved by
the lexical evidence, as is Poebel's reading an-zág (*ZA*, *37*, 247); see *CAD*, E, 79 s.v.
*elât šamê*.

other hand ki-úr does not occur, so far as we know, in Sumerian literature, is not listed in the vocabularies, and what would have been its Akkadian equivalent (*išid erṣetim*) is not attested either. Compare, however, kur-úr, Poebel, *ZA*, *37* (1927), 245, 248; and see for general references, Sjöberg, *Nanna-Suen*, 175. Cf. also the duplicate line Cb 16.

*67 A 14.      ki-a zà-ba mu-un-ma-al-la-šè
   C rev. 12. ki-a zà-bi-a mu-un-< ma-al-la-[šè> II]
         When it rests over the farthest reaches of the earth, (C: dto.)

Cf. the duplicate line Cb 17. Notice that this line is repeated twice more in text A without the subject element -n- in the verbal chain.

*68 C rev. 13. ki-a gaba-ba mu-un-< ma-al-la-[šè> II]
         When it rests over the surface of the earth, dto.

Cf. the duplicate line Cb 18. As is the case with some of the phrases in the preceding lines, the constituents of ki-a gaba-ba are part of a common stock of words used in various combinations describing topographical features. The Akkadian equivalent of the present phase is *irat erṣetim*; other phrases are: gaba-a = *irat mê* "edge of the water," gaba-kur-ra = *irat šadî* "flanks of the mountains," gaba-kur-ra = *irat erṣetim* "edge of the netherworld;" see, for these and other Akkadian references, *CAD*, *I/J*, 186 f. In Sumerian alone: gaba-hur-sag-gá "'breast' of the mountains," van Dijk, *SGL*, *2*, 17; gaba-ki-duru₅-a "edge of the river, bank" and gaba-a-ab-ba "surface of the ocean," Sjöberg, *Nanna-Suen*, 54 n. 15. For syllabic spellings see Falkenstein, *ZA*, *55* (1963), 35.

*69 C rev. 14. kur ní-ri-a mu-un-< ma-al-la-[šè > II]
         When it rests over the awe-inspiring mountains, dto.

This line could be the substitute for the missing line about Elam, above, *62. For ní-ri "awe-inspiring" cf. also ní-huš-ri "awful terror" (Römer, *Königshymnen*, 105) and ní-su-zi-ri "awe-inspiring glow" (Sjöberg, *Nanna-Suen*, 65:11, 68). Cf. also the duplicate line Cb 19. For the possible reading im-ri-a in our passage see Å. Sjöberg, *Heidelberger Studien*, 203, wherein the entire passage is quoted.

*70 C rev. 15. kur anₓ'-na mu-un-< ma-al-la-[šè> II]
         When it rests over the high mountains, dto.

Unfortunately the key word both in the present line and in the duplicate Cb 20 is partly destroyed. For the suggested reading BÀD = anₓ = *elû* cf. kur BÀD-na, hur-sag BÀD-na = *šadû elû* quoted in *CAD E*, 110 s.v. *elû* lexical section. anₓ is, then, a variant of an = *elû*, *šaqû*.

*71 C rev. 16. kur á'-diri mu-un-< ma-al-la-[šè> II]
         When it rests over the powerful(?) mountains, [dto.]

All that is left of the duplicate line Cb 21 is [...] di-bi mu-un-<ma-al-la-šè>. The meaning in both lines is obscure.

*72 C rev. 17. kur-ra an da-ma-al-la-šè mu-un-ma-al-la-šè an ní-b[i nam-dúb$^{II}$]
When it rests over the mountains and over the wide sky, the sky itself trembles. $^{dto.}$

The -šè in the middle of the line seems to be redundant but it is present also in the duplicate Cb 22.

### Stanza VI

(A: ki-ru-⌈gú⌉ ⌈VI⌉-kam-ma)

| Lines | Texts | |
|---|---|---|
| | A | C |
| 73 | | |
| 74 | | |
| 75 | | |
| 76 | | |
| 77 | | |
| 78 | | |
| 79 | | |
| 80 | | |
| 81 | | |
| 82 | | |
| 83 | | |
| 84 | | |
| 85 | | |
| 86 | | |
| 87 | | |
| 88 | | |
| 89 | | |
| 90 | | |
| 91 | | |

*73 A 15.     [ši]-mah-en ši-mah-en
You are likewise exalted, you are likewise exalted!
C rev. 18. za-e mah-me-en za-e mah-me-en
C rev. 19. [za-e e]-lum-ma-e-me-en a$^{me-en}$ za-e mah-me-en!
e-lum-ma za-e mah-me-en
You are the Dignitary, you are the Father (?), you are exalted, Dignitary, you are exalted!

For the translation "likewise" of the preformative ši- in text A see Jacobsen, AS, 16, 73, and for a detailed discussion see Falkenstein *ZA, 38* (1944), 69 ff. Its use here is intended to match the greatness of Enlil with that of his deeds. The change to za-e in text C probably came about because the original meaning of ši- had been forgotten by the neo-Babylonian period. The verbal use of mah in text A is perculiar, but not altogether unique; cf. aša i-mah-me-en "You alone are exalted," *The Exaltation of Inanna*, 134. With Akkadian translation it occurs in an-na za-e mah-me-en za-e mah-me-en = *ina šamê at-ta și-i-ri at-ta și-ra-at*, BRM, *4*, 8:1 f.

The translation of C rev. 19 is uncertain. The role of -ma in e-lum-ma(-e) is unknown, and the translation a = "father" is tentative; cf. also line *1. For -me-en! (not me-nu-ú) see Kramer, *JCS, 23* (1970), 10. The line seems to be an expanded, partly syllabic, version of C rev. 18.

*74 A 16.  $^d$mu-ul-líl ši-mah-en
Enlil, you are likewise exalted!

*75 A 17.  $^d$[mu]- $^{\ulcorner}$ul $^{\urcorner}$-líl kur-kur-ra ši-mah-en
Enlil of the Foreign Lands, you are likewise exalted!

C rev. 20. umun kur-kur-ra za-e <mah-me-en> $^{II}$
King of the Foreign Lands, you are exalted! $^{dto.}$

*76 C rev. 21. umun du$_{11}$-ga-zi-dè za-e <mah-me-en> $^{II}$
Master of the Fulfilled Speech, you are exalted! $^{dto.}$

The orthography zi-dè (instead of zi-da) in this epithet is uncommon. It perhaps reflects retention of the vocative postposition -e; see Sjöberg, *Nanna-Suen*, 18.

*77 C rev. 22. $^d$mu-ul-líl a-a ka-nag-gá za-e <mah-me-en> $^{II}$
Enlil, Father of the Nation, you are exalted! $^{dto.}$

*78 A 18.  sipa sag-gíg-ga ši-mah-en
C rev. 23. sipa sag-gíg-ga za-e <mah-me-en> $^{II}$
Shepherd of the Black-headed, you are (A: likewise) exalted!
(C: $^{dto.}$)

*79 C rev. 24. i-bí-du$_8$ ní-te-na za-e <mah-me-en> $^{II}$
The One Inspecting for Himself, you are exalted! $^{dto.}$

*80 C rev. 25. am erín di-di za-e <mah-me-en> $^{II}$
The Warrior Who Leads the Troops, you are exalted! $^{dto.}$

*81 C rev. 26. ù-lul-la ku-ku za-e <mah-me-en> $^{II}$
The One Who Feigns Sleep, you are exalted! $^{dto.}$

*82 C rev. 27. umun$^e$ $^d$am-an-ki-ga za-e <mah-me-en> $^{II}$
The Lord Enki, you are exalted! $^{dto.}$

*83 C rev. 28. ur-sag ᵈasal-lú-hi za-e <mah-me-en> ᴵᴵ
The Warrior Asalluhi, you are exalted! ᵈᵗᵒ·
*84 C rev. 29. umun ᵈen-bi-lu-lu za-e <mah-me-en> ᴵᴵ
The Lord Enbilulu, you are exalted! ᵈᵗᵒ·
*85 C rev. 30. ur-sag ᵈmu-zé-eb-ba-sa₄-a za-e <mah-me-en> ᴵᴵ
The Warrior Mudugasa'a, you are exalted! ᵈᵗᵒ·
*86 C rev. 31. umun ᵈdi-ku₅-mah-aᵃ za-e <mah-me-en> ᴵᴵ
The Lord Dikumah, you are exalted! ᵈᵗᵒ·

In the next few lines the order in both text A and text C is disrupted; for A 19 f. see *104 f.; for C rev. 32 ff. see notes to *87.

*87 A 21. mušen ši-bi-ta a-e àm-šú-šú
The bird 'pours out' a wailing from its throat,
C rev. 40. mušen ši-bi-ta i-lu ši-bi-ta é-a-na šú-šúᴵᴵ
The bird, from its throat, 'pours out' a wailing, from its throat over his house, ᵈᵗᵒ·

The translation of A 21 is suggested by Jacobsen. ši is the Emesal form of zi = *napištu* "throat" (Emesal Voc. II 189). a-e as the sound of wailing occurs also in the first line of text A (*41). For šú-šú = "to pour out (here: voice)" compare gù--dé-dé = "pour out the voice, shout."
The significance of the bird is not clear; the next line clarifies which bird is referred to (*88). The house over which it 'pours' its wailing is probably the house of the man of Nippur. The structure of this line is peculiar; it may be another result of a broken Vorlage; cf. notes to *89. For mušen compare the following forms: mu-sa₄-a (in the Emesal text *CT*, *42*, 3 v 5 [Falkenstein, *ZA*, *55*, 52 n. 156]), mu-še dingir-re-e-ne (*TRS*, 72:83) = [mu]-sa, dingir-ra-àm (*SLTN*, 26, rev. 8 = *Creation of the Pickaxe*, 83 ), mu-še mu-še-na (copy B of *The Coronation of Ur-Nammu*, 25 f.) and mu-sig₅ (ibid. in copy C; both from Ur; see Hallo, *JCS*, *20* (1966), 139 ff.). In the light of these forms one should question whether the form mušen is not an Emesal borrowing in Emegir and mu-sa₄-a, vice versa, an Emegir borrowing in Emesal. Such an exchange of roles apparently occurred also in "Emegir" kalam = "Emesal" ka-na-áǵ(a) (cf. notes to *4).
From line C rev. 32 on, text C and text A differ in their arrangements; see notes to *88–*90 and to *103 f.

*88 A 22. mušen gì[r-g]i-lu ši-bi-ta a-e àm-šú-šú
The *girgilu*-bird "pours out" a wailing from its throat,

For mušen gìr-gi-lu cf. Hh XVIII 266 (*MSL*, *8/2*, 138) and *CAD*, *G*, s.v. *girgilu*. The present line offers yet another variation to the various logographic combinations employed in the writing of the bird's name. Also in the present line the determinative is written before the name whereas in the other cases it is written after it. The statement in *CAD*, *G*, 86 s.v. *girgilu* that there is no connection between this bird and a city near Nippur (or a part of Nippur) called Girgilu is disproved by the occurrence of the name of that place with the postdeterminative mušen in TMH, 5, 24 obv. i 4. In this case, however, it is written with HA, i.e. an ungunified GIR (ref. courtesy Th. Jacobsen). In a kudurru of Nazimaruttaš (written in Akkadian) the *girgilu* bird is described as the messenger of Enlil (MDP, 2, pl. 17 iv 3) and it is owing mainly to this fact that we interpret the Sumerian gìr-gi-lu also as standing for this bird and not for the laughing bird *ṣajāhu* which shares the same logogram in Hh XVIII 265 (*MSL*, *8/2*, 138). For the poetic structure of the couplet *87/*88 see notes to *22 and compare also *Lamentation over Ur*, 237/238.

*89 C rev. 41. še-še gig ér gig i-lu še-bi-ta$^{II}$
           42. um-ma-šú-šú ......
           Bitter crying, bitter tears, wailing from its throat it
           "pours out," [dto.]

It is doubtful whether the first section of line 42 is indeed the predicate of line 41. The former contains portions from three different lines; see notes to *90, *104, and *105. The latter seems corrupt. Both are probably the result of a broken source; cf. also notes to *41 and *87.

še-še seems to be syllabic writing for $\text{še}_8\text{-še}_8 = bakû$.

*90 A 23.      mu-lu ka-na-ága-da ba-da-gur-ra-na
     C rev. 42. ...... ka-naga$_x$(NAG)-da .....
           Since the Master turned away from the nation,

Line A 23 is a clause dependent on A 24 (*91), which ends with -ta "since." As observed in notes to *89, line C rev. 42 contains portions from three different lines, but only the portion belonging to the present line is quoted here.

gur is interpreted *sakāpu* "to cast down" in the partial duplicate of our line, *SBH*, 46, obv. 41 f.: mu-lu ka-naga$_x$-da ba-an-da-gur-ra-e líl-lá-da <bí-in-ku$_4$> = [*be-lum*] *šá ma-a-ti is-ki-pu ana za-qi-qi* <*ú-tir-ru*> "The master who cast down his land turned it into a haunted place" (cf. *CAD*, *Z*, 59 s.v. *zaqīqu*). A similar motif of casting down Nippur occurs in *SK*, 5, ii 41 ff. For the replacement of the early spelling ka-na-ága by ka-nag-gá and ka-naga$_x$ in the late periods see *Kultlyrik*, 140.

*91 A 24. sag-gí[g-g]a-na gú-z[à-g]a bí-íb-lá-a-ta
   And from the Black-headed, the head lolls (lifeless) over the shoulder.

   About gú--lá and gú-zà--lá see Kramer, AS, 12, 41:224, Falkenstein, *ZA*, *48* (1944), 81 f. and OBGT, 15, 17 (*MSL*, *4*, 124). Jacobsen thinks that, contrary to *CAD*, *E*, s.vv. *edēru*, *egēru*, the translation *ni-en-gu-ru-um* in OBGT is correct. Our line forms one unit with *90.

## Stanza VII

(A: ki-ru-gú ⌈VII⌉-kam-ma)

| Lines | Texts |
|-------|-------|
|       | A     |
| 92    |       |
| 93    |       |
| 94    |       |
| 95    |       |
| 96    |       |
| 97    |       |
| 98    |       |

*92 A 25. gud-sún [e-l]um gud-sún mu-zu kur-kur-šè
   Wild Bull, Dignitary, Wild Bull, when your name is over the foreign lands,
*93 A 26. kur-gal a-a ᵈmu-u[l-líl]l gud-sún mu-zu kur-kur-šè
   Great Mountain, Father Enlil, Wild Bull, when your name is over the foreign lands,
*94 A 27. sipa sag-gíg-ga gud-sún mu-zu kur-kur-šè
   Shepherd of the Black-headed, Wild Bull, when your name is over the foreign lands,
*95 A 28. mu-zu kur-ra mu-un-ma-al-la-šè
   When your name rests over the mountains,
*96 A 29. kur elamᵏⁱ-ma m[u-u]n-ma-al-la-šè
   When it rests over the mountains of Elam,
*97 A 30. an-na úr-ba mu-un-ma-a[l-l]a-šè
   When it rests over the horizon,
*98 A 31. ki-a zà-ba mu-ma-al-la-šè
   When it rests over the farthest reaches of the earth.

## Stanza VIII

(A: ⌜ki⌝-ru-gú VIII-kam-ma)

| Lines | Texts | | | | | |
|---|---|---|---|---|---|---|
| | A | B | C | Cd | Ce | Ci |
| 99 | | | | | | |
| 100 | | | | | | |
| 101 | | | | | | |
| 102 | | | | | | |
| 103 | | | | | | |
| 104 | | | | | | |
| 105 | | | | | | |
| 106 | | | | | | |
| 107 | | | | | | |
| 108 | | | | | | |
| 109 | | | | | | |
| 110 | | | | | | |
| 111 | | | | | | |
| 112 | | | | | | |
| 113 | | | | | | |
| 114 | | | | | | |
| 115 | | | | | | |
| 116 | | | | | | |
| 117 | | | | | | |
| 118 | | | | | | |

*99   A 32.      me-na-šè me-na-šè
    B ii 1.      mi-na-še mi-na-še
    C rev. 44. me-na-šè me-na-šè
             How long? how long?

In text C this line is the catchline, which means it is the incipit line of the third tablet of the C series. It follows the fourth section of text C (= stanza VI) which implies that text C does not repeat the refrain stanza V (= VII = IX). Notice the inconsistency in the orthography of text B: in its first line (*28), the present expression is spelled mi-na-ši.

*100 A 33   ᵈmu-ul-líl me-na-šè
     B ii 2. mu-le-el mi-na-še
          Enlil, how long?
*101 A 34.   ᵈmu-ul-líl kur-kur-ra me-na-šè
          Enlil of the Foreign Lands, how long?
     B ii 3. kur-gal a-a ᵈen-líl-lá mi-na-še
          Great Mountain, Father Enlil, how long?

Notice the logographic (Emegir!) usage in the B line; the same orthography, with the exception of a-a, occurs also in B i 3 (*31). The sections A 32–35 and B ii 1–4 (*99–*102) are duplicates, except for this line.

*102 A 35.   sipa sag-gíg-ga me-na-šè
   B ii 4.   sa-pa sa-gi-ki-ga mi-na-še
            Shepherd of the Black-headed, how long?

The form sa-pa for sipa or su₈-ba is peculiar. About the possibility of reading GÍG as gikki$_x$ see Krecher in *Heidelberger Studien zum alten Orient* (= Falkenstein AV, 1967), p. 98 n. 14.

*103 B ii 5.      gu sa-an-zu-a du bi-du-la
                 You, who covered your neck and head wtih a cloth,
   C rev. 32. mu-lu sag-zu-a túg ba-e-dul!-la$^{II}$
                 You, Master who covered your head with a cloth, $^{dto.}$

Line Cd 50 reads: mu-lu sag-zu-a túg bi-dul-la èn-šè = *šá qa-qa-ad-ka ṣu-bat tu-kat-ti-mu.* Cf. also Ce 9 and Ci 14. About the syllabic spellings see pp. 31, ff., 41. As shown by sag-zu-a, the verb dul with the meaning "to cover" governs the locative case.

*104 A 19.      gú-zu úr-ra ba-e-ni-mar-ra ši-mah-en
   B ii 6.      gu-zi ú-ra bi-ni-ma-ra
   C rev. 33.   gú-zu úr-ra ba-e-ne-mar-ra$^{II}$
   C rev. 42b.  gú-zu úr-ra ba-e-ne-mar-ra$^{II}$
                (You,) who placed you neck between your thighs, (A: you
                are likewise exalted!) (C: $^{dto.}$)

The duplicates of this line are Ce 10, Ci 18, and Cd 51. The latter is accompanied by an Akkadian translation: *ki-šad-ka ina su-ni-ka taš-ku-na.* The prefix bi- in the B line is, as can be gleaned from the other recensions, a contraction of ba-e-. On the infix -e- of the second person see notes to *32. About the syllabic spellings of B see pp. 34, 37, 39, and 41.

Taking line A 19 out of its position in stanza VI and inserting it (and A 20) in this position, namely within stanza VIII, is dictated by the B recension. That the evidence of B is weightier than that of A is clear from several considerations; the connection between the two halves of A 19 (and of A 20) is not clear. An exclamation exalting Enlil (ši-mah-en) would not be expected after a line describing how Enlil ignores the plight of his people. Rather, one would expect a rhetoric question "until when?" This is precisely what is found in the Cd line quoted above. Furthermore, in stanzas VIII and X of text A, which are construed on a pattern almost identical with that of stanza VI, the refrain is repeated only five times—in the first four lines of the stanza. The main theme of the stanza is treated in two or four lines in the fifth to eighth lines of the stanza. If lines A 19–20 were left in stanza VI they would destroy this pattern and lengthen the refrain part of the stanza. They belong, it seems, in the thematic part of stanza VIII.

In the present line the last portion of C rev. 42 is quoted; the other portions of that line are quoted in *89 and *90, cf. notes ad loc.

*105 A 20.      šà-za èn-tar-bi ši-mah-en
               (You,) who takes counsel (only) with yourself (lit. "the one who asks his heart"), you are exalted!
    C rev. 39.  šà-zu èn-tar-bi mušen ši-bi-ta[II]
               (You,) who takes counsel only with yourself .... [dto.]

For quoting A 20 out of its original place in stanza VI see notes to *104. For translation of the second half of C rev. 39 see *87; it is obvious that the two halves of this line do not belong together. Similarly, C rev. 42 contains portions from three different lines; see notes to *89. Notice that this line is absent from the duplicates Cd, Ce, and Ci.

The image of lines *104/*105 is that of a person squatting and burying his "neck" (i.e. head) between his thighs; Enlil does not wish to see or hear the plight of his people. Lines *106–*107, and especially the Akkadian translation of line Cd 53 (see notes to *107), are further elaborations of this theme.

*106 C rev. 34.  šà-zu [gi]pisan-gin$_x$ èm-ba-e-šú-a[II]
               (You,) who covered your heart as (one covers) a basket, [dto]

An Akkadian translation of this line is offered in Cd 52: *lib-ba-ka kima pi-sa-an-nu tak-tu-mu.* Cf. also Ce 11 and Ci 20 (only traces left). On the prefix see Jacobsen AS, 16, 76, 81 n. 11.

*107 C rev. 35.  e-lum mu-uš-túg[geštug]-zu úr-ra mi-ni-íb-ús-si[a II]
               Dignitary, you leaned your ear on your lap, [dto.]

Cf. Cd 53: e-lum-e mu-uš-túg[geštug]-zu úr-ra mi-ni-íb-ús-sa èn-šè = *kab-tu šá ú-ba-na-ti-ka ina uz-ni-ka taš-ku-nu.* Notice that the Akkadian line is not a translation of the Sumerian; it simply introduces a new element into the motif of Enlil's ignoring his people. Translate: "Dignitary, you put your finger into your ear."[13] The mistranslation can perhaps be explained by the scribe's inadvertently skipping from the Sumerian line Cd 53 to the Akkadian translation of the next Sumerian line; this kind of mistake can be readily understood since the word *uznu* obviously occurred

---

13. Notice that in his translation of the Cd section in *The Intellectual Adventure of Ancient Man* (1946), 154, Th. Jacobsen translated only the Akkadian part of Cd 53. He privately suggested that the Sumerian version of this line originally could have been ... mu-uš-túg[geštug]-zu úr šu-si mi-ni-ib-ús-sa, but 𒋗𒋛 (šu-si) was erronously read 𒁉 which eventually resulted in the present version.

in both Akkadian lines—the translation of Cd 53 and that which he actually copied. Deimel's translation ús = šakānu (ŠL, 211, 60k) quotes the present Cd line as the only reference, but since the Akkadian line is not a translation of the Sumerian his equation should be ignored (but cf. *200).

*108 A 36.   š[à-b]a ᵘNAGAᵍᵃ·ᵐᵘšᵉⁿ-e šà-ab su$_x$-ud mu-un-ak-e
      B ii 7. ša [su]-ta mu-na-ka ša-pa ú-ga-e
              In (Nippur's) midst, the raven makes the heart unfathomable,

The B line is divided between two rubrics, but in the wrong order; the order of its two halves should be reversed thus: ša-pa ú-ga-e ša su-ta mu-na-ka. For šà su$_x$-ud cf. SBH, I (p. 130), 6 f.: umun kur-kur-ra šà sú-ud-da-ke₄ = be-lum ma-ta-a-tú li-ib ru-ú-qu "King (Akk. lord) of the foreign lands, fathomless heart;" see also van Dijk, SGL, 2, 95. On ugaᵐᵘšᵉⁿ see Hh XVIII 348 (MSL, 8/2, 152) and Hg D 350 (ibid. 176). On su$_x$(BU)-ud cf. notes to *13.

*109 A 37.   ᵘNAGAᵍᵃ·ᵐᵘšᵉⁿ-e [inim] ᵈmu-ul-líl-lá-šè šà su$_x$-ud mu-
              un-ak-e
              At the command of Enlil, the raven makes the heart fathomless,
      B ii 8. ú-ga-e i-ni-im mu-le-la-ke < ?>
              The raven, at the command of Enlil ...

The B lines seem to contain an unfinished sentence. Notice the deviation in B from standard Emesal: i-ni-im (which reflects the Emegir form) instead of e-ne-èm.

*110 A 38.  e-lum mu-lu ka-na-ága-da ba-da-sal-la-[x]
              Dignitary, the one who oppressed the nation,

The reading sal is doubtful; cf. however, SBH, 46, 43 f.: sag-gíg-ga-na ba-an-da-sal-la-e = šá ṣal-mat qa-qa-du ú-ma-az-zu-ú "who oppresses his Black-headed." See also Hallo, in Studies Presented to A. Leo Oppenheim (1964), 98, n. 28.

*111 A 39.  e-lum ᵈmu-ul-líl sag-gíg-ga-ni ba-da-lá-e-en-na
              Dignitary Enlil, his Black-headed are being reduced(?)

The interpretation of lá (with the infix -da-) as "reduce, decrease" is uncertain; cf., however, the occurrence of -da-lá in Gordon, Sumerian Proverbs, 1.43 (see his notes ad loc.), and 1.84.

*112 C rev. 36.  ᵈmu-ul-líl šu-zu-ta šu sá-a nu-ma-alⁱⁱ
                  Enlil, a hand equal to your hand does not exist, ᵈᵗᵒ·

Cf. *ASKT*, 21:59 f.: gašan-mèn šu-mu-ta šu sá-a nu-ma-al =
*be-lé-ku iš-ti qa-ti-ia qa-tu šá iš-ša-an-na-nu ul i-ba-áš-ši* (cf. Schollmeyer,
MVAG, 13/4, 16). An Emegir duplicate of this line is *SK*, 28:12 which,
however, is not accompanied by an Akkadian translation. We introduce the
section C rev. 36–38 at this point and not immediately after C rev. 35 (*107)
since the connection of this section to the preceding lines in text C is not
obvious and, at any rate, would not justify interrupting stanza VIII.

*113 C rev. 37. ᵈmu-ul-líl me-ri-zu-ta me-ri sá-a nu-ma-al$^{II}$
            Enlil, a foot equal to your foot does not exist, ᵈᵗᵒ·

Cf. *ASKT*, 21:63 f.: gašan-mèn me-ri-mu-ta me-ri sá-a nu-ma-
al = *be-lé-ku it-ti še-pe-ia še-pu šá iš-šá-an-nu-na ul i-ba-áš-ši* (cf. Schollmeyer loc. cit. and the duplicate Emegir line *SK*, 28:13, also *CT*, *42*, 3 vi 33).

*114 C rev. 38. za-ra dìm-me-er sá-a nu-è-a$^{II}$
            No god equal to you comes forth, ᵈᵗᵒ·

For the succeeding line in text C, namely rev. 39, see *105.

*115 B ii 9. el-lu-um-lu sa-an-du na-am-ta-ba-ra-e
            Dignitary, no man may come out to confront you.

The following analysis of this line was suggested by Th. Jacobsen: e-lum
mu-lu sag-du nam-ta-ba-ra-è. In our tentative translation we suggest
taking sag-du--è as a compound verb with the meaning "to come out head
first > to confront." This interpretation also fits well with the theme of the
last three lines (*112–*114).

The verb è = *waṣû* frequently occurs with the vetitive preformative
nam- (see notes to *62 and Jacobsen, AS, 16, 74) and with the prefix bara-
(Jacobsen, ibid.); see simply *ŠL*, 381:251d. The occurrence of both in the
same verbal chain is unusual; also, we cannot explain the appearance of the
preformative within the verbal chain and not at its head. For sa-an = sag see
p. 35 for el-lu-um-lu see p. 41. The germination in el-lu-um is unique.

*116 B ii 10. a-a mu-le-el ka-na-da gi-ú
            Father Enlil, return to the land!

The appearance of this line before a division line in text B is perhaps
meant to anticipate the theme of the next section in text B (*126 ff.). ka-na-
da = ka-na-ága-da with elision of the intervocalic /ǧ/; see p. 37. gi-ú is
syllabic spelling for gi₄-ù; see *126 f. In those lines, however, gi₄ is rendered
ki in text B. The use of the postposition -da with the verb gi₄ is uncommon;
ordinarily the terminative -šè is used. Or translate "turn away from the
land," i.e., stop harrassing it?

*117 C rev. 42. um-ma-šú-šú ka-naga$_x$-da gú-zu úr-ra ba-e-ne
                mar-ra$^{II}$

This line is a haphazard compilation of elements from three different lines; see *89, *90, and *104.

*118 C rev. 43. sag-gíg-ga-na gú-e ge₄-bi de₅-de₅-ga[II]
His Black-headed ... (Nippur's) girls are being pushed (?) [dto.]

This line is the last in text C; it is followed by a catchline (*99) and a colophon; see p. 58.

## Stanza IX

(A: ki-ru-gú IX-kam-ma)

| Lines | Texts A |
|-------|---------|
| 119   |         |
| 120   |         |
| 121   |         |
| 122   |         |
| 123   |         |
| 124   |         |
| 125   |         |

*119 A 40. gud-sún e-lum gud-sún mu-zu kur-kur-šè
Wild Bull, Dignitary, Wild Bull, when your name is over the foreign lands,

*120 A 41. kur-gal a-a ᵈmu-ul-líl gud-sún [mu-zu] kur-kur-šè
Great Mountain, Father Enlil, Wild Bull, when your name is over the foreign lands,

*121 A 42. sipa sag-gíg-ga [gu]d-sún mu-zu kur-kur-šè
Shepherd of the Black-headed, Wild Bull, when your name is over the foreign lands,

*122 A 43. mu-zu kur-ra mu-ma-al-[la-š]è
When your name rests over the mountains,

Notice the absence of the subject element -n- from the verbal chain, as against A 11 (*62) and A 28 (*95).

*123 A 44. kur elam[ki]-ma mu-un-ma-al-la-šè
When it rests over the mountains of Elam,

*124 A 45. an-na úr-b[a] mu-ma-[al]-la-šè
When it rests over the horizon,

Notice the absence of the subject element -n- from the verbal chain, as against the duplicate A lines 13 (*65) and A 30 (*97).

*125 A 46. ki-a zà-[ba] [m]u-ma-al-la-šè
        When it rests over the farthest reaches of the earth.

### Stanza X

### (A: ki-ru-gú X-kam-ma)

| Lines | | Texts | | | |
|---|---|---|---|---|---|
| | A | B | D | Da | Db |
| 126 | | | | | |
| 127 | | | | | |
| 128 | | | | | |
| 129 | | | | | |
| 130 | | | | | |
| 131 | | | | | |
| 132 | | | | | |
| 133 | | | | | |
| 134 | | | | | |
| 135 | | | | | |
| 136 | | | | | |
| 137 | | | | | |
| 138 | | | | | |
| 139 | | | | | |
| 140 | | | | | |
| 141 | | | | | |
| 142 | | | | | |
| 143 | | | | | |
| 144 | | | | | |
| 145 | | | | | |
| 146 | | | | | |
| 147 | | | | | |
| 148 | | | | | |
| 149 | | | | | |
| 150 | | | | | |
| 151 | | | | | |
| 152 | | | | | |

*126 A 47.    šà-ab gi₄-ù [šà-ab] gi₄-ù
    B ii 11. ša ki-ú ša ki-ú
        Restore (your) heart, restore (your) heart!

The Akkadian translation of the verb $gi_4$ in our context (see notes to *140) suggests that the verb should be interpreted as an intransitive, thus implying that the appeal is addressed to the heart of Enlil. It is clear, however, from the employment of the verb *saḫāru* that the translation is incorrect since that verb is otherwise unattested as translating $gi_4$. The implication of this appeal is that when Enlil is angry his heart is not in its proper place and its restoration marks pacification. This idea is more expressly stated in *SBH*, 30, rev. 6 f.: *lib-ba-ka lib-bi um-mi a-lit-tú ana áš-ri-šú li-tur*; for translation, duplicates and further references see *CAD*, *A*/1, 340 s.v. *ālidu* and Bergmann, *ZA*, 57 (1965), 42. The appeal for restoration of the heart appears at the end of letters (addressed to superiors) and at the end of eršaḫunga prayers; see M. Civil, in *Studies Presented to A. Leo Oppenheim* (1964), 89, Bergmann, loc. cit., and Hallo, *JAOS*, *88* (1968), 84:56.

*127 A 48.      $^d$mu-ul-líl šà-ab $gi_4$-ù
    B ii 12.      mu-le-el ša ki-ú
                Enlil, restore (your) heart!
*128 A 49.      $^d$mu-ul-líl kur-kur-ra šà-ab $gi_4$-ù
                Enlil of the Foreign Lands, restore (your) heart!
    D 1.        [e-lum-e umun kur-kur-ra šà-ab g]$i_4$-ù g[$i_4$-ù]
                Dignitary, King of the Foreign Lands, restore (your) heart,
                restore!
*129 D obv. 2.   [umun $du_{11}$-ga zi-da šà]-<ab $gi_4$-ù $gi_4$-ù>
                Master of the Fulfilled Speech, restore (your) heart,
                restore!
*130 D obv. 3.   [$^d$mu-ul-líl a-a ka-nag-gá š]à-<ab $gi_4$-ù $gi_4$-ù>
                Enlil, Father of the Nation, restore (your) heart, restore!
*131 A 50.      sipa sag-gíg-ga šà-ab $gi_4$-ù
                Shepherd of the Black-headed, restore (your) heart!
    D obv. 4.   [sipa sag-gìg-ga] šà-<ab $gi_4$-ù $gi_4$-ù>
                Shepherd of the Black-headed, restore (your) heart, restore!
*132 D obv. 5.   [ur-sag i-bí-$du_8$ ní]-te-en šà-<ab $gi_4$-ù $gi_4$-ù>
                The Warrior, the One Inspecting for Himself, restore (your)
                heart, restore!

ní-te-en instead of the usual ní-te-na is also attested in Cc 8 (*54).
Haa 12 (*243) has ní-te-en-na.

*133 D obv. 6.   [umun am erín-na] di-di šà-<ab $gi_4$-ù $gi_4$-ù>
                The Lord, the Warrior Who Leads the Troops, restore
                (your) heart, restore!
*134 D obv. 7.   [ur-sag ù-lul]-la ku-ku šà-<ab $gi_4$-ù $gi_4$-ù>
                The Warrior Who Feigns Sleep, restore (your) heart,
                restore!

*135 D obv. 8.   [umun ᵈ]am-an-ki šà-<ab-gi₄-ù gi₄-ù>
                 The Lord Enki, restore (your) heart, restore!

*136 D obv. 9.   ur-sag ᵈasal-lú-hi šà-<ab gi₄-ù gi₄-ù>
                 The Warrior Asalluhi, restore (your) heart, restore!

*137 D obv. 10a. umun ᵈen-bi-lu-lu šà-<ab gi₄-ù gi₄-ù>:
                 The Lord Enbilulu, restore (youɪ) heart, restore!

*138 D obv. 10b. ur-sag ᵈmu-zé-eb-sa₄-a šà!-<ab gi₄-ù gi₄-ù>
                 The Warrior Mudugasa'a, restore (your) heart, restore!

This epithet was accidentally omitted by the scribe who realized his mistake only after he had written the next line. The order of the epithets being canonical, he had to add this line in the space normally reserved (and left blank) for the refrain. To indicate that the two half-lines should be separated, he inserted two small wedges. The šà at the end of the line is written KI.

*139 D obv. 11. umun ᵈdi-ku₅-mah-àm šà-<ab gi₄-ù gi₄-ù>
                The Lord Dikumah, restore (your) heart, restore!

The function of the copula -àm in this line is not clear.

*140 A 51.      šà-ab gi₄-ù gi₄-ù e-ne-ra tuku-àm
                "Restore (your) heart, restore" belongs to him,

     B ii 12.   mu-le-el ša ki-ú
         13.    i-ni-ra tu-ku-a
                "Enlil, restore your heart!" belongs to him,

     D obv. 12. šà-ab gi₄-ù gi₄-ù dè-ra-an-tuku-a
          13.   *lib-bu tu-ra-am* ɪɪ *liq-qa-bi-ka*
                Sum.: Let "Restore (your) heart, restore!" belong to you,
                Akk.: Let "Return, o heart, return!" be said to you,

Line B ii 12 is repeated here because, it seems, B ii 13 is dependent on it (see *127). The ɪɪ mark in the Akkadian line of D stands for the repetition of the verb. A duplicate of the D lines is Da 30 f. (cf. Langdon, OECT, 6, 1 ff.): šà-ab gi₄-ù gi₄-ù de-en-na-an-tuku-a = *lib-bu na-ás-hi-ra* ɪɪ *liq-qa-bi-šum*: Let 'O heart, turn around, dto.' be said to him." On the incorrectness of the translation see notes to *126.

The personal pronoun of the third person in B ii 13 shows an /i/ vowel. The same form is attested in *Ur-Nammu* 3/54. The initial sign of the pronoun in text A looks as if it has been erased both in line 51 and 52 (*141). This may indicate that some irregularity existed concerning the initial vowel. At any rate, before the Akkadian translation was introduced into a-ab-ba hu-luh-ha, the initial vowel of e-ne-ra ("to him") was lost (cf. also Ca 50 ff.). The loss of that vowel caused the scribes in the late periods to interpret the remaining NE-(ra) as the jussive preformative dè- which figures predominantly in Emesal texts and is usually translated into Akkadian by the third person precative passive (see Jacobsen, *AS*, *16*, 72 f.). This misunderstanding resulted in the employment of the N stem precative in the Akkadian translations of the D versions. Elision of the /m/ of the final -àm also facilitated the misunderstanding.

e-ne-ra tuku-àm "it belongs to him" is a new form of the refrain "it is thine/mine." Normally it occurs without the verb tuku but simply in the form of the pronoun followed by the genitive postposition and the copula; cf. za-a-kam bí-in-du$_{11}$-ga, *The Exaltation of Inanna*, 122, 133; with the dative postposition: za-(e-)ra; in the first person: gá-a-kam, (Hallo and van Dijk, YNER, 3, 94 f.). Cf. also the passage from *Enheduanna Hymn B* in which $^{d}$inanna za-kam = *ku-ma ištar*, Sjöberg, *RA*, *60* (1966), 92. Finally, cf. za-e bí-du$_{11}$ in *202 f.

It is clear that the present function of tuku was not understood by the neo-Assyrian and Seleucid scribes. It is hard to say, however, why they translated it as *qabū*; did they, like Deimel (*ŠL*, 574, 10), take it as a variant of dug$_4$? Several other such translations of tuku, all neo-Assyrian and Seleucid, are quoted by Deimel, ibid.

*141 A 52.    šà-ab hun-ù hun-ù e-ne-ra tuku-à
              "Calm down (your) heart, calm down!" belongs to him,
   B ii 14.    [ša h]u-mu hu-mu
              Calm down (your) heart, calm down!
   D obv. 14. šà hun-gá-ú hun-gá dè-ra-an-tuku-a
        15. *lib-bu nu-ha-am* II *liq-qa-bi-ka*
              Sum.: "Calm down (your) heart, calm down!" belongs to
                 you,
              Akk.: Let "Calm down (your) heart, calm down!" be said
                 to you,

The duplicate Da 32 has the same variants as Da 30 (see notes to *140). Its Akkadian translation reads (Da 33): *lib-bu nu-uh nu-uh* < *liq-qa-bi-ka* > "Let 'Calm down (your) heart, calm down!' be said to you." For general remarks on the translation see notes to *140. The gá in the form hun-gá-ù (notice that in the second verb the -ù is omitted) is, in all probability, used as a phonetic indicator intended to effect the pronunciation /huǧ/ for the preceding syllable; cf. notes to *41.

*142 B ii 15.   [mu-lu ši]-iš-ku-ra-ka
   B ii 16.   [xxx] mu-na-bé
             [The man of] prayers says [prayers] (?)
   D obv. 16. mu-lu siskur$_x$-ra-ke$_4$ siskur$_x$-ra dè-ra-ab-bé
        17. *šá ik-ri-bi ik-ri-bi liq-qa-bi-ka*
             Let the man of prayers say prayers to you,

Line D 16 is duplicated by Db 50. The B lines suggest a syllabic rendering of the D line, but it would be difficult to fit the missing signs at the beginning of the lines into the broken space if we assume that the lines do not start to the left of the vertical division line.

Notice that by inertia the verb *liqqabika* "let be said to you" in the Akkadian translation was carried over from the preceding lines, which resulted in a senseless Akkadian sentence. The mistake is duly corrected in the next line (*143). Notice also that in the B version the Sumerian verb is construed with a prefix mu-. It may well be that in the D versions the preformative dè- was carried over from the preceding lines by way of "harmonizing" the text. That it occurred at an early stage (if this is indeed the case) is clear from the duplicate lines Db 50 and 52 (Middle Assyrian). Db 51 and 53, reserved for Akkadian translation, are left blank.

On [ši]-iš-ku-r(a) = siskur$_x$ see p. 36.

*143 D obv. 18. mu-lu a-ra-zu-ke$_4$ a-ra-zu dè-ra-ab-bé
         .19. *šá tés-li-ti tés-li-ti liq-bi-ka*
         Let the man of supplications make supplications to you,

In this line the scribe dutifully corrected the mistake in the Akkadian translation—from *liqqabika* in *142 to *liqbika* here; see notes to *142 and cf. the duplicate Db 52.

*144 D obv. 20. an-uraš-a ki-še!-gu-nu-ra
         Heaven and earth, place of the spotted barley (?)

The meaning of this line, as well as its significance here, is not clear; for a discussion see Falkenstein, *ZA*, *52* (1957), 72 ff. (Add to his references: *SK*, 11, rev. v 2.) še-gu-nu is discussed in detail by Landsberger, *JNES*, *8* (1949), 281 f. with literary references. One may compare ki-še-gu-nu to ki-sum-ma "place of onions" which occurs in non-literary contexts; cf. Y. Rosengarten, *Le concept sumérien de consommation dans la vie économique et religieuse* (1960), 29 with n. 1 and passim.

The present line opens a section which seems to resemble a "genealogy of Enlil" (see van Dijk, *SGL*, *2*, 151 and *AcOr*, *28*, 6 ff.), but due to its fragmentary shape it is difficult to assess its exact nature.[14]

*145 D obv. 21. [x]-lum?-ma?-zu ᵈen-ki ᵈnin-ki
         Your . . . . . Enki and Ninki,

Restore, perhaps, [a-a e]-lum-ma-zu "Your dignified parents"; cf. however, a-a ugu-zu ᵈen-ki ᵈnin-ki siskur = *a-bu a-lid-ka* ᵈII ᵈII

---

14. It does not seem likely that we are dealing with the goddess Gunura, the daughter of Ninisina; see *Kultlyrik*, 123.

*ik-ri-bi*, Langdon, *BL*, no. 208, rev. 12 f. (/) Mark E. Cohen has called my attention to this text. Cf. also pp. 49f.

**\*146 D obv. 22.** [mud]na ki-ága-zu ama-gal ᵈnin-líl
Your beloved wife, the Great Mother Ninlil,

Cf. mudna ki-ága-zu ama-gal ᵈnin-líl a-ra-zu = *hi-ir-tum na-ram-ka um-mu* GAL-*tum* ᵈII *tes-li-ti*, Langdon, l. 14 f. For mudna, nitlam = *hīrtu* see *CAD*, *H*, s.v. *hīrtu*.

**\*147 D obv. 23.** [egí ni]n!-gal-zu ga-šà-an-kè[šᵏⁱ-ke₄]
The princess, your big sister, Nin-Keš,

For the restoration see Krecher, *Kultlyrik*, p. 61, VIII 13* and p. 208. Only traces of the sign before GAL are left, but they are not NIN. For egí = *rubâtu* see the references ibid., 155. Nin-Keš is described here as Enlil's sister, but she is also identical with Gašanhursag (= Ninhursag) who is Enlil's wife; see *Kultlyrik*, 208 and Falkenstein, *ZA*, *55* (1962), 25 n. 96. Notice the spelling ga-šà-an for ga-ša-an.

**\*148 D obv. 24.** [inim?]-ma-dè-dè ga-ša-an [nibruᵏⁱ]
The herald(?), Nin-Nibru

For the restoration see *CT*, *42*, 3 rev. iv 11 and *SBH*, I, rev. 23. The restoration is tentative, however, since in neither of these lines is inim complemented by -ma. Indeed, no verb inim--dé-dé can safely be estab-lished since whenever a phonetic indicator is provided, it shows the reading to be gù; cf., however, inim--du_{II}-du_{II}, YNER, 3, 79 and notes to *174. For Nin-Nibru see *Götterepitheta*, 416 and Emesal Voc. I 9. For inim--dè-dè = *šassā'itum* see Langdon, OECT, 6, 3:10 f.

**\*149 D obv. 25.** [uku]-uš kala-ga-zu umun ᵈ[nin-urta]
Your strong soldier, the lord Ninurta,

Ninurta's appellative is maškim kala-ga (see Römer, *Königshymnen*, 66 n. 225) but the sign following the break is definitely uš. For a possible reading dag-ga (instead of kala-ga) see Falkenstein, *JAOS*, *72* (1952), 43 n. 21.

**\*150 D obv. 26.** [sukk]al-mah-zu [kingal ᵈnusku]
Your "grand vizier," the commander Nusku,

For the restoration see Langdon, *BL*, no. 208, rev. 16. For Nusku as "grand vizier" and commander (kingal = *mu'irru*) of Enlil see van Dijk *SGL*, *2*, 122 ff., 130 f., and Lu, I, 110 f. (*MSL*, *12*, 96).

**\*151 D obv. 27.** [dumu] ki-ága-zu [gašan-an-na-ke₄]
**\*152 D obv. 28.** [umun]-si-[gal umun-guruš-a-ke₄]

The restoration of lines *151 and *152 is according to the suggestion of W. W. Hallo, on the basis of TCL 6 57: obv. 3, 7; *BL* 70 = *BL* 92 obv. 7.

## Stanza XI

### (A: ki-ru-gú XI-kam-ma)

| Lines | Texts | | |
|-------|-------|------|------|
|       | A | Ea | Eb |
| 153 |  |  |  |
| 154 |  |  |  |
| 155 |  |  |  |
| 156 |  |  |  |
| 157 |  |  |  |
| 158 |  |  |  |
| 159 |  |  |  |
| 160 |  |  |  |
| 160a |  |  |  |
| 161 | skipped |  |  |
| 162 | skipped |  |  |
| 163 | skipped |  |  |
| 164 | skipped |  |  |
| 165 | skipped |  |  |
| 166 | skipped |  |  |
| 167 | skipped |  |  |
| 168 | skipped |  |  |
| 169 | skipped |  |  |
| 170 | skipped |  |  |
| 171 |  |  |  |

*153 A 53. am al-ná te mu-un-zi-zi
        The Wild Ox is asleep, when will he rise?
   Ea 1. [am al-n]á te nu-un-zi-zi
      2. [*be-lum*] *šá ṣal-lu mi-nam la i-te-e*[*b-bi*]
        The Wild Ox (Akk.: who) is asleep, why does he not rise?

See the duplicates Eb 19 ff.: am al-ná te nu-um-zi-zi: te-nu-[xxx] = *be-lum šá ṣal-lu mi-nam la i-da-ab-*[*x*] (21) *be-lum šá ṣal-lum mi-nam la i-te-eb-bi*. For a possible restoration of Ea 20 (*i-da-ab-*[*bu-ub*]) see *CAD*, Ṣ, 67 s.v. *ṣalālu* (bilingual section).

The meaning "when?" for te is suggested by Th. Jacobsen. It seems that the discrepancy between the Old Babylonian text A and the Seleucid texts Ea and Eb concerning the verb (positive vs. negative) stems from the fact that the unfamiliar particle te was known only with the meaning "why?" in the late periods, the meaning "when?" having been forgotten. The scribes were compelled, therefore, to insert the negative preformative nu- so that the sense of the line within the framework of the composition be retained. The same discrepancy between the A and E versions obtains throughout the stanza.

The general sense conveyed by this line is that the plight of Enlil's people is ascribed to his indifference towards them, an attitude symbolized by his sleep. (Is this concept the origin of Enlil's seventh epithet, "he who sleeps a false sleep?")

The theme of the "Sleeping Enlil" is treated in the following passage (*IV, R*, 23 no. 1 i 26–31): [mu-lu] ná-a e-lum mu-lu ná-a èn-šè ba-an-ná-a = [šá] ṣal-lu be-lum šá ṣal-lum a-di ma-ti ṣa-lil; kur-gal a-a ᵈmu-ul-líl-lá mu-lu ná-a èn-šè = KUR-ú GAL-ú a-bu ᵈII šá ṣal-lum a-di mat; sipa na-ám-tar-tar-ra mu-lu ná-a èn-šè = re-'u mu-šim ši-ma-a-ti šá ṣal-lum a-di mat.

*154 A 54. ᵈmu-ul-líl al-ná te mu-un-zi-zi
        Enlil is asleep, when will he rise?
  Ea 3. [ᵈmu]-ul-líl-lá am al-ná[....]
     4. ᵈNINNU be-lum ša ṣal-lu mi-nam la i-te-eb-[bi]
        Sum.: Enlil, the Wild Ox is asleep, why does he not rise?
        Akk.: Enlil, the Lord who is asleep, why does he not rise?

For the identity of ᵈNINNU with Enlil see *Götterepitheta*, 429. On p. 47 we called attention to the fact that text Ea always translates am by *bēlu*. Cf. the duplicate Eb 22.

*155 A 54a. alim-ma al-ná te mu-un-zi-zi
        The Dignitary is asleep, when will he rise?
  Ea 5. alim-ma am al-ná te <nu-un-zi-zi>: kab-tu be-lum šá
      ṣal-lu mi-na[m la i-te-eb-bi]
      The Dignitary, Wild Ox (Akk.: who) is asleep, why does he not rise?

Cf. the duplicate line Eb 23. Line A 54a was inadvertently omitted by the scribe and added on the left edge after the colophon had already been written. The latter counts seventy lines whereas the text proper contains seventy-one lines, including the present one. The place where the line belongs is shown by a ruled line continuing over to the left edge between lines 54 and 55. For similar cases see l. *6, Kramer, *JCS*, *4* (1950), 206 n. 45 and Hallo, *JCS*, *24* (1971), 39 n. 1. For alim-ma see notes to *174; similarly see *9 ff.

*156 A 55. nibru^ki-a dur-an-ki-ri te mu-un-zi-zi
          In Nippur, over the Duranki, when will he rise?
     Ea 6. a-a ^dmu-ul-líl-lá urú-na nibru^ki te <nu-un-zi-zi>:
          *a-bi* ^dNINNU *a-lu ni-ip-pu-[ru]*
          Sum.: Father Enlil, in his city Nippur why does he not rise?

Cf. Eb 24. Duranki (lit. "Bond of Heaven and Earth") is an epithet of Nippur or one of its sectors; cf. *Königshymnen*, 247. For the postposition -ri "over" see notes to *13.

*157 A 56. nibru^ki ki nam-tar-tar-ri te mu-un-zi-zi
          Over Nippur, the Place of Fate-deciding, when will he rise?

The employment of the reduplicated form of the verb in this epithet of Nippur is uncommon, but it occurs also in *189. The Akkadian translation of this phrase is found in *KAR*, 375 ii 60 f.: [x]-zé-bi ki na-ám-tar-ra-[ke₄] = [x]-*zé-eb a-šar šim-tum iš-ša-mu-[ú]*; notice that the Akkadian is not a literal translation of the Sumerian; cf. also notes to *153.

The compound verb nam--tar occurs as early as Eannatum (Sollberger, *Système Verbal*, 243). The Akkadian translation of the verb always offers the figura etymologica *šimtam šâmu* quoted above. Perhaps this is the origin of the lexical entry tar = *šá-a-mu* in *CT*, *12*, 35 i 1 (Nabnitu IV). For other occurrences of the verb see Zimmern, *ZA*, *39* (1930), 272; Falkenstein, *SGL*, *1*, 103, and cf. especially the discussion by Jacobsen, *ZA*, *52* (1957), 101 n. 13. Eb 25 reads at this point alim-ma = *kab-tu* [....]

*158 A 57. é ši ka-na-ág-gá mu-ma-al-la-ri te mu-un-zi-zi
          Over the temple which he set up for the life of the land, when
          will he rise?

The Akkadian translation of this line occurs in Eb rev. 2: é *šá ana na-piš-tum ma-a-tim iš-sak-nu*. The "temple which he set up for the life of Sumer" is a reference to the Ekur, as is clear from the *Hymn to Enlil*, 69: sahar-bi zi kalam-ma zi kur-kur-ra-ka "Its (Nippur's) ground is the life of Sumer, the life of the foreign countries;" the Ekur is Nippur's temple par excellence. Enlil's attribute en zi-kalam-ma (*Götterepitheta*, 307) is probably derived from the same concept.[15]

*159 A 58. ši kur-kur-ra mu-ma-al-la-ri te mu-un-zi-zi
          Over (the temple) which he set up for the life of the foreign
          countries, when will he rise?

15. For a temple bearing the same name in Zabalam see *RLA*, *2*, 489; for the correct reading ZA.SUH.UNU^ki = zabalam^ki (and not Hallab) see Falkenstein–Matouš, *ZA*, *42* (1934), 148 f. For é zid-ka-nag-gá(?) in Kullab see *RLA*, ibid.

This line contains, it seems, another reference to the Ekur; compare
*Hymn to Enlil*, 69, quoted in notes to *158.

*160 Ea 7. é-kur-ra é šà-ge-pà-da [ᵈmu-ul-líl-lá(?)]
    8. *šá* É II *bi-it i-tu-ut kun-nu lìb-ba-[x]*
        Sum.: The Ekur, the temple chosen by the steadfast heart (of
            Enlil)
        Akk.: The Ekur, the temple of the choice of the steadfastness
            of his (?) heart,

Cf. Eb rev. 4 and *SBH*, 5:22. The Akkadian line is divided in two, with a
scribal note inserted between the two halves; see *161.

Line *160 contains yet another epithet of the Ekur; for further references
see *Kultlyrik*, 81. é šà-ge-pà-da is also the name of a temple built by
Šu-Suen for Šara in Umma; see his building inscriptions nos. 4, 8, and 9
(references in Hallo, *HUCA*, *33* [1962], 37 f.). For ᵈnin-šà-ge-pà-da see
UET, 8, 18 (Ur-Nammu). šà-pà-da-DN "called by the heart of DN"
occurs in royal titles of the early periods, from Eannatum to Ur III, as part of
the official titulary, sometimes with šà qualified by an adjective; see Hallo,
*Royal Titles*, 134. The Akkadian *itūt kun libbi* is attested once in the prism of
Tiglatpileser I and several times in royal inscriptions of the late periods; see
*CAD*, I/J, 317 s.v. *itūtu* A for references. Our line is not quoted there but
it is quoted in *AHw*, 407 s.v. *itūtu* A.

*160a Ea 8 (a). 34 MU.MEŠ GUD.MEŠ
             34 lines skipped.

This line is inscribed between the two halves of the Akkadian line Ea 8.
For the scribal custom of skipping lines see Meissner, *OLZ*, *11* (1908),
405 ff., where he identifies from duplicates some of the lines skipped in *SBH*
texts. The lines skipped by the scribe of Ea can be partly retrieved in text Eb,
for which see the following lines. The unknown lines are not brought into
consideration in the numbering of the lines of the Composite Text.

*161 Eb rev. 5. é-ki-ùr-ra-AŠ é ᵈnin-líl-lá-ke₄
            The Ekiur, the temple of Ninlil,

The reading and the syntactic function of AŠ are not clear. About the Ekiur
see *RLA*, *2*, 322. This temple is also recorded in the map of Nippur (Kramer,
*From the Tablets of Sumer* [1956], 274). Some further references are é-gi₄-a-
mah ki-ùr-ra (YBC, 4705:5; letter of Sin-iddinam to Ninisina, reference

courtesy of W. Hallo); van Dijk, *AcOr*, *28*, 27 n. 67a (geographic name?); Frankena, *Tākultu*, 125:149; Kramer, *PAPS*, *107* (1963), 503:64, and *JCS 18* (1964), 44, both referring to *CT*, *42*, 13:63 f.), and C. J. Gadd, *Iraq*, *22* (1960), 164. Cf. also *CAD*, *D*, s.v. *durušsu*.

**\*162 Eb rev. 6. é-nam-ti-la-AŠ é ᵈmu-ul-líl-la-ke₄**
The Enamtila, the temple of Enlil,

See *RLA*, *2*, 369 about this "House of Life."

**\*163 Eb rev. 7. é-MI-tum-ma-al-AŠ éᵈnin-líl-la-ke₄**
The EMItummal, the temple of Ninlil, ˙

For the reading tum-ma-al (and not íb-) see E. I. Gordon, *BASOR*, *132* (1953), 29 n. 18, and Sjöberg, *JCS*, *13*, 59. On the Tummal inscription see Sollberger, *JCS*, *16* (1962), 40 ff. Kramer, *The Sumerians* (1963), 46 ff. For é-MI *Kultlyrik*, 110 f.

**\*164 Eb rev. 8. šà é-dimₓ-ma-AŠ *qe-reb-šu-ma* éᵈmu-ul-líl-la-ke₄**
In the Edimma, the temple of Enlil,

About the reading and possible meaning of dimₓ (LÚ + GAM) see *MSL*, *2*, 78 to 632 and *Kultlyrik*, 83. The Akkadian gloss may have been inserted here because of this line's deviation from the pattern set by the preceding ones. This temple epithet occurs also in line \*266.

**\*165 Eb rev. 9. ma-nun-mah-àm ᵈmu-ul-líl-lá-[ke₄]**
The Main Storehouse of Enlil

The function of the copula -àm is not clear. ma-nun is the Emesal form of gá-nun "storehouse," see also \*45.

**\*166 Eb rev. 10. ká še-nu-ku₅-AŠ ᵈmu-ul-líl-lá-[ke₄]**
The Gate of Uncut Barley

The Gate of Uncut Barley is one of the gates of the Ekur and not of the city (these are called KÁ.GAL = abul; see \*168). Leaving the barley uncut at this gate seems to have been a matter of religious obligation; in *The Curse of Agade*, 125 f., Naram-Sin is accused of having committed an act of sacrilege by cutting the barley at this gate. For further references see Falkenstein, *ZA*, *57* (1965), 98 f.

**\*167 Eb rev. 11. i₇-ninnu-AŠ ᵈmu-ul-líl-lá-[ke₄]**
The Ninnu-canal of Enlil,

This canal may be one of the two moats simply marked *hi-ri-tum* in the
Nippur map (nos. 17, 18; see notes to *161).

*168 Eb rev. 12. abul-mah ᵈmu-ul-líl-lá-[ke₄]
               The Glorious Gate of Enlil,

The Glorious (City)-Gate is a gate in the southwest wall of Nippur,
marked on the map of Nippur (no. 11; see notes to *161). For the reading
abul (KÁ.GAL) see *CAD, A,* s.v. *abullu,* but cf. Sjöberg's suggested reading
abulla in *RA, 60* (1966), 91.

*169 Eb rev. 13. abul-la ki ᵈutu-è-a[....]
         14.  <    > *a-šar ṣi-it* ᵈUTU<    >
               Sum.: The Eastern (lit. "place of sunrise") Gate,
               Akk.: Place of sunrise,

The Eastern Gate is not shown on the Nippur map (see notes to *161), but
it can be the Nanna Gate or the Uruk Gate, both in the southeast wall of the
city (nos. 13 and 14). For the third gate in that wall see *170.

*170 Eb rev. 15. abul-la i-bí urí[ᵏⁱ-šè]
               The Gate Facing Ur,

The Gate Facing Ur is in the southeast wall of Nippur and is shown on the
Nippur map (no. 15; see notes to *161). Notice the rendering of the name in
Emesal and the omission of the possessive suffix (due to haplology i-bí-bi >
i-bí?).

*171 Ea 9.  umun ka-nag-gá é-dàra-an-na
      10.  *be-lum ma-a-tú ana* É II
               King of the land, (Akk. from [?]) Edara'anna,

The location of Edara'anna ("House of the Heavenly Ibex") is not known,
but Babylon is a possibility, cf. *RLA, 2,* 266 and notes to *261. For further
literary references to this temple see *RLA,* ibid. to which add *SBH,* 5, obv.
23, and cf. *ŠL,* 100:13.
    dàra-an-na is an epithet of Enki: see Jacobson, *Tammuz,* 7, 22 and cf.
his epithet dàra-nun-na (*Götterepitheta,* 287). Compare also the name of
the Uruk ruler en-nun-dàra-an-na, *The Sumerian King List* iii 29
(Jacobsen, AS, 11 [1939], 90 f.).

## Stanza XII

### (A: ki-ru-gú xii-kam-ma)

| Lines | Texts | | | |
|-------|-------|---|----|----|
|       | A     | B | Ea | Eb |
| 172   |       |   |    |    |
| 173   |       |   |    |    |
| 174   |       |   |    |    |
| 175   |       |   |    |    |
| 176   |       |   |    |    |
| 177   |       |   |    |    |
| 178   |       |   |    |    |
| 179   |       |   |    |  ? |
| 180   |       |   |    |    |
| 181   |       |   |    |    |
| 182   |       |   |    |    |
| 183   |       |   |    |    |
| 184   |       |   |    |    |

*172 A 59.     am ná-dè dè-en-zi-zi
              The sleeping Wild Ox, let him rise!
    Ea 11.    am du₇-du₇ te nu-um-zi-zi
        12.   *be-lum mut-tak-bu mi-na la i-te-eb-ba*
              The goring Wild Ox, why does he not rise?

Cf. Eb rev. 16 f. In both texts, Ea and Eb, the present line follows a division line. In text E, as far as can be judged from the remaining parts of Ea, a new string of Enlil's attributes starts at this point. But the theme is a mere repetition of the theme of the previous section, whereas the new theme of text A is absent from text Ea. This leads to the conclusion that the present sections in Ea (11 ff.) and in Eb (rev. 16 ff.) are roughly the parallels of stanza XII of A. But just as the theme of stanza XI ("when will he rise?") is distorted in the E texts (see notes to *153), so is the theme of stanza XII ("let him rise!"). The result is a third theme ("why does he not rise?") which in the late versions Ea and Eb runs through the two stanzas. The replacement of ná-dè by du₇-du₇ cannot be readily explained. On *nakābu* see the Glossary sub du₇-du₇.

*173 A 60.     ᵈmu-ul-líl ná-dè dè-en-zi-zi
              The sleeping Enlil, let him rise!
    Ea 13a.   ᵈmu-ul-líl-lá am du₇-du₇ te <nu-um-zi-zi> :
              Enlil, the goring Wild Ox, why does he not rise?

The grammatically unwarranted -lá in the Ea-line appears also in Ea 6 (*156) and in Ea 14a (*175). The line marked Ea 13a is the first half of Ea 13. The second half, marked Ea 13b, is quoted in *174. The same applies to Ea 14a (*175) and Ea 14b (*176). The two halves are separated by Glossen-keil's. All that is left of Eb 18 is a ZU sign which indicates that it is not a duplicate of Ea 13a. The duplicate is probably Eb rev. 19 (mistakenly marked 20 in the autographed copy).

*174 A 61.    alim-ma ná-dè dè-en-zi-zi
             The sleeping Dignitary, let him rise!
  Ea 13b. alim-ma am du₇-du₇ te <nu-um-zi-zi>
             The Dignitary, goring Wild Ox, why does he not rise?

The duplicate of this line is probably Eb rev. 20. The -ma in the A line is grammatically unjustified and is probably intended to indicate the reading alim for the preceding sign. Such phonetic complements were introduced already in the Old Sumerian period; see, e.g., é-an-na-túm lú inim-ma-sì-ga ᵈnin-gír-su-ka-ke₄ "Eannatum, the one given command by Ningirsu" (Sollberger, *Corpus*, Eannatum 2 vi 14–16). In late texts redundant elements abound in the orthography and not all can be accounted for. As a rule we do not indicate their function except for the cases in text C 9 ff. (*9 ff.) where the complements are written above the line in small characters.

*175 Ea 14a. a-a ᵈmu-ul-líl-lá umun kur-kur-ra:
             Father Enlil, King of the Foreign Lands,

As observed on p. 27, the E recensions share with text A the tradition of Enlil's attributes. Yet, whereas text A always mentions three attributes, the E texts in the present section elaborate on them and quote five. In text Ea they are arranged in three lines (11, 13 f.) and in Eb in five (rev. 16–22). The refrain is missing in this line and the next; see also *195 f. Cf. Eb rev. 21.

*176 Ea 14b. alim-ma umun nibru^{ki}
             Dignitary, Lord of Nippur,

Cf. the duplicate Eb rev. 22.

*177 A 62. gud-niga á-gur-gur-ra dè-en-zi-zi
             Among the rebellious, fattened bulls, let him rise!

For the reading ŠE = niga, nigu, or nigan see *JNES*, 4 (1945), 156 nn. 6–7; Proto Ea 690 (*MSL*, 2, 83); Sᵃ Voc. Ad 9' (*MSL*, 3, 84); Hh XIII 2 (*MSL*, 8/1, 7), and its Nippur forerunner 1 (ibid. 83). gud-niga is translated *ma-ru-ú* in Hh XIII 303 (ibid. 44). For the etymology of niga etc. see Landsberger, *MSL*, 3, 213 to 690.

á-gur "obstinate, rebellious" (lit. "limb twisting") in connection with bulls and oxen is well attested in literary texts; see Falkenstein, *GSGL, 1*,

26, 27 n.2; *SGL,1*, 131; *ZA*, *56* (1964), 52; van Dijk, *SGL*, *2*, 141, and
Heimpel, *Tierbilder in der sumerischen Literatur*, Studia Pohl, 2 (Rome, 1968),
95. Here the form is reduplicated to denote plural.

*178 A 63.  udu en-zi šà-gada-lá-a-da dè-en-zi-zi
                Among the choice sheep of the linen-clad priest, let him rise!
       Ea 15.  e-zé èm-kú-e šà-gada! (text: BA)-lá-a-ta
           16.  *şe-e-nu ina a-kal-lu lìb-bi a-di la in-ni-[x]*
                Sum.: With the fattened sheep of the linen-clad priest, let
                him rise!

Cf. the duplicate line Ea 23 (with the adjoining fragment, *SBH*, p. 152):
[e]-zé èm-[kú-e] šà-gada! (text: NA?)-lá-a. From the two E versions it
becomes clear that the Seleucid scribes did not understand the term šà-
gada-lá, whose proper Akkadian translation is *lābiš kitê* "linen-clad priest"
(Lu IV, 99 = *MSL*, *12*, 131). This resulted in copying gada (KÁD) as BA in
text Ea (collated from a photograph) and as NA(?) in Eb. The Akkadian translation of Ea speaks volumes to that effect: not having understood the Sumerian
(which may have been corrupted already in his Vorlage), the scribe tried a
verbatim translation of whatever he did understand. Thus he translated šà by
*libbi* and kú (which is part of a designation of a kind of sheep) by *a-kal-lu*
(collated from a photograph), i.e. "food", a form otherwise unattested
(except in *179) with a geminated /l/. The *ina* is completely out of place,
but it is not repeated in the next line. We cannot make any sense out of the rest
of the Akkadian line. e-zé èm-kú-e of text Ea, on the other hand, shows
that at least at this point text Ea relied on a tradition different from that of A.
The form is the Emesal equivalent of udu-niga (Emesal Voc. II 90); cf.
also the remarks concerning gud-niga in notes to *177.

For šà-gada-lá see *CAD*, *G*, s.v. *gadalallû*, and Falkenstein, *ZA*, *56*
(1964), 68, and *SGL*, *1*, 99. Notice the absence of the refrain from Ea 15 and
17 (*178 f.) For the replacement of -da (in A) by -ta (in E) see Poebel, *GSG*,
§ 37.

*179 A 64.  ud$_x$ ne-èm-àr-ra-kú-a-da dè-en-zi-zi
                Among the grist-fed goats, let him rise!
       Ea 17.  e-zé èm-kú-e kú-a-t[a]
           18.  *şe-e-nu a-kal-lu ina a-kal-lu*
                Sum.: Among the fattened sheep, fed ⟨on grist(?)⟩

In this line, as in the preceding one, the traditions of A and Ea differ on
the animal mentioned; the latter simply repeats the same animal. On the
other hand, it seems that the designation of the food on which the sheep
mentioned here are fed has been omitted from the Ea line. In Emegir this
line would read: udu-niga ⟨x⟩-kú-a-ta (translation above) where the
⟨x⟩ symbolizes the omitted element. In this line, as in the previous one, the

Akkadian line seems to be a word-by-word rendering, and it does not constitute a full sentence; see in general notes to *178.

For the reading $ud_x$ (= UZ) see Hh XIII 192a (*MSL, 81, 28*) with notes; for ne-èm(= níg)-àr-ra = *mundu* "grist, fine flour," see Oppenheim, *Eames Collection*, 61ª and *AHw* s.v. *mundu*.

The assumed duplicate of the present line, Eb rev. 24 is fragmentary.

*180 A 65. gukkal-guru$_x$(E.íB)-lá-lá-da dè-en-zi-zi
        Among the fat-tailed, banded sheep, let him rise!

   Ea 19. gukkal-íB-lá-a-ta te nu-um-zi-zi
      20. *gu-uk-kal-lum ina* UK-*ba-ti-šú a-li-lum mi-nam la i-te-eb-ba*
        Sum.: Among the fat-tailed, banded sheep, why does he not rise?
        Akk.: The fat-tailed sheep whose tail is tied, why does he not rise?

It seems that guru$_x$ (= E.íB) should be connected with $^{kuš}$E.íB = *misarru*, *mēzehu* "leather strap," Hg to Hh XI 172 (*MSL, 7, 151*; for the reading guru$_x$ see *AHw* s.v. *misarru*). gukkal-guru$_x$-lá = *zibbānu* is a fat-tailed sheep (gukkal < kun-gal) on which a band was tied (guru$_x$-lá) for marking, cf. Hh XIII 26 (*JNES, 4* [1945], 156; *MSL, 8/1, 9, CAD, G* s.v. *gukkallu*). The Akkadian translation of the term implies only a large tail, but not marking, cf. *CAD, G*, ibid. The leather determinative is omitted in our line possibly because the band used on the sheep was not a leather one. The spelling íB for E.íB, attested in the Ea line above is also attested in the entry Hh XIII 26.

UK-*ba-ti-šú* in the Akkadian version of Ea may be a scribal error for *zib-ba-ti-šú*. (The reading UK is certain.) *a-li-lum* may be an otherwise unattested *parīs* adjective formation from *alālu* "to tie, suspend." Line Ea 20 seems to be another case of a verbatim translation in text Ea (see notes to *178 f.): *zib!-ba-ti-šú* "its tail"—perhaps a corruption of *zibbānu*—reflects íB-lá, whereas *a-li-lum* might reflect a second lá which may have been in the source of text Ea, just as it is found in text A, marking the plural.

*181 B iii 1. [...... ti]-in-zi-zi
     .... let him rise!

*182 B iii 2. [...n]i-ib-ru du-ra-an-ki-ra-ka
     .... of Nippur, the Bond of Heaven and Earth,

About the Duranki see notes to *155. For other syllabic spellings of nibru$^{ki}$ and dur-an-ki see Bergmann, *ZA, 56* (1964), 8 f. The extra -ra- is enigmatic.

*183 B iii 3. a-li-ma-ha nu le-el-di ti-in-zi-zi
        The sleeping, exalted Dignitary, with the wind let him rise!

The translation of this line is suggested by Th. Jacobsen, who analyzes it as follows: alim maha ná líla-da dè-en-zi-zi. nu for ná is attested in one manuscript of S[b] II 374 (*MSL, 3,* 152, note ad loc. and *MSL, 8/1,* 55 n. 1 and 66 n. 1.). For the sandhi form see p. 42.

Introducing B iii 1 ff. at this point is motivated by the identity of its refrain with that of A stanza XII; Nippur and the Duranki, however, are not mentioned in that stanza of text A.

**\*184 B iii 4. i-ni-ma-ni-lu-i-lu**
            His words: "Wailing, wailing."

This line is the syllabic rendering of inim-a-ni i-lu i-lu (notice that it contains a case of sandhi, see p. 42). Two ruled lines over and under this line separate it from the preceding and succeeding lines respectively. They indicate that it is the incipit line of a section, probably a refrain section which is to be recited at this point. As suggested above, pp. 22 f., text B is extra-canonical since it served only as an aid in teaching (or memorizing) a-ab-ba hu-luh-ha for recitation. Apparently a well-known section had to be recited at this point so there was no need to write it down entirely and the incipit line was sufficient. In fact, a stanza beginning with these words (in standard Emesal orthography: e-ne-èm-mà-ni etc.), and in which the subsequent lines begin e-ne-èm DN etc., occurs in the Old Babylonian text *CT, 42,* 15 ii 9 ff. The same line (also in standard Emesal orthography) is entered in the neo-Assyrian catalogue *IV, R,* 53, 19 as the incipit of a balag. Cf. also TCL, 6, 48 rev. 4.

Notice that i-ni-ma reflects the Emegir form inim and not the Emesal form quoted above. Compare the spelling i-lu in this line with ì-lu in B i 6 (\*41).

Stanza XIII

(A: ki-ru-gú XIII-kam-ma)<br>(F: ki-ru-gú IX-kam-ma)

| Lines | Texts | | | |
|---|---|---|---|---|
| | A | D | Ea | F |
| 185 | ⌉ | | ⌉ | ⌉ |
| 186 | | | | |
| 187 | | | | |
| 188 | ⌉ | ⌉ | | |
| 189 | | | | |
| 190 | | | | |
| 191 | | | | |

*185 A 66.  am zi-ga u₆-di àm-du₁₁
            The rising Wild Ox will look hither,
    Ea 21.  [.....] u₆!-di-ga àm-zé-[x]
        22. [.....] ì-x-du₁₁(?)
    F 1.    am zl-g[a₁₁₁à]m-d[u₁₁]

The two Ea lines are unclear. u₆ is written PI.É and zé-[x] may be a mis-
application of an Emesal form to the Emegir du₁₁ (cf. zé-eb = dùg, zé-èm
= duh etc.), although the horizontal wedge which follows suggests neither
EB nor ÈM. Ea 22 seems to be Sumerian, but the second sign could not be
identified, and the meaning remains obscure; cf. also *186 f. where the
Sumerian lines in Ea do not end and probably continue below. For a general
characterization of text F which begins at this line with stanza IX see pp. 23 ff.

In text A this line opens stanza XIII with a note of optimism: Enlil will
certainly look favorably upon his people, an act which will mark the end of
the suffering. In the next stanza (preserved only in D and F) this note of
hope gives way to a hymnal praise of Enlil (see p. 27).

*186 A 67.      ᵈmu-ul-líl z[i-g]a u₆-di àm-du₁₁
                The rising Enlil will look hither,
    Ea 23a. [......] ⌈zi-ga⌉(?)
    F obv. 2. a-a ᵈmu-[ul-líl z]i-ga u₆-di [àm-du₁₁]
             The rising Father Enlil will look hither,

The traces of Ea 23 show two Glossenkeil's dividing the line into two
halves (see also notes to *173). Since the second half of the line (23b) belongs
structurally *after* line A 67 (see *187 with notes), we assume that Ea 23a is the
parallel of A 67. The traces of the line suggest zi-ga which means the
sentence ends in the line below, in that part of the tablet which is broken off;
cf. also *185 and *187.

*187 Ea 23b. ⌈alim-ma am zi-ga-àm u₆⌉-[x]
             The dignitary is the rising Wild Ox, he will look hither,

In this line, as in the preceding ones in Ea (21–23a = *185 f.), the sentence
is completed in the line below, which is broken off. In stanzas XI–XIII text A
uses the third set of Enlil's attributes (see p. 47). Accordingly, the attribute
alim would have been expected after A 67 (*186; cf. also *155 and *174).
Its absence may be due to an inadvertent omission, as is suggested by its
presence in the Ea line.

*188 A 68.      nibruᵏⁱ dur-an-ki-ri u₆-di àm-du₁₁
                Over Nippur, the Bond of Heaven and Earth, he will look
                hither,
    D rev. 2. [nibru]ᵏⁱ-a[........]-ta

Reintroducing D at this point is based on the evidence of the succeeding lines; as D rev. 4 f. parallels A 69 (*189), it is reasonable to assume that D rev. 2 is the parallel of A 68, although neither of the D lines forms an exact parallel of the respective A lines. For the Duranki see notes to *156. About the postposition -ri see notes to *13.

*189 A 69.    nibru$^{ki}$-a ki nam-tar-tar-ri u$_6$-di àm-du$_{11}$
     D rev. 3. [nibru]$^{ki}$-a [ki nam-tar-t]ar-ra-ta
          4. [. . . . . . .] a-[šar ši-m]a-a-tú iš-šim-mu
          Over (D: from[?]) Nippur, the Place of Fate-deciding.

The D line does not contain a verb; it is probably part of a list of geographic features or the like, of the kind quoted in *161 ff. For Nippur, the place of fate-deciding, see notes to *157; about the postposition -ri see notes to *13.

*190 D rev. 5. [. . . . .]-ib-ba ki
          6. [. . .]á(?)-mar ri-ri: *ana iga-re-tu*

This line (or lines) is too fragmentary to allow any translation. The reading of the Akkadian words is uncertain.

*191 A 70.    mu-e-tu$_x$-tu$_x$-bé-en-dè-en    mu-e-g[i$_{16}$-i]l-gi$_{16}$-il-
          dè-en
     D rev. 7. ba-e-tu$_{10}$-tu$_{10}$-ba-en-dè ba-e-gi$_{16}$-li-ìm-mà-e-dè
          You have overwhelmed us, you have destroyed us.

A close parallel offering an Akkadian translation is *SBH*, I, 54 f.: a-a $^d$mu-ul-líl ba-e-tu$_{10}$-tu$_{10}$-be$_8$-en-na ba-e-gi$_{16}$-li-ìm-mà-e-dè = *a-bi* $^d$II *iṭ-ṭah-ha-a: it-tak-ma-ri uh-tal-li-qa*; for translation of this passage see *CAD, H*, 37 s.v. *halāqu*. For the reading tu$_x$ (HÚB) cf. Proto-Ea 622 (*MSL*, 2, 77). The duplicates show that tu$_x$ and tu$_{10}$ (HUB) can interchange; therefore the meaning *kummuru* "overturn" of tu$_{10}$-tu$_{10}$ (Geller, *AOTU, 1*, 315:13 f.) can be extended to tu$_x$-tu$_x$ as well. Cf. also van Dijk, *SGL, 2*, 12 with n. 7. For other occurrences see Sjöberg, *ZA, 54* (1961), 62 f.

The three duplicates of this line vary most significantly in the suffixes of the verbs. We interpret the suffixes as those of the first person plural with the confusion stemming from the fact that already in the Old Babylonian period (the date of text A) the distinction between first person plural inclusive -enden and first person plural exclusive -de(n) started to disappear (see Jacobsen, AS, 16, 100). Yet, texts A and D use the former after the first verb and all three versions of this line use the latter after the second verb, a situation which can hardly be dismissed as a coincidence.

Notice that instead of $gi_{16}$-il-$gi_{16}$-il in text A, the late duplicates use $gi_{16}$-li-ìm which is more common both in the early and in the late periods. For references for na-àm-$gi_{16}$-li-ìm (Emesal Voc. III 57) etc. see *Kultlyrik*, 205 f. About the possible connection between Emesal $gi_{16}$-li-ìm and Emegir ha-lam see Poebel, *GSG*, §82, and Falkenstein, *Das Sumerische*, 31. Notice also gul: gilim = hul:halam. Another case of g-h connection is làl-har = làl-gar (*lalgaru* = "wisdom"), Civil, *RA*, *60* (1966), 92.

The present line (which is the last one in text A) strikes a discordant chord with the rest of the stanza, whose atmosphere is optimistic (see notes to *185). It is intended, perhaps, to sum up the contents of the composition up to this point.

Stanza XIV

| Lines | Texts | | |
|---|---|---|---|
|  | A | D | F |
| 192 | I | I | I |
| 193 |  |  |  |
| 194 |  |  |  |
| 195 |  |  |  |
| 196 |  |  |  |
| 197 |  |  |  |
| 198 |  |  |  |
| 199 |  |  |  |
| 200 |  |  |  |
| 201 |  |  |  |

*192 A catchline. am zi-ga-ni an-né [nam]-ús
    D rev. 8.    am zi-g[a-n]i an-ná nam-[ús]
         9.    [....] *ti-bu-ut-su šá-mu-ú en-de-et*
    F obv. 3.    am zi-g[a-n]i an-né nam-[ús]
                 The Wild Ox, his rising reached up to the sky,

On an-né--ús see the literature quoted in *CAD*, *E*, 139 s.v. *emēdu* and also *The Curse of Adage* 42 and *Hymn to Enlil* 78. On the assertative preformative nam- see notes to *62.

The stanza division in D agrees with that of A: in the latter this is the catchline, which means it is the first line of stanza XIV, whereas in the former it follows a division line which marks a new section. The division in text F is different: the present line is the third of stanza IX. This line also starts a new theme: Enlil has finally responded to the pleadings of his people, and his rise seems to be a formidable event in which both the earth and the sky are affected.

*193 D rev. 10. [ᵈmu-u]l-líl am! zi-ga-àm an-⟨na nam-ús⟩
           Enlil is the rising Wild Ox, he reached up to the sky,
     F obv. 4.  ᵈmu-ul-[líl] zi-ga-ni an-né na[m-ú]s
           Enlil, the Wild Ox, his rising reached up to the sky.

The text in D has Á instead of AM. Since the two are so similar, it would not be too far-fetched to assume a mistake on the part of the scribe or the copyist. The change in the syntactical pattern of D is curious; it deviates from the pattern set by the preceding lines of D.

*194 D rev. 11. [alim-ma] am zi-ga-àm an-⟨na nam-ús⟩
           The Dignitary is the rising Wild Ox, he reached up to the
           sky,

For the restoration of the line cf. Ea 13b (*174).

*195 D rev. 12. a-a ᵈmu-ul-líl umun kur-kur-ra
           Father Enlil, King of the Foreign Lands,

Notice that in *195 f. the main theme of the present section (The rising wild ox, his rising . . .) is not repeated. The structure of D rev. 8–13 (*192–*196) is similar to that of Ea 11–14b (*172–*176): in both sections two Enlil attributes are added without repeating the main theme of the section.

*196 D rev. 13. alim-ma umun nibruᵏⁱ-a
           The Dignitary, Lord of Nippur,

See notes to *195. This line is followed by a division line, for which there is no counterpart in the F recension. We follow the latter's arrangement.

*197 D rev. 15. umun e-ne-èm-mà-ni an-e nu-íl-e
           16. šá be-lu a-mat-su šá-mu-ú ul ina-aš-šu-ú
           The Lord, his word the sky cannot bear,

The Sumerian line is marked 15 by mistake of the copyist, but since he proceeded from here in regular order, we do not depart from his numbering; actually it is line 14. On the concept of the "word" of Enlil see Nötscher, *Ellil*, 46 f. and *RLA*, 2, 384.

*198 D rev. 17. ᵈmu-ul-líl e-ne-èm-mà-ni ki nu-íl-e
           18. šá ᵈII a-mat-su KI-tim ul ina-aš-ši
           Enlil, his word the earth cannot bear,

*199 D rev. 19. umun šu ašaₓ-ni an-e nu-íl-e
20. *šá be-lu ti-ri-iṣ qa-ti-šú šá-mu-ú ul ina-aš-šu-ú*
Sum.: The lord, his unique hand the sky cannot bear,
Akk.: The Lord, the stretching of his hand the sky cannot bear,

F obv. 5. e-lum-e šu-ni tab-ba-bi an-né na[m-ú]s
The Dignitary, the grasp of his hands reached up to the sky,

For the reading ašaₓ (AŠ) see Proto Ea 98 (*MSL, II*, 42). The translation šu ašaₓ = *tiriṣ qāti* (and similarly me-ri ašaₓ = *tiriṣ šēpi* in *200) is questionable. To the best of our knowledge, nowhere is ašaₓ rendered by *tarāṣu* or *tirṣu* except in these two cases; *tarāṣu* translates mainly lá, but also several other Sumerian verbs (see Deimel, *ŠL, 3 Teil, Band 2*: Akkadisch-sumerisches Glossar 477). On the other hand, šu ašaₓ "single hand" in D strikes a significant contrast with šu tab-ba "joining of hands, grasp" in the F line. The latter is translated *kepû ša šēpi* in *CT, 12*, 46 ii 41 (Nabnitu XXII), whereas tùn tab is translated *kepû ša qāti* (ibid. 40), which may be a mistake. Compare also *The Exploits of Ninurta* (lugal-e) XII 5: šu-zu ašaₓ-àm nu-mu-un-ši-in-zi = *qa-at-ka iš-te-in la taš-šá-a* "Your single hand you do not raise."

Although the D and F lines differ in their contents, their structure is practically identical, and they both deal with Enlil's hand supporting the sky. The same difference between the two texts exists in the next line (*200). Compare the cliché "Who is broad enough to embrace the earth?" (Hallo, *IEJ, 12* [1962], 20 n. 33).

*200 D rev. 21. ᵈmu-ul-líl me-ri ašaₓ-ni ki nu-íl-e
22. ⟨         ⟩ me-ri ús-sa-na ⟨         ⟩
23. ⟨         ⟩ ši-ki-in še-pe-ʳeˡ ⟨         ⟩
24. [ᵈᴵᴵ] *ti-ri-iṣ še-pe-šú* KI-[-*tim ul ina-aš*]-*ši*
Sum.: Enlil, his unique foot (var. planted foot) the earth cannot bear,
Akk.: Enlil, the stretching (var. putting) of his foot the earth cannot bear,

F obv. 6. ᵈmu-ul-líl-le me-ri gub-ba-bi ki-[e] n[am-ú]s
Enlil, the treading of his foot abutted the earth,

On the differences between the D and F versions see notes to *197. Text D itself displays two versions which differ only in one item. To indicate that line 22 (and its translation, 23) is only a variant, the relevant phrase is inscribed immediately below its parallel in the main text, with the translation of the variant following immediately below. The last line of this four-line section contains the Akkadian translation of the main text line; in the transliteration this order has been maintained. On the incorrectness of the Akkadian translation see notes to *199.

One can only speculate which of the two D versions in the present line is the original. Perhaps the variant was the version in one of the scribe's sources, whereas another source, namely the one incorporated in the main text, had undergone a process of "harmonization." Thus in the poetic couplet D 19/21 the second stich was modified to duplicate the first in all aspects for the contrast šu:me-ri. This may explain why there are no variants in the first stich. For another possible case of "harmonization" in text D see notes to *144. Line D 24, the last legible line of that text, is followed by a division line.

*201 F obv. 7. am zi-ga-ni an-né ba-ab-ús
The Wild Ox, his rising reached up to the sky.

This line seems to repeat line F 3 (*192) with slight variations; since in the next two stanzas of text F (X and XI) the last line repeats the first line in part (9/19 = *202/*212; 21/34 = *213/*224), it is conceivable that text F has undergone a stanza rearrangement prior to which line 3 (*192) was the first in the present stanza; that line is also the first line in stanza XIV in the A recension.

## Stanza XV

### (F: ki-ru-gú X-kam-ma)

| Lines | | Texts | | |
|---|---|---|---|---|
| | F | Fa | Fba | Fbb |
| 202 | | | | |
| 203 | | | | |
| 204 | | | | |
| 205 | | | | |
| 206 | | | | |
| 207 | | | | |
| 208 | | | | |
| 209 | | | | |
| 210 | | | | |
| 211 | | | | |
| 212 | | | | |

*202 F obv. 9. za-e bí-du₁₁ za-e bí-du₁₁
You threatened, you threatened,

See notes to *142.

*203 F obv. 10. ù-mu-un-e kur-kur-ra za-e bí-du$_{11}$
King of the Foreign Lands, it is you who threatened,

*204 F obv. 11. èm-e a-ba mu-un-gul za-e-mèn mu-e-gul-gul
Who destroyed everything? It is you who destroyed!

Compare *BA*, 5, 683:13 f.: an-nim a-ba mu-un-gul = *šá-me-e man-nu i-bu-ut*. Is an-nim "Akkadianized" Sumerian, or should it be translated "the high sky?" It is doubtful whether any significant difference should be sought between the single and the reduplicated forms of the verb in the F line; cf. also *abātu* and *ubbutu*, *CAD*, *A/1*, 41 ff.

*205 F obv. 12. èm-e a-ba mu-un-sì za-e-mèn mu-e-sì-sì
Who razed everything? It is you who razed!

As in the preceding line, there is no discernible difference between the single and the reduplicated forms of the verb. Compare for this line *BA*, 5, 683:15 f.: ki-a a-ba mu-un-sì = *er-ṣe-tim man-nu is-pu-un*.

*206 F obv. 13. $^{d}$mu-ul-líl é zi-da gi-sig mi-ni-ku$_4$-ku$_4$
Enlil, a well-founded house you turned into a reed hut,

Cf. the duplicate Fa 38 f.: umun ka-nag-gá $^{d}$mu-ul-líl é zi-da gi-sig-ga mi-ni-íb-ku$_4$-ku$_4$ = *be-el ma-a-tú* $^{d}$II É.MEŠ *ki-na-a-tum a[na kikkiši tutter]* (restoration by Falkenstein, *ZA*, 57 [1965], 111). A duplicate is partly preserved in *BA*, 5, 683:18. Similarly cf. *BA*, 5, 618:25 f.: é zi mu-un-gul-e mu-lu zi mu-un-tu$_{10}$-bé-eš mu-un-ug$_5$-[xx] = [b]*i-ta-a-ti ki-na-a-ti i-bu-ut*? *a-mi-le-e ki-nu-ti* [. . . . .]. The sign followed by a question mark is written TE; *CAD*, *A/1*, s.v. *abātu* A (bilingual section) transliterates *-ut* but it could be a mistake for *-tu* as well. The plural form *i-bu-tu* can be compared with the plural form of the Sumerian verb tu$_{10}$ in the second half of the line, although gul, translated by *i-bu-tu*? is in the singular.

*207 F obv. 14. du$_5$-mu mu-lu zi-da-ke$_4$ ki mu-ni-ri-ri
The son of an honest man ran away(?),

Cf. the duplicates of this line; Fa 40 f.: $^{d}$mu-ul-líl du$_5$-mu mu-lu zi-da ri[. . .] = $^{d}$II *ma-ri ki-nim* [. . .]; Fba 13 f.: [. . . . . . . .]-ra ki mu-ni-íb-ri-[ri] = [. . . . *ki*]*-nu-tim uṭ-ṭi-tam ú-[laq]-qit*; Fbb 27 f.: [. . . .] mu-lu zi-da-ra ki mu-ni-íb-ri-[ri] = [. . . .*k*]*i-nu-tim uṭ-ṭi-tam ú-tá[m*?*-mid*?]; cf. also Fba 20, (in notes to *210): *ú-ṭi-tum ú-ṭam-mi-[id]*. It seems that *uṭṭitam utemmudum* is an Akkadian idiom whose meaning is roughly equivalent to that of ki--ri-ri. ri is translated *ummudu* ("to lean") in *RA*, *6* (1907), 132 i 6 (*á* = A = *nāqu*) and it occurs with that meaning in *The Curse of Agade*, 109. This meaning does not fit very well into the context of the present F line; we can compare, however, [a]b-ba ki-ri-a-šè dumu-ni-ir kin bí-in-gi₄ "[A f]ather sent to a far off place for his son," Kramer, *Two Elegies*, line 1, (restored from *SEM*, 134). The translation of ki--ri-ri "to run around, run away" is suggested for the present F line by Th. Jacobsen; the meaning may be secondary, derived from the primary one which occurs in *210. For ri-ri = *luqqutum* (Fba) cf. notes to *210.

*208  F obv. 15. ᵈmu-ul-líl túg-gal-gal šed_x-dè ba-e-gam
                        Enlil, the (wearer of) fancy garments you killed by freezing,

For šed_x (A.MÙŠ.DI) as a graphic variant of šed₇, see also *The Curse of Agade*, 213. For duplicates of this line see Fba 15 f.; Fbb 29 f.; *SBH*, 43, obv. 5; Thureau-Dangin, *Rituels accadiens*, 28:4 f., and *SBH*, 44, rev. 33 f.: túg-gal-gal-la šed₇-dè ba-e-gam = *la-biš ṣu-ba-a-ti ra-bu-ú-ti ina ku-ṣi it-mi-it* (*CAD*, Ṣ, 225 s.v. *ṣubātu* emends to *ušmīt*; neither version seems to be correct, however, as the Sumerian verb is in the second person; in the other duplicates except F the Sumerian verb is rendered in third person).

*209  F obv. 16. gána-ni gána da-ma-al-la šà-mar-re ba-e-gam
                        He whose fields are wide fields, you killed by hunger,

The duplicates of this line are Fba 17 f.: gána!-ni gána! da-ma-al-la šà-mar-ra[...] = *šá me-riš-ti ra-pa-áš-ti ina bu-bu-ti* [....]; *SBH*, 43, obv. 6; *SBH*, 44, rev. 35 f.; *Rituels accadiens* 28:6 f.; K.6930:3 (Bezold, *Catalogue*, 2, 819).

*210  F obv. 17. ki ri-ri-ra ki mu-ni-tar
                        To the picker (of vegetables) from the earth, the earth stopped (producing),

Cf. Fba 19 f.: ⌈ki⌉ [xx]-ra ki mu-ni-íb-[tar] = *ana eš-x-*[.....] *ú-ṭi-ṭim ú-tam-mi-*[*id*]. In spite of the breaks and the orthographic variants it is clear that the Akkadian line employs *uṭṭitam utemmudum* to translate ki--tar whereas in line 14 (notes to *207) text Fba uses this Akkadian idiom to translate ki--ri-ri. The origin of the confusion seems obvious, namely, the occurrence of ki--ri-ri in both lines. There is little doubt, however, that the two cases of ki--ri-ri should be kept apart. In line *207 the suggested meaning is "to run around, to run away." In the present line ri-ri is a nomen agentis preceded by the direct object ki. For ri-ri (-g) = *laqātu* "to pick" see A. Salonen *Agricultura Mesopotamica* (*AASF*, B, *149*, 1968), 420. For ki--ri-ri cf. the passage quoted by van Dijk, *SGL*, *2*, 47: tu-gur₄ᵐᵘˢᵉⁿ-gin_x ki im-ri-ri-g[e-e]n which should be translated: "Like a turtle dove you pick from the ground." For tu-gur$_4$$^{mušen}$ = "turtle dove" see Landsberger, *WO*, *3* (1966), 267.

*211 F obv. 18. pú-sag-bala-e-ra pú-sag mu-ni-tar
        To the drawer of water, the water hole cut off (its supply),

Cf. Fba 21 f.: pú-sag-⌐ri-ri⌐-ra pú-sag mu-ni-íb-[tar] = *ana mu-par-re-e šaṭ-pi šat-pi ú-šá-ab-re-e-[ma]*. The last word seems to be an Š form of *berû, barû* "to be hungry;" the Akkadian thus paraphrases the Sumerian: by cutting of the water for irrigation, the water hole starves the water drawer. About *šaṭpu* and *issû* see Güterbock, *AfO*, *13*, 50; cf. also Hallo, *HUCA*, *33* (1962), 10 n. 73. The term pú-sag also occurs at the beginning of Old Babylonian mathematical texts, see Thureau-Dangin, *Textes mathématiques babyloniens* (1938) 11 ff. and 242.

The other duplicate of this line, Fa 42 f., is fragmentary.

*212 F obv. 19. za-e bí-du$_{11}$ ši-im-diri-ge-en
        You threatened, but you exceeded your threats.

For the preformative ši- see notes to *73; for a similar theme see line *34.

Stanza XVI

(F: ki-ru-gú XI-kam-ma)

| Lines | Texts | | |
|---|---|---|---|
|  | F | Fc | Fd |
| 213 | ⌐ | | |
| 214 | | | |
| 215 | | | |
| 216 | | | |
| 217 | | ⌐ | |
| 218 | | | ⌐ |
| 219 | | | |
| 220 | | | |
| 221 | | | |
| 222 | | | |
| 223 | | | |
| 224 | ⌊ | ⌊ | ⌊ |

*213 F obv. 21. za-e mah-mèn za-e mah-mèn
        You are exalted, you are exalted!

Cf. this hymnal cliché in *73 ff. The form -mèn is Emesal for -me-en; see the Glossary s.v. -mèn.

*214 F obv. 22. umun-e kur-kur-ra za-e mah-mèn
         King of the Foreign Lands, you are exalted!

*215 F obv. 23. an-e a-ba mah-mèn za-e-mèn mah-mèn
         In heaven, who is exalted? It is you who are exalted!

For a similar passage with the same apparent deviation from the syntactic pattern (a-ba mah-àm would be expected), see Sjöberg, *Nanna-Suen*, 168: 24 f. and his comment, p. 177.

*216 F obv. 24. ki-e a-ba mah-mèn za-e-mèn mah-mèn
         On the earth who is exalted? It is you who are exalted!

Cf. notes to *215.

*217 F obv. 25. ù-mu-un zà-an-na ù-mu-un zà-ki-⌈ke₄⌉
         Lord of all heaven, lord of the entire earth,

The section F 25–33 (*217–*223) is duplicated by *SK*, 101:4–13 (text Fc) and, starting from F 26, also by *CT*, *15*, 10:15–21 (text Fd; translated by Falkenstein, *SAHG*, 76 f.).

We interpret zà(-g) "border" in a wider sense, namely the area circumscribed by the border, the entire territory within it; compare Akk. *itû* (*CAD*, I/J, 315) sub mng. 3 and Hebrew גְבוּל (*geḇūl*). For zà-an-na with a different meaning see Römer, *Königshymnen*, 63 n. 171. Cf. also ki-a zà-ba, *67, *98, *125.

*218 F obv. 26. kur ᵈutu-è-a-ta kur ᵈutu-šú-a-šè
         From the country of sunrise to the country of sunset,

Cf. the duplicate lines Fc 6 f. and Fd 15. This phrase (which with the next line forms a complete sentence here) is not uncommon. Further duplicates are *SBH*, 47, 19 f. (with Akkadian translation); Ur-Ninurta hymn no. *28, 4, and rev. 5 (Falkenstein, *ZA*, *49* [1949], 116; see *Königshymnen*, 3 for cataloguing); *Enki and the World Order*, 191 and *PBS*, *10/4*, 8:7 (with partial Akkadian translation); Letter Prayer H, 5 (Hallo, *JAOS*, *88* [1968], 82); and Bur-Sin, *31d, rev. 12 (Hallo, *BiOr*, *23* [1966], 247). For Akkadian references see *CAD*, Ṣ, 217 s.v. *ṣītu* especially sub mngs. 1c 3′–4′. Cf. also the Hebrew כי ממזרח שמש ועד מבואו גדול שמי בגוים (Malachi 1:11, similarly Psalms 50:1 and 113:3) and Phoenician וכך בימתי בכל גבל עמק אדך לממצא שמש ועד מבאי ... (Azitawadda A II 1–3 = H. Donner-W. Röllig, *Kanaanäische und aramäische Inschriften*, *1* no. 26).

*219 F obv. 27. kur-ra ù-mu-un nu-mu-un-ti za-e ù-mu-un
         ab-ak
         In no country is there a king; only you exercise kingship,

Cf. the duplicate Fc 8: [kur-r]a ù-mu-un nu-un-ti za-e ù-mu-un ab(gloss: a-[ ])-ak-me-en, and Fd 16: kur-ra ù-mu-un nu-um-ti za-e ù-mu-un ab-DA-me-en. The Fd line is translated by Falkenstein, *SAHG* 77 ".... gibt es im Lande keinen Herren—du allein bist der Herr." This translation essentially repeats his earlier translation of the passage (*ZA*, *48* [1944], 102), in which he reads èš-da which, he explains, is a variant of aš-da = "allein." He ignores, however, the duplicate Fc 8 which clearly has a small A (followed by a break) under the AB. The new duplicate of this line, namely text F, has an unquestionable AK both in the present and in the next line.

Our translation umun--ak "to exercise kingship" is based on the context; cf. nam-en--ak = *bêlu* "to exercise rulership" (*CAD*, *B*, s.v. *bêlu* Jestin-Lambert, *Thésaurus*, *2*, 41); *šarrūta epēšu*, *CAD*, *E*, 219 f.

*220 F obv. 28–29. ᵈmu-ul-líl kur-kur-ra ga-ša-an nu-mu-un-ti
                   dam-zu ga-ša-an ab-ak
                   Enlil, in all the lands there is no queen, only your wife
                   exercises queenship,

Cf. the duplicates; Fc 9: [ᵈm]u-ul-líl kur-kur-ra ga-ša-an nu-mu-un-ti dam-zu ga-ša-an ab-ak; Fd 17: ᵈmu-ul-líl kur-kur-ra ga-ša-an nu-um-ti dam-zu ga-ša-an ab-DA. Both duplicates remain loyal to the variants they display in the preceding line, with the exception of the gloss A, written below AB in Fc 8 but absent from Fc 9. For general commentary on the translation see notes to *219. On the translation ga-ša-an--ak "to exercise queenship" cf. ibid. and nam-nin--ak, *Lamentation over Ur*, 383; Jestin-Lambert, *Thésaurus*, *2*, 42. For the translation ga-ša-an = "queen" see Sᵇ I 364 (*MSL*, *3*, 128).

*221 F obv. 30–31. im an-na a ki-a ᵈmu-ul-líl eškiri dìm-mi-ir-
                   r[e-ne] za-e-da ša-mu-e-da-ma-al
                   It is you, Enlil, who holds the rain of heaven, the water
                   of the earth and the halter of the gods,

This line is restored from two duplicates which offer some variants. Fc: (10) ꜥeꜣ-lum im an-na a ki-a (11) ᵈmu-ul-líl eškiri (gloss: eš-ki-ri) dìm-me-er-re-ne [za]-e-da ša-mu-e-da-ma-al "Dignitary, the rain of heaven, the water of the earth—Enlil, it is you who holds the halter of the gods." The other duplicate, Fd, has: (18) e-lum im an-na a ki za-da ša-mu-e-da-gál (19) ᵈmu-ul-líl eškiri dingir-re-ne za-da ša-mu-e-da-gál. "Dignitary, it is you who holds the rain of heaven, the water of the earth; Enlil, it is you who holds the halter of the gods."

In F 30–31 the whole line constitutes one syntactical unit. This is clear not only from the structure of the sentence but also from its inclusion in one rubric (which had to be divided into two lines, the bottom one indented). In text Fc, line 10 adds e-lum at its beginning, thus turning the line into an elliptical sentence. Text Fd also adds e-lum at the beginning of the sentence but it also inserts a verb at the end of line 18 thus turning lines 18–19 into two independent sentences.

For the reading eškiri (ŠIBIR) see the gloss eš-ki-ri in Fc 11 and cf. *ŠL*, 412, 2. As the etymology éš-kiri₄ implies, it means "nose-rope (lead-rope, halter)," used here in a transferred meaning; see *CAD*, Ṣ, s.v. *ṣerretu* A. The semantic connection between eškiri, šibir (both U + EN × GÁNA-*tenû*) and buruₓ (EN × GÁNA-*tenû*) is well demonstrated in *The Coronation of Ur-Nammu*, 17: šibir-buruₓ ukù-dagal-lu-a . . . hé-lah₄-lah₄-e "the staff and crook for directing the numerous people" (Hallo, *JCS, 20* [1966], 139 ff.). For further references to eškiri see Proto-Ea 418 (*MSL, 2*, 64 and *MSL, 3*, 203 ad loc.); W. G. Lambert, *BASOR*, 169, 63; Falkenstein, *BaghMitt, 3*, 30; van Dijk, *SGL, 2*, 69 with n. 27 and especially his numerous references in *MIO, 12* (1966), 70 ff.

On the preformative ša- see Jacobsen, AS, 16, 73 and, in detail, Falkenstein, *ZA, 48*, 69 ff. Notice the Emegir usages dingir and gál in Fd.

*222 F obv. 32. mu-lu gu mú-mú-mèn mu-lu še [mú-mú-mèn]
      Lord, you are the grower of legumes, you are the grower
      of barley,

The line is restored from Fd 20 (which adds a-a ᵈmu-ul-líl at the beginning of the sentence). Fc 11 shows some interesting variants: [a]-a ᵈmu-ul-líl mu-lu gu mú-mú-mú mu-lu še mú-mú-mú. Van Dijk's interpretation of mú-mú-mú as a triple verb (he quotes the Fc line, *SGL, 2*, 130) is to be rejected on the basis of the two duplicates: as indicated by the F line, mú is a variant of the suffix -me-en. (On triple verbs see H. Radau, BE, 29/1 and A. Falkenstein, *GSGL, 2*, 63 n. 1.) This suffix also appears as -mu in some copies of *The Exaltation of Inanna*, 67, 81, 121, and 135, see YNER, 3, 40 f.

gu and še appear in a parallelism indicating "fertility, abundance" or the like; cf. Hallo, *JNES, 18* (1959), 55 f. and the text quoted by him, ibid. 60 f., no. A 7557:4 f. Compare also the following passage in *CT, 36*, 27:6 ff.: gu nì-kala mú-mú še nì-kala mú-mú/šul-gi é-kur-ra ú-a-bi na-nam/gu-bi gu na-nam še-bi še na-nam "The grower of first quality legumes, the grower of first quality barley/Šulgi is the provider of the Ekur./Its legumes are (first quality) legumes, its barley is (first quality) barley" (Šulgi G; siglum of J. Klein).

*223 F obv. 33. [ᵈ]mu-ul-líl me-lám-zu engur-ra kua mu-[ni-
      ib-šèg-šèg]
      Enlil, your glow boils the fish in the fresh waters.

The restoration of this line is based on Fc 13: [$^d$m]u-ul-líl me-lám-zu engur-ra (gloss: im-gu-ra) kua mu-ni-ib-šèg-šèg. In Fd 21 the verb is šeg$_6$-šeg$_6$. Cf. *SBH*, 56, obv. 66 f. (quoted by Poebel, *ZA*, *38* [1929], 83 f.): me-lám-mu engur-ra kua mu-ni-íb-šeg$_6$-[šeg$_6$] = *me-lám-mu-ú-a ina ap-si-im nu-ni* [*ušabsalu*]. Strictly speaking, text Fd has the "correct" form of the verb (IZI.IZI = "to boil, roast") but confusion with šèg-šèg (A.AN–A.AN = "rain") is not uncommon; see Poebel, ibid. and Falkenstein, *ZA*, *49* (1949), 322. For the reading kua (HA) see S$^a$ 38 (*MSL*, *3*, 17). In translating engur "fresh waters" we rely on Jacobsen's remark (*JNES*, *5* [1946], 139 n. 21) that ". . . *apsû* denotes the sweet waters of the underground water-bearing strata of Mesopotamia, waters which may be reached when one digs down deep . . . but which also appear in pools and marshes where the surface of the plain naturally dips down below the water table. As *apsû* is used in Akkadian, so is engur and its approximate synonym abzu . . . in Sumerian." Obviously the passage cannot refer to the underground sweet waters, and it is the marshes, pools, etc. which are meant. Notice the gloss im-gu-ra in Fd, and compare the spelling an-gur$_x$ (=ENGUR) in UET, 8, 16:8. The idea of fish being boiled in their natural habitat by the powerful glow of a god is also brought up in a Šamaš hymn, Schollmeyer, *Šamaš*, no. 1 ii 43 f.

*224 F obv. 34. za-e ma[h-mèn]
     You are exalted!

For the restoration of this line see *213.

### Stanza XVII
### (F: ki-ru-gú XII-kam-ma)

| Lines | Texts |
|-------|-------|
|       | F     |
| 225   | broken |
| 226   | broken |
| 227   | broken |
| 228   | broken |
| 229   | broken |
| 230   | broken |
| 231   | broken |
| 232   |   |
| 233   |   |
| 234   |   |
| 235   |   |
| 236   |   |

*225-*231 F rev., 3 lines missing at the top + lines 1–4.

Of these seven lines, three are completely missing and of the first four lines only a few signs are preserved.

*232 F rev. 5. [. . . . . . .] mu-bi [še àm-š]a₄
. . . . . . .  that young man is mourning,

For the restoration compare the second stich of the couplet, *233. The cliché *232/3 is commonly used in laments, as shown by the many duplicates quoted by Krecher, *Kultlyrik*, 78 (to which add *SBH*, 4:56 ff.); cf. also *44 ff.

*233 F rev. 6. [. . . . . .] ge-bi še à[m-š]a₄
[. . . . . .] that young girl is mourning,

*234 F rev. 7. [n]iʔ u₈ al-lu u₈ al-tuš
[. . .] "woe!" has increased, "woe!" has settled in,

The translation of this and the following lines is tentative. For u₈ as a wailing cry (Akk. *uʾa*) see *ŠL*, 494, 2 and *MSL*, 2, 29 f. This cry is rendered in a variety of spellings, the most common of which are u₈-a, ú-a, ù-a and ù-u₈-a; a long list of references is offered by Krecher, *Kultlyrik*, 114 f. with notes 333–342; see now also Kramer, *ANET*³, 652 n. 3. For lu = "much" in various combinations and in exclamations see Sjöberg, *Nanna-Suen*, 17 f. and M. Lambert, *OrNS*, 30 (1961), 88 ff.

*235 F rev. 8. [gu]dʔ àm-me u₈ al-lù u₈ al-gi₆
[. . . .] says, woe! There is trouble, woe! It is dark!

For "trouble" and "darkness" occurring in the same contexts see for example, AN.GI₆ GAR-*an* AN.GI₆ *du-luh-hu-ú* "There will be an eclipse, an eclipse (predicts) trouble," Thompson, *Reports of the Magicians*, 112:5 (quoted by *CAD*, D, 178 s.v. *duluhhû*), and, from the Commentary to *Enuma* ᵈ*Anu* ᵈ*Enlil*: AN.GI₆ = *du-lu-uh-hu-ú* (*CAD*, ibid.). *dalāhu* is the common Akkadian translation of lù. The lexical entry an-ta-lù = *adāru šá* ᵈ*Sin* is dismissed by A. Goetze, *JCS*, 1 (1947), 251 f. as learned etymology, artificially created from *antalū* which is the late form of OB *namtallum* < *namtal-a "division, separation."

*236 F rev. 9. [. . . . . a]ma-a a-di-di-in
[. . . . .] in the bedroom (sheʔ) walks around in despair.

With the subject apparently missing, this line does not lend itself to an effective translation. We base our translation mainly on *SBH*, 6, rev. 7 f.: ama-ni na-an-ku₄-ku₄ na-an-di-di = *ina maš-ta-ki-šá i-dal i-te*-NI-*šú* (read *i-te-rib!-šú*?) "Into her room she enters, she wanders;" (the Akkadian translation reversed the order of the two verbs). ama in the F-line and in the *SBH* passage is to be understood as a variant of ama₅. Notice that *CAD*, D, s.v. *dâlu* sub mng. 1b "to wander around in despair," quotes two passages in which this verb is attested in connection with *dalāhu*, and cf. notes to *235.

## THE ERŠEMMA

| Lines | | Texts | | | | Lines | | | Texts | | | |
|---|---|---|---|---|---|---|---|---|---|---|---|---|
| | F | G | Haa | Hab | Ia | | G | Haa | Hab | Hb | Hc | Ia |
| 237 | I | I | I | I | | 271 | I | | | | | |
| 238 | | | | Skipped | | 272 | | | | | | |
| 239 | | | | Skipped | | 273 | | | Skipped | | | I |
| 240 | | | | Skipped | | 274 | I | | Skipped | | | |
| 241 | | | | Skipped | | 275 | | | Skipped | | | |
| 242 | | | | Skipped | | 276 | | | Skipped | | | |
| 243 | | | | Skipped | | 277 | | | Skipped | | | |
| 244 | | | | Skipped | | 278 | | | Skipped | | | I |
| 245 | | I | | Skipped | | 279 | | | Skipped | | | |
| 246 | | | | Skipped | | 280 | | | Skipped | | | |
| 247 | | | | Skipped | | 281 | I | | Skipped | | | |
| 248 | | | | Skipped | | 282 | | | Skipped | | | |
| 249 | | | | Skipped | | 283 | | | Skipped | | | |
| 250 | | | | Skipped | | 284 | | | Skipped | | | |
| 251 | | | | Skipped | | 285 | | | Skipped | | | |
| 252 | | | | Skipped | | 286 | | | Skipped | | | |
| 253 | | I | | Skipped | I | 287 | | | Skipped | I | | |
| 254 | | I | | Skipped | I | 288 | I | | Skipped | I | I | |
| 255 | | | | Skipped | | 289 | | | Skipped | | | |
| 256 | | | | Skipped | | 290 | | | Skipped | | | |
| 257 | | | | Skipped | I | 291 | | | Skipped | | I | |
| 258 | | | | Skipped | I | 292 | I | | Skipped | | | |
| 259 | | | | Skipped | | 293 | | | Skipped | | | |
| 260 | | | | Skipped | | 294 | | | Skipped | | | |
| 261 | | | | Skipped | | 295 | I | | Skipped | | | |
| 262 | | | | Skipped | | 296 | | | I | | | |
| 263 | | I | I | Skipped | | | | | | | | |
| 264 | | I | | | | | | | | | | |
| 265 | | | | | | | | | | | | |
| 266 | | | | | | | | | | | | |
| 267 | | | | | | | | | | | | |
| 268 | | | | | | | | | | | | |
| 269 | | | | | | | | | | | | |
| 270 | | I | | | | | | | | | | |

*237 F rev. 11. ⌜dil⌝-[mu]-un nigín-ù uru!-zu u₆ ga-e-du₁₁
       12. [erasure] IGI.DU ga-e-du₁₁
    G 1.        dilmun nigín-ù urú-zu u₆ ⌜di⌝-[du₁₁]
    Haa 5.      dilmunᵏⁱ nigin-na urú-zu u₆ gá-e-dè
       6.       *kab-tum:* ᵈ*en-líl na-ás-hi-ram-ma ana* URU-*ka tu-ur*: URU-*ka
                hi-iṭ-ṭi*
                Sum.: "Dignitary turn around and look at your city!" let
                me say,
                Akk.: Dignitary (var. Enlil), turn around and return to
                your city (var. survey your city)!

Cf. the duplicate line Hab 27: dilmunᵏⁱ nigín-ù urú-zu u₆ ga-e-du₁₁
= *kab-tum na-as-hi-ram-ma* URU-*ka hi-i-iṭ.* Texts Haa and Hab are from the
duplicate texts *IV, R², 28* 4 rev. and *SBH,* 46 respectively (see Meissner,
*OLZ, 11* [1908], 405; Krecher, *Kultlyrik,* 184). Text Hab preserved only
the first and last lines of the text; the 49 intervening (Sumerian) lines were
"skipped" (see notes to *238).
The interpretation of this line and the following ones is suggested by Th.
Jacobsen. u₆, it seems, is a contracted form of u₆-ù. The verbal form ga-e-
du₁₁ "Let me say (to him?)" of the Old Babylonian text F has changed into
gá-e-dè ("weak form") in the neo-Assyrian text Haa. Text G, on the other
hand, uses the preformative dè- (see Jacobsen, AS, 16, 72 f.), but in the
present line the traces suggest di-, which may be a syllabic spelling.
For dilmun (dilmunᵏⁱ in late texts) = *kabtu* see *AHw* s.v. *kabtu* and
compare aratta = *kabtu,* ibid.
The position of F rev. 11 immediately after the stanza XII rubric suggests
that it is a catchline. The partly erased line F rev. 12 is followed by three
erased lines and the rest of the reverse is uninscribed. This evidence—
erasures and uninscribed space—suggests that F rev. 9 is the last line of the
balag, and F rev. 11 is the catchline for the eršemma. It seems that the scribe
wrote five lines of the eršemma immediately after the last stanza of the balag
before realizing that the entire eršemma could not fit into the remaining space.
He therefore erased four (or, rather, three and one-half) lines, leaving the
first line as a catchline, and presumably began a new tablet. Text G is the Old
Babylonian edition of the eršemma. Its 34 lines occupy a separate tablet. For
the occurrence of the incipit line of the eršemma in the neo-Assyrian catalogue
see above, p. 18.

*238 G 2.   alim-ma dilmun nigín-ù urú-zu u₆ [dè-du₁₁]
    Haa 7. alim-ma dilmunᵏⁱ nigin-na ⟨urú-zu u₆ gá-e-dè⟩
              "Dignitary Enlil, turn around and look at your city!" let me
              say,

Text Hab introduces at this point (line 29) the scribal note 42(?) MU.MEŠ
GU₄.UD. MEŠ "42(?) lines skipped." As already observed by Meissner (*OLZ, 11*,
[1908], 405), the duplicate text Haa shows that not 42 but 49 lines were
skipped (not counting the Akkadian translations). Cf. also p. 47 n. 3.

*239 G 3.  ù-mu-un kur-kur-ra-ke₄ nigín-ù urú-[zu u₆ dè-du₁₁]
   Haa 8.  umun kur-kur-ra nigin-na ⟨urú-zu u₆ gá-e-dè⟩
           "King of the Foreign Lands, turn around and look at your
           city!" let me say,

The break at the end of the G line allows for only a short restoration,
based on G 20 (*272).

*240 G 4.  ù-mu-un du₁₁-ga zi-da nigín-ù urú-[zu u₆ dè-du₁₁]
   Haa 9.  umun du₁₁-ga zi-da nigin-na ⟨urú-zu u₆ gá-e-dè⟩
           "Master of the Fulfilled Speech, turn around and look at
           your city!" let me say,

*241 G 5.  ᵈmu-ul-líl a-a ka-na-ág-gá [nigín-ù urú-zu u₆] dè-
           [du₁₁]
   Haa 10. ᵈmu-ul-líl a-a ka-nag-gá nigin-na ⟨urú-zu u₆
           gá-e-dè⟩
           "Enlil, Father of the Nation, turn around and look at your
           city!" let me say,

*242 G 6.  sipa sag-gíg-ga nigín-ù urú-[zu u₆ dè-du₁₁]
   Haa 11. sipa sag-gíg-ga nigin-na ⟨urú-zu u₆ gá-e-dè⟩
           "Shepherd of the Black-headed, turn around and look at
           your city!" let me say,

*243 G 7.  i-bí-du₈ ní-te-na nigín-ù urú-[zu u₆ dè-du₁₁]
   Haa 12. i-bí-du₈ ní-te-en-na nigin-na ⟨urú-zu u₆ gá-e-dè⟩
           "The One Inspecting for Himself, turn around and look at
           your city!" let me say,

*244 G 8.  am erín-na di-di nigín-ù urú-[zu u₆ dè-du₁₁]
   Haa 13. am erín-na di-di nigin-na ⟨urú-zu u₆ gá-e-dè⟩
           "The Warrior Who Leads the Troops, turn around and look
           at your city!" let me say,

*245 G 9.  ù-lul-la ku-ku nigín-ù urú-[zu u₆ dè-du₁₁]
   Haa 14. ù-lul-la ku-ku nigin-na ⟨urú-zu u₆ gá-e-dè⟩
           "The One Who Feigns Sleep, turn around and look at your
           city!" let me say,

*246 Haa 15. ᵈam-an-ki nigin-na ⟨urú-zu u₆ gá-e-dè⟩
           "Enki, turn around and look at your city!" let me say,

*247 Haa 16. ur-sag ᵈasal-lú-hi nigin-za ⟨urú-zu u₆ gá-e-dè⟩
"The Warrior Asalluhi, turn around and look at your city!"
let me say,

*248 Haa 17. umun ᵈen-bi-lu-lu nigin-na ⟨urú-zu u₆ gá-e-dè⟩
"The Lord Enbilulu, turn around and look at your city!" let
me say,

*249 Haa 18. ur-sag ᵈmu-zé-eb-ba-sa₄-a nigin-na ⟨urú-zu u₆
gá-e-dè⟩
"The Warrior Mudugasa'a, turn around and look at your
city!" let me say,

*250 Haa 19. umun ᵈdi-ku₅-mah-a nigin-na ⟨urú-zu u₆ gá-e-dè⟩
"The Lord Dikumah, turn around and look at your city!" let
me say,

*251 Haa 20. ur-sag ᵈuta-uₓ-lu nigin-na ⟨urú-zu u₆ gá-e-dè⟩
The Warrior Uta-ulu, turn around and look at your city!" let
me say,

ᵈuta-uₓ(GIŠGAL)-lu, the divine Cloudy Day (or South Storm) is an
epithet of Ninurta; see *ŠL*, 381:146; *TRS*, 10:63; *CT*, *24*, 6 ii 34 (an =
*anum* I 205); *CAD*, *E*, s.v. *erpu* and cf. Jacobsen, *JAOS*, *88* (1968), 105.

*252 Haa 21. umun an-uraš-a-ra nigin-na ⟨urú-zu u₆ gá-e-dè⟩
"Lord of Heaven and Earth, turn around and look at your
city!" let me say,

*253 G 10. urú-zu nibruᵏⁱ-zu nigín-ù [urú-zu u₆ dè-du₁₁]
Haa 22. ⌜urú⌝-zu nibruᵏⁱ-ta nigin-na ⟨urú-zu u₆ gá-e-dè⟩
"Toward (Haa: from) your city, (G: your) Nippur, turn
around and look at your city!" let me say,

The use of the possessive pronoun after Nippur in text G is unusual, but
note the same variant between *SK*, *2*, 8 i 26 and YBC 9838:21 (YNER, 3,
49 n. 4.).

*254 G 11. še-eb é-kur-ra-ta nigín-ù [urú-zu u₆ dè-du₁₁]
"From the brickwork of the Ekur turn around and look at
your city!" let me say,
Haa 23. še-eb é-kur!-ra-ta ki-ùr é-nam-ti-la
"From the brickwork of the Ekur, the foundation of the
Enamtila,"

Translating ki-ùr = "foundation" (*duruššu*) is justified by the parallelism
with še-eb. One cannot exclude the possibility, however, that Ninlil's

temple é-ki-ùr is intended; cf. above *161 f. The é-nam-ti-la in Assur is
explained in the "Götteradressbuch" as *bīt balāṭi* = *bīt ᵈgula*, see Frankena,
*Tākultu*, 126:171. For recent references to Enamtila see Römer, *Königshymnen*, 253 f.

*255 Haa 24. še-eb zimbirᵏⁱ-ta nigin-na ⟨urú-zu u₆ gá-e-dè⟩
                   "From the brickwork of Sippar turn around and look at your
                   city!" let me say,

*256 Haa 25. èš é-babbar-ra! é-di-ku₅-kalam-ma
                   "The shrine Ebabbar, Edikukalama,"

   Four temples by the name é-babbar ("White House") are listed by
*RLA*, *2*, 263; two of them, belonging to Šamas and Ištar respectively, were
in Sippar. W. Moran privately suggested, however, that there was only
one such temple in Sippar in which both deities were worshipped. Since
each of the five cities mentioned in lines *253–*263 is followed by the names
of two of its shrines, it is presumably the Sippar temple which is intended in
the present line (Sippar is mentioned in *255).

   é-di-ku₅-kalam-ma ("Temple of the Judge of the Nation") is probably
an epithet of the é-babbar, with reference to Šamaš, the divine judge. Two
other temples by that name existed in Babylon and Isin, see Edzard, *ZwZw*,
158, n. 842; Hallo, *JNES*, *18* (1959), 56.

*257 Haa 26. še-eb TIN.TIR.KI-ta nigin-na ⟨urú-zu u₆ gá-e-dè⟩
                   "From the brickwork of Babylon turn around and look at
                   your city!" let me say,

*258 Haa 27. še-eb é-sag-íl-la e-tùr-kalam-ma
                   "The brickwork of Esaĝila, Eturkalama"

   é-sag-íl-la ("Temple, the Raised Head") is Marduk's temple in Babylon
and one of the most important ones in Babylonia; see Unger, *RLA*, *1*, 353 ff.
Extensive archaeological and philological discussions can be found in F. Wetzel
and F. H. Weissbach, *Das Hauptheiligtum des Marduk in Babylon Esagila
und Etemenanki* (WVDOG, 59 [1938]). é-tùr-kalam-ma ("Temple, the
Corral of Sumer") is Ištar's temple in Babylon; see *RLA*, *2*, 482 f.

*259 Haa 28. še-eb bàd-SI.AB.BAᵏⁱ-ta nigin-na ⟨urú-zu u₆ gá-e-
                   dè⟩
                   "From the brickwork of Borsippa turn around and look at
                   your city!" let me say,

*260 Haa 29. še-eb é-zi-da-ta é-mah-ti-la
                   "From the brickwork of Ezida and Emahtila,"

é-zi-da ("Well Founded Temple"), Nabû's temple in Borsippa, had a counterpart in Assur bearing the same name. According to *RLA*, *1*, 188, the name of the latter is explained as *bīt napišti māti* ("House of the Life of Sumer"). The foundation of the Ekur in Nippur is also called "the life of Sumer"; see notes to *158. é-mah-ti-la ("Magnificent House of Life") is a cella in the Ezida (*RLA*, *2*, 360).

*261 Haa 30. še-eb é-te-mén-an-ki é-darà-an-na
              "The brickwork of Etemenanki and Edara'anna,"

The é-temen-an-ki ("Temple, Basis of Heaven and Earth") is the great ziqqurrat in the Esaĝila complex in Babylon; see WVDOG, 59 (cf. notes to *258). On the various spellings of the name see ibid. 79 n. 3. temen = "foundation (of a building), basis (of a building, throne)" is discussed by Falkenstein, *OrNS*, *35* (1966), 236 ff.

Mentioning Edara'anna together with Etemenanki suggests that the former, like the latter, is in Babylon; cf. notes to *171.

This line disrupts the pattern mentioned in notes to *256, whereby each of the five cities enumerated in *253–*263 is followed by two of its temples. Babylon and two of its shrines are mentioned in *257 f.

*262 Haa 31. [še-eb] ì-si-in^ki-na-ke₄ nigin-na ⟨urú-zu u₆ gá-e-
              dè⟩
              "From the brickwork of Isin, turn around and look at your
              city!" let me say,

*263 Haa 32. [še-eb] é-gal-mah é-raba-ri-ri
              "The brickwork of Egalmah and Erabariri,"

é-gal-mah ("Glorious Temple") is the great temple of Ninisina in Isin, also known as é-ᵈnin-in-si-na (Kraus, *JCS*, *3* [1949], 60). In the "Götteradressbuch" from Assur é-gal-mah is glossed as *bītu rabû ṣīru* = *bīt* ᵈ*gula* (Frankena, *Tākultu*, 126:128). On the identity of ᵈNinisina with ᵈGula see Kraus, op. cit., 64. More recent references to the Egalmah can be found in Krecher, *Kultlyrik*, 83, 85, 232, and in Falkenstein, *BaghMitt*, *2* (1963), 32 n. 139; cf. also below, line *270.

On é-rab-ri-ri ("Temple, Pillory Which Clamps Down") see *RLA*, *2*, 458. On raba see Sᵇ II 332 (*MSL*, *3*, 149): raba = *rappu*; Hh IV 56 f. (*MSL*, *5*, 154): ᵍⁱˢrab-gal, ᵍⁱˢrab-tur-tur = *maluṭṭu* (all = "pillory, neck-stock," or the like). For further references see Römer, *Königshymnen*, 164 f., Civil, *JAOS*, *88* (1968), 13; and especially Landsberger's detailed discussion in *The Date Palm and its By-products* (1967), 27 n. 80. raba is used with šu--ri-ri in the following passage from Ur-Ninurta hymn *27:23: sig-ta igi-nima-šè kalam-ma rab(LUGAL)-ginₓ šu hé-em-ri-ri-e "From below to above may you clamp down on the land like a pillory" (Falkenstein, *ZA*, *49* [1949], 106; also quoted by Landsberger), and similarly in *Išme-Dagan and Enlil's Chariot*, 14 (Civil, p. 4). The Akkadian occurrence of *rappu* with *lāṭu* is the equivalent of the Sumerian occurrence of r a b with šu-ri-ri, but they do not occur in bilingual texts.

*264 G 12. ki-ùr ki-gal-ta nigín-ù [urú-zu u$_6$ dè-du$_{11}$]
    "From the Ekiur, the Great Place, turn around and look at your city!" let me say,

The ki-ùr ("Floor?") mentioned here is no doubt Ninlil's temple in Nippur, from which the é is often dropped. For the occurrence of this temple with the epithet ki-gal see Falkenstein, *SGL*, *1*, 33.

*265 G 13. du$_6$-kù ki-kù-ta nigín-ù [urú-zu u$_6$ dè-du$_{11}$]
    "From the Duku, the Holy Place, turn around and look at your city!" let me say,

According to Jacobsen, *JNES*, *5* (1946), 141, the Holy Mound du$_6$-kù was located somewhere on the eastern horizon. Apparantly, this hill, always green and rich in vegetation, had a miniature copy in Nippur, which is referred to in our line. For recent references see *Kultlyrik*, 83.

*266 G 14. šà é-dim$_x$-ma-ta nigín-ù [urù-zu u$_6$ dè-du$_{11}$]
    From within the Edimma turn around and look at your city!" let me say,

About this part of the Ekur see notes to *164.

*267 G 15. é-ká-mah-ta nigín-ù [urú-zu u$_6$ dè-du$_{11}$]
    "From the Ekamah turn around and look at your city!" let me say,

The é-ká-mah ("Temple, Magnificent Gate") is, perhaps, part of the Ekur (*RLA*, *2*, 320); see now also *Kultlyrik*, 82. At Ur the abulla-mah (KÁ.GAL-mah) was the site of a ritual in which Rim-Sin played an important role; see Gadd, *Iraq*, *22* (Woolley MV, 1960), 157 ff. and cf. Levine and Hallo, *HUCA*, *38* (1967), 48 n. 24.

*268 G 16. é-gá-nun-mah-ta nigín-ù [urú-zu u$_6$ dè-du$_{11}$]
    "From the Main Storehouse turn around and look at your city!" let me say,

A gá-nun-mah ("main storehouse") is known to have existed in Nippur as well as in other cities, but our line seems to be the only reference to the one in Nippur; see *RLA*, *2*, 278, *3*, 142 ff., Falkenstein, *ZA*, *56* (1964), 121, and

Krecher, *Kultlyrik*, 82; cf. also *CAD*, *G*, s.v. *ganūnmāhu* and *ganūnu* A. The é is probably intended to indicate the sacred nature of the Nippur structure.

\*269 G 17.  ma-mu-šú-a-ta nigín-ù u[rú-zu $u_6$ dè-du$_{11}$]
"From the Gagiššua turn around and look at your city!" let me say,

ma-mu-šú-a is the Emesal form of gá-giš-šú-a, a shrine of Ninlil in Nippur. It is described in CTL, 49 as the fifth temple of Ninlil, in Nippur. The name can be interpreted as "Shrine, the Stool" (from $^{giš}$šú-a = *littu*), or "Shrine, Covered Sky" (from mu = giš = *šamû* Emesal Voc. II 1 and šú = *katāmu*). This shrine may be identical with é-gán-giš-šú = *bīt išid māti* = *bīt* $^d$*Nin-líl*, "Götteradressbuch" 148 (Frankena, *Tākultu*, 125).

\*270 G 18.  ma é-gal-mah-ta nigín-ù u[rú-zu $u_6$ dè-du$_{11}$]
"From the shrine Egalmah turn around and look at your city!" let me say,

On the Magnificent Temple see notes to \*263.

\*271 G 19.  še-eb urí$^{ki}$-ma-ta nigín-ù urú-z[u $u_6$] dè-du$_{11}$
"From the brickwork of Ur turn around and look at your city!" let me say,

\*272 G 20.  še-eb larsam$^{ki}$-ma-ta nigín-ù urú-zu [$u_6$] dè-du$_{11}$
"From the brickwork of Larsa turn around and look at your city!" let me say,

\*273 G 21.  urú a-du$_{11}$-ga a-gi$_4$-a-zu!
    Haa 33.  [urú] a-du$_{11}$-ga a-gi$_4$-a-za
         34.  [*ālu*] *šá naq-rù-ú šá-nu-u* : *a-hu-lap tu-ur-šú*
         Your destroyed, flooded city (Akk. var.: woe, turn to it!)

It seems that the entries a-du$_{11}$-ga = $e_{11}$ = *naqāru*, a-gi$_4$-a = a-gar-ra = *šanû*, Emesal Voc. III 65 f. (see correction, *MSL*, *5*, 195), are derived from the same literary tradition as our line, in which the two expressions are associated; cf. also notes to line \*274. The basic meaning of *šanû* seems to be "to flood, immerse," as suggested by the Sumerian (cf. also Jacobsen, *Tammuz*, 329). The meaning "to dye (cloth, by immersing in paint)" (Landsberger, *MSL*, *4*, 33 ad Emesal Voc. III 66 and *JCS*, *21* [1967], 169) is secondary. For actual flooding of fields in the Ur III period, see Sauren, *Topographie der Provinz Umma*, Heidelberg, 1966, 76, 200 f.

In the Akkadian variant a-gi$_4$-a is interpreted as a = *ahulap* and gi$_4$ = *tāru*. The Sumerian line can also be translated "Your smitten, ruined city," from a-du$_{11}$-ga = *mahāṣu* and a-gi$_4$-a = *naqāru ša āli*, K. 2055 obv. 15 (*RA*, *18* [1916], 190 = Antagal).

*274 G 22.   a-du$_{11}$-ga a-ta gar-ra-zu
    Haa 35. nibru$^{ki}$ a-du$_{11}$-ga a-ta mar-ra-za
        36. ⟨          ⟩ *šá naq-ru-u ana me-e sa-lu-u*
    G      Your destroyed (city), inundated by water,
    Haa    In your destroyed Nippur, inundated by water,

Notice the Emesal usage in Haa as against Emegir in G. These forms are entered in the Emesal Voc. III 67: a-mar-ra = a-gar-ra = A.MEŠ *rahāṣu*. This entry follows immediately after the two mentioned in the preceding line (*273; cf. notes ad loc.). It should be observed, however, that the Akkadian verb used in our line (*salû*) differs from that of the Emesal Voc. entry, whereas in *273 the Akkadian verbs used are precisely those of Emesal Voc. III 65 f. The data from Emesal Voc. concerning lines *273 f. seem to refute Langdon's claim that the Akkadian translation is a misunderstanding (*Babyloniaca*, *2*, 156 n. 2 [1907]). The allusion to inundation here may be metaphorical; see Finkelstein, *JAOS*, *86* (1966), 361 n. 23.

The literary pattern of the couplet *273/*274 resembles that of *21/*22; see notes ad loc, and cf. lines *275–*280.

*275 Haa 37. urú a-du$_{11}$-ga a-gi$_4$-a-za
         In your destroyed, flooded city,

*276 Haa 38. zimbir$^{ki}$ a-du$_{11}$-ga a-ta ⟨mar-ra-za⟩
         In your destroyed Sippar, inundated by water,

*277 Haa 39. urú a-du$_{11}$-ga a-gi$_4$-⟨a-za⟩
         In your destroyed, flooded city,

*278 Haa 40. TIN.TIR.KI a-du$_{11}$-ga a-ta ⟨mar-ra-za⟩
         In your destroyed Babylon, inundated by water,

*279 Haa 41. urú a-du$_{11}$-ga a-gi$_4$-⟨a-za⟩
         In your destroyed, flooded city,

*280 Haa 42. ì-si-in$^{ki}$-na a-du$_{11}$-ga a-ta ⟨mar-ra-za⟩
         In your destroyed Isin, inundated by water,

*281 G 23.   urú še ku$_5$-da ki-lá-a-zu
    Haa 43. urú še ku$_5$-da ki-lá-lá-a-zu
        44. *a-lum šá še-um ip-par-su-šú uṭ-ṭi-tum iš-šaq-lu-šu*
        Sum.: Your city whose harvested barley is weighed out
            (separately by the kernel),
        Akk.: The city from which barley is cut off, wheat is weighed
            out (by the kernel),

The picture presented here is that of a city under siege in which food has become very expensive and is very carefully weighed.

It seems that the translator misunderstood the Sumerian idioms and provided a word-by-word translation. The rendering of ki = *uṭṭitum* here and in *207 and *210 is problematic. Did the scribe connect it with gig?

*282 G 24.    [èm]-kú nu-kú-a u₄-zal-zal-la-ri
     Haa 45. èm-kú nu-kú-e u₄-zal-zal-la-ri
         46. *ak-ki-lu ina la a-ka-li uš-tab-ru-u*
         The gluttonous man carries on without eating,

Cf. YBC 3537:10 (unpubl.) nu-kú-e lú-kú-e nu-un-sum = *ul ta-ak-kal ana a-ki-li ul ta-nam-din* "You do not eat, but to a glutton you do not give."

*283 G 25.    dam tur-ra-ke₄ dam-mu mu-ni-ib-bé
     Haa 47. dam tur-ra-ke₄ dam-mu mu-ni-íb-bé
         48. *šá mu-us-sà ṣi-ih-ru mu-ti-ma i-qab-bi*
         Sum.: The wife of a young man there (= in the city) says "My husband!"
         Akk.: She whose husband is young says "My husband!"

*284 G 26.    dumu tur-ra-ke₄ dumu-mu mu-ni-ib-bé
     Haa 49. dumu tur-ra-ke₄ dumu-mu mu-⟨ni-íb-bé⟩
         The son of a young man there says "My son!"

It seems that this line was construed as the second leg of couplet whose first leg is the preceding line. (The couplet dam/dumu is quite common; cf., e.g., *16/*17.) But this line is not convincing, as the son of a young man would be expected to say "My father!" and not "My son!" This confusion may be the reason for the absence of an Akkadian translation here.

*285 G 27.    ki-sikil-e šeš-mu mu-ni-ib-bé
     Haa 50. ki-sikil-mu šeš-mu mu-⟨ni-íb-bé⟩
         51. *ar-da-tum a-hi-mi ⟨i-qab-bi⟩*
         The (Haa: my) maiden there says "My brother!"

For a possible reading sis for šeš see Sollberger, *OrNS, 24* (1955), 18.

*286 G 28.    urú-ta ama-gan-e dumu-mu mu-ni-ib-bé
     Haa 52. urú ama-gan-mu dumu-mu mu-⟨ni-íb-bé⟩
         53. *ina a-li um-mi a-lit-tu ma-ri-mi ⟨i-qab-bi⟩*
         In the city, the (Haa: my) mother who gives birth there says "My child!"

*287 G 29.    dumu bàn-da a-a-mu mu-ni-ib-bé
     Haa 54. dumu bàn-da a-a-mu mu-⟨ni-íb-bé⟩
         55. *mar-tum ṣi-hir-tum a-bi-mi ⟨i-qab-bi⟩*
         The young girl there says "My father!"

Text Hb (*SBH*, 70 obv. 1–14) starts at this line. For dumu-bàn-da =
"young girl" see also Falkenstein, *ZA, 57* (1965), 78.

*288 G 30.    tur-e al-è mah-e al-è
    Haa 58. tur-e al-è mah-e ≪e≫ al-è
        59. *ṣi-iḫ-ru i-maḫ-ḫi ra-bu-ú i-maḫ-ḫi*
            Young and old are raging,

Cf. the duplicates Hb 4 f. and Hc 28 f. It seems that the Akkadian line of
Hb differs from that of Haa; in the beginning of the former [x]-*ṣal-al*-[x] can
be read. The end of the line agrees with that of Haa 58.

tur//mah (*ṣiḫru//rabû*) are used here in hendiadys with the meaning
"everybody," cf. *CAD, Ṣ*, 184 s.v. *ṣiḫru* 2c. It seems that when the verb è
occurs with the meaning *maḫû*, the prefix al- is favored; see *AHw* s.v.
*maḫû*.

In texts Haa and Hb the present line comes after *292 (Haa 56/57, Hb 2/3);
the arrangement of text G is followed here.

*289 Haa 60. nibru^{ki} tur-e al-è mah-⟨e al-è⟩
            (In) Nippur young and old are raging,
    Cf. the duplicate Hc 30.

*290 Haa 61. TIN.TIR.KI tur-e al-è mah-⟨e al-è⟩
            (In) Babylon, young and old are raging,

*291 Haa 62. ì-si-in^{ki}-na tur-e al-è mah-⟨e al-è⟩
            In Isin, young and old are raging,
    Cf. the duplicate line Hc 32.

*292 G 31.    e-sír-e gub-ba mu-un-sar-re-da₄
    Haa 56. e-sír-ra gub-ba mu-un-sar-re-e-dè
        57. *šá ina su-qi iz-za-az-zu uš-taḫ-mi-ṭú*
            Those standing in the streets were being chased away,

Cf. the duplicate lines Hb 2 f. On the durative aspect of the -e- of the
suffix see Jacobsen, *AS*, 16, 98 and Yoshikawa, *JNES, 27* (1968), 251 ff.
    The present line is translated by *CAD, H* s.v. *ḫamāṭu* B (p. 65): "they have
made restless those who were standing in the street."

*293 G 32.    gal₄-la-bi ur-e àm-da-ab-sur₅
    Haa 63. gal₄-la-bi ur-re an-da-ab-sur₅
        64. *qal-la-šu kal-bu uš-qa-lil : na-ak-ru it-ta-ši*
            Their genitals the dogs (carried) hanging (from their mouths)
            (Akk. var.: the enemy carried away),

The duplicate Hb 7 f., only partly preserved, records the verb as [uš]-ta-qal-lil (from šuqallulu, t form). It also offers the same variant as in Haa. This line is discussed by Meissner, BAW, 1, 24 f. and Heidel, AS, 13, 31 ff. The variant in the Akkadian translation is based on the interpretation ur₅, ur = nakru and LÁ (sur₅) = našû. For sur₅, lá = šuqallulu, našû see Gordon, Sumerian Proverbs, 2.66 n. 7.

*294 G 33.   ság-bi mu-bar-re àm-da-ab-lá
    Haa 65.   ság-bi mu-bar-ra an-da-ab-lá
         66.   [sap]-hu!-us-su bar-bar-ru ú-šaq-lil
               Sum.: Their scattered remains are set aflame(?)
               Akk.: Their scattered remains the wolves (carried) hanging
                     (from their mouths),

Cf. the duplicate Hb 9 f.: ság-bi mu-bar-ra an-da-ab-[x] = sà-ap-hu-us-su-šu [xxx] uš-ta-qal-lil. Our translation of the Sumerian line is based on the assumption that mu-bar-re/ra is the Emesal form of giš-bar-ra = girru "fire" (cf. CAD, G, s.v. girru B and its translation of our line, ibid., B, s.v. barbaru). This interpretation is perhaps supported by the lexical entry [izi]-lá = šutāhuzu ša išāti (CAD, A, 183). ság = saphūtu probably denotes "that which has been scattered." In our context it is the scattered remains of the corpses, parts of which were carried away by dogs (*293). saphussušu in Hb is problematic. [Cf. now ság-du₁₁-ga, Sjöberg, ZA, 63, 25.]

It seems that the an- prefix in Haa is a phonetic variant of the àm- prefix attested in G, perhaps a partial assimilation due to the immediate proximity of the dental /d/: cf. *29, *31, *33, and *293.

It is difficult to reconcile the Akkadian and Sumerian versions of this line. Perhaps under the influence of the preceding line, where dogs are mentioned, the translator mistook mu-bar-re for ur-bar-ra = barbaru "wolf," and proceeded to translate lá = šuqallulu just as he did (appropriately) in the previous line.

*295 G 34.   ešemen-ba líl ba-e-sù
    Haa 67.   ešemen líl-lá-àm e-si
         68.   me-lul-ta-šu zi-qi-qam im-ta-la
               Sum.: Their playgrounds (G: you) have filled with storms,
               Akk.: His (Enlil's) games filled with ghosts,

sù(-g) (in G) is a variant of si(-g) (Haa, Hb 11); cf. si-ga-àm var. sù-sù-ga-àm = ma-la-a-ti, CT, 16, 46:187 f. For ešemen (lit. "skip rope") = mēlultu ("dancing, games") and other terms for games see Landsberger, WZKM, 56 (1960), 121 ff., Civil, JNES, 23 (1964), 9, and Römer, Königshym-nen, 173 f. Cf. also uru-ba KI.E.NE.DI (= ešemen)-bé mir i-in-si

"A tempest has filled the dancing of its city," *The Exaltation of Inanna*, 49. Text Hb 12 has *me-lul-la-šu*.

**\*296 Haa 69. e-sír la-la-bi nu-gi₄-gi₄**
      70. *su-ú-qu šá la-la-a la áš-bu-ú*
      Sum.: The streets (Akk.: which) are not sated.

Having skipped "42" lines, text Hab resumes at this line, and is identical with Haa (see notes to \*238).

*ašbu* in Haa 70 is first person, but it does not make much sense; *šebû*, third person stative (from *šebû* "to become sated") would have been expected. For references to la-la- - gi₄-gi₄ "to satisfy, fulfill" and its Akkadian equivalents see *AHw* s.v. *lalû*, *CAD*, Ṣ, s.v. *ṣajāhu*, Sjöberg, *Nanna-Suen*, 174 and Hallo and van Dijk, YNER, 3, 83.

The present line seems to be an integral part of the eršemma and its omission from text G may be due to an oversight. The figure 34 in the line count of the text refers to the number of lines actually copied, regardless of the number of lines in the Vorlage. This is true also of text A where the figure 70 does not include the line accidentally omitted and then added on the left edge; see notes to \*155.

Our translation and interpretation of the Akkadian line (pace Sjöberg, *Nanna-Suen*, 174: *sūquša lalâ lā ašbu*) is based on Hb 14: *su-ú-qu šá la-la-šú la [šebû (?)]*. It indicates clearly that *šá* is not a feminine pronominal suffix attached to *sūqu* but a relative pronoun introducing a relative clause.

THE COMPOSITE TEXT IN CONNECTED TRANSLATION

### Stanza II

  **\*1.** Oh, you angry dwelling(?), father(?), your angry heart, until when will it not be pacified?
      Father Enlil, until when will he not calm down? King of the Foreign Lands, until when will he not calm down?
      Father Enlil, ᵈⁱᵗᵗᵒ Master of the Fulfilled Speech, ᵈⁱᵗᵗᵒ
      Father Enlil, ᵈⁱᵗᵗᵒ Enlil, Father of the nation, ᵈⁱᵗᵗᵒ
  **\*5.** Father Enlil, ᵈⁱᵗᵗᵒ Shepherd of the Black-headed, ᵈⁱᵗᵗᵒ
      Father Enlil, ᵈⁱᵗᵗᵒ The One Inspecting for Himself, ᵈⁱᵗᵗᵒ
      Father Enlil, ᵈⁱᵗᵗᵒ The Warrior Who Leads the Troops, ᵈⁱᵗᵗᵒ
      Father Enlil, ᵈⁱᵗᵗᵒ Who Feigns Sleep (lit. Who Sleeps a False Sleep), ᵈⁱᵗᵗᵒ
      Dignitary, the Warrior Asalluhi, ᵈⁱᵗᵗᵒ
  **\*10.** The Great Warrior, the Lord Enbilulu, ᵈⁱᵗᵗᵒ
      The Dignitary, the Warrior Mudugasa'a, ᵈⁱᵗᵗᵒ
      The Great Warrior, the Lord Dikumah, ᵈⁱᵗᵗᵒ

Since that day, since that day long ago, <sup>ditto</sup>

Since that night, since that night long ago, <sup>ditto</sup>

*15. Since that year, since that year long ago, <sup>ditto</sup>

Since the day the wives were delivered unto the enemy, <sup>ditto</sup>

Since the day the sons were delivered unto the enemy, <sup>ditto</sup>

... since the wife died, <sup>ditto</sup>

The wife died; since the wife died, <sup>ditto</sup>

*20. The son died; since the son died, <sup>ditto</sup>

To devastate your city, the shepherd rampaged in the Holy of Holies like a wild ox. <sup>ditto</sup>

To devastate Nippur, the shepherd rampaged in the Holy of Holies like a wild ox. <sup>ditto</sup>

To devastate Babylon, the shepherd rampaged in the Holy of Holies like a wild ox. <sup>ditto</sup>

Since he (Enlil) swept away the temple tower like a big reed mat, <sup>ditto</sup>

*25. The onlooker is saying "Woe, my house! Where is it? Woe, my city! Where, oh where is it?" <sup>ditto</sup>

The onlooker is saying "Woe, my baby! Where is it? Woe, my big son! Where, oh where is he?" <sup>ditto</sup>

Oh, bitter hostility and crying, how long will it go on like this? <sup>ditto</sup>

## Stanza III

How long, Enlil, how long, until when prayers, until when will he not be pacified? (Var. Enlil, how long ... how long?)

(Enlil,) like a cloud over the horizon, where will you alight from there? (var. how long? <sup>ditto</sup>)

*30. Like a cloud over the horizon, Great Mountain Enlil, how long? <sup>ditto</sup>

Great Mountain Enlil, where will you alight from there?

As much as you have promised, you killed, <sup>ditto 16</sup>

That which you promised, you have accomplished, <sup>ditto 17</sup>

Whatever you promised, you have exceeded, <sup>ditto</sup>

*35. You have finished with your cursed place. <sup>ditto</sup>

A shepherd who would not lie down he installed over the sheep, <sup>ditto</sup>

A shepherd who does not fall asleep he placed on guard, <sup>ditto</sup>

Grass which is not grown (i.e. weeds) he grew in the steppe, <sup>ditto</sup>

Father Enlil, reeds (for lamentation flutes) which had not been there (?) proliferate in the high steppe.

*40. The Great Mountain Enlil, like a cloud over the horizon, where will he settle down from there?

16. Var. That which you have promised, you have fulfilled,

17. Var. Wherever you promised, you have reached; where will you alight from there?

## Stanza IV

A wailing, oh, a wailing, oh, could he only hold back the lament![18]
Lord of my city, Great Mountain Enlil, a wailing, oh![19]
Lord of my city, Great Mountain, lord . . . a wailing, oh![20]
Over the shack, this young man is shedding tears,[21]
*45. A dirge over the storehouse, this girl is mourning,
This young man is shaking in tears,[22]
This girl is shaking in tears, (var. [ditto])
This girl is crying.

## Stanza V

Wild bull, Dignitary, Wild Bull, when your name is over the foreign
    lands,
*50. King of the Foreign Lands, Wild Bull,
Master of the Fulfilled Speech, Wild Bull,
Enlil, Father of the Nation, Wild Bull,[23]
Shepherd of the Black-headed, Wild Bull,[24]
The One Inspecting for Himself, Wild Bull,
*55. The Warrior Who Leads the Troops, Wild Bull,
The One Who Feigns Sleep, Wild Bull,
The Lord Enki, Wild Bull, [ditto]
The Warrior Asalluhi, Wild Bull, [ditto]
The Lord Enbilulu, Wild Bull, [ditto]
*60. The Warrior Mudugasa'a, Wild Bull, [ditto]
The Lord Dikumah, Wild Bull, [ditto]
When your name rests over the mountains, the sky itself
    trembles; [ditto]
The sky itself trembles, the earth itself shivers. [ditto]
When it rests over the mountain of Elam,
*65. When it rests over the horizon, [ditto]
When it rests over the "foundation of the earth," [ditto]

18. Var. A wailing, it is a wailing, a lament is not set up, a lament is not set up, a lament is not set up.
19. Var. Lord of my city, there is a wailing, a lament is not set up, [ditto]
20. Var. Lord of my city, there is a wailing over your Splendor, a lament is not set up, [ditto]
21. Var. Over the shack he is shedding bitter tears, [ditto]
22. Var. This young man is bitterly shaking in tears, [ditto]
23. Var. Great Mountain, Father Enlil, Wild Bull, when your name is over the foreign lands,
24. Var. Shepherd of the Black-headed, Wild Bull, when your name is over the foreign lands,

When it rests over the farthest reaches of the earth, <sup>ditto</sup>
When it rests over the surface of the earth, <sup>ditto</sup>
When it rests over the awe-inspiring mountains, <sup>ditto</sup>
*70. When it rests over the high mountains, <sup>ditto</sup>
When it rests over the powerful (?) mountains, <sup>ditto</sup>
When it rests over the mountains and over the wide sky, the sky itself [trembles. <sup>ditto.</sup>]

## Stanza VI

You are the Dignitary, you are the Father (?), you are exalted, Dignitary, you are exalted![25]
Enlil you are likewise exalted!
*75. King of the Foreign Lands, you are exalted! <sup>ditto</sup>[26]
Master of the Fulfilled Speech, you are exalted! <sup>ditto</sup>
Enlil, Father of the Nation, you are exalted! <sup>ditto</sup>
Shepherd of the Black-headed, you are (var. likewise) exalted! <sup>ditto</sup>
The One Inspecting for Himself, you are exalted! <sup>ditto</sup>
*80. The Warrior who Leads the Troops, you are exalted! <sup>ditto</sup>
The One Who Feigns Sleep, you are exalted! <sup>ditto</sup>
The Lord Enki, you are exalted! <sup>ditto</sup>
The Warrior Asalluhi, you are exalted! <sup>ditto</sup>
The Lord Enbilulu, you are exalted! <sup>ditto</sup>
*85. The Warrior Mudugasa'a, you are exalted! <sup>ditto</sup>
The Lord Dikumah, you are exalted! <sup>ditto</sup>
The bird pours out a wailing from its throat, [27]
The *girgilu*-bird pours out a wailing from its throat,
Bitter crying, bitter tears, wailing from its throat it pours out, <sup>ditto</sup>
*90. Since the Master turned away from the nation,
And from the Black-headed, the head lolls (lifeless) over the shoulder.

## Stanza VII

Wild bull, Dignitary, Wild Bull, when your name is over the foreign lands,
Great Mountain, Father Enlil, Wild Bull, when your name is over the foreign lands,
Shepherd of the Black-headed, Wild Bull, when your name is over the foreign lands,

25. Var. You are likewise exalted, you are likewise exalted!
26. Var. Enlil of the Foreign Lands, you are likewise exalted!
27. Var. The bird, from its throat, pours out a wailing, from its throat, over his house, <sup>ditto</sup>

*95. When your name rests over the mountains,
    When it rests over the mountains of Elam,
    When it rests over the horizon,
    When it rests over the farthest reaches of the earth.

## Stanza VIII

    How long? how long?
*100. Enlil, how long?
    Enlil of the Foreign Lands, how long [28]
    Shepherd of the Black-headed, how long?
    You, Master, who covered your (var. neck and) head with a cloth, [ditto]
    You, who placed your neck between your thighs, (var. you are likewise
        exalted!) [ditto.]
*105. You, who take counsel only with yourself, you are exalted!
    You, who covered your heart as (one covers) a basket, [ditto]
    Dignitary, you leaned your ear on your lap, [ditto]
    In (Nippur's) midst, the raven makes the heart fathomless,
    At the command of Enlil, the raven makes the heart fathomless.
*110. Dignitary, the master oppressed the nation.
    Dignitary Enlil, his Black-headed are being reduced(?).
    Enlil, a hand equal to your hand does not exist, [ditto]
    Enlil, a foot equal to your foot does not exist, [ditto]
    No god equal to you comes forth, [ditto]
*115. Dignitary, no man may come out to confront you.
    Father Enlil, return to the land!
*117. (Untranslated)
    His Black-headed . . . (Nippur's) girls are being pushed(?)

## Stanza IX

    Wild bull, Dignitary, Wild Bull, when your name is over the foreign
        lands,
*120. Great Mountain, Father Enlil, Wild Bull, when your name is over the
        foreign lands,
    Shepherd of the Black-headed, Wild Bull, when your name is over the
        foreign lands,
    When your name rests over the mountains,
    When it rests over the mountains of Elam,
    When it rests over the horizon,
*125. When it rests over the farthest reaches of the earth.

28. Var. Great Mountain, Father Enlil, how long?

## Stanza X

Restore (your) heart, restore (your) heart!
Enlil, restore (your) heart!
Dignitary, King of the Foreign Lands, restore (your) heart![29]
Master of the Fulfilled Speech, restore (your) heart, restore!
*130. Enlil, Father of the Nation, restore (your) heart, restore!
Shepherd of the Black-headed, restore (your) heart, restore!
The Warrior, the One Inspecting for Himself, restore (your) heart, restore!
The Lord, the Warrior Who Leads the Troops, restore (your) heart, restore!
The Warrior Who Feigns Sleep, restore (your) heart, restore!
*135. The Lord Enki, restore (your) heart, restore!
The Warrior Asalluhi, restore (your) heart, restore!
The Lord Enbilulu, restore (your) heart, restore!
The Lord Mudugasa'a, restore (your) heart, restore!
The Lord Dikumah, restore (your) heart, restore!
*140. "Restore (your) heart, restore!" belongs to him,[30]
"Calm down (your) heart, calm down!" belongs to him (var.: to you),
Let the man of prayers say prayers to you,[31]
Let the man of supplications make supplications to you.
Heaven and earth, place of the spotted barley(?)
*145. Your . . . Enki and Ninki,
Your beloved wife, the Great Mother Ninlil,
The princess, your big sister, Nin-Keš,
The herald, Nin-Nibru,
Your strong soldier, the lord Ninurta,
*150. Your "grand vizier," the commander Nusku,
*151. Your beloved child, Gašananna,
*152. The great governor, Umunguruša,

## Stanza XI

The Wild Ox is asleep, when will he rise?[32]
Enlil is asleep, when will he rise?[33]

29. Var. Enlil of the Foreign Lands, restore (your) heart!
30. Var. "Enlil, restore your heart (var.: restore)!" belongs to him, (var.: let belong to you,)
31. Var. [The man of] prayers says [prayers],
32. Var. The Wild Ox is asleep; why does he not rise?
33. Var. Enlil, the Wild Ox, is asleep; why does he not rise?

*155. The Dignitary is asleep, when will he rise?[34]
In Nippur, over the Duranki, when will he rise?[35]
Over Nippur, the Place of Fate-deciding, when will he rise?
Over the temple he set up for the life of the land, when will he rise?
Over (the temple) he set up for the life of the foreign countries, when will he rise?
*160. The Ekur, the temple chosen by the steadfast heart (of Enlil)
*160a. "34 lines skipped"
The Ekiur, the temple of Ninlil,
The Enamtila, the temple of Enlil,
The Emitummal, the temple of Ninlil,
In the Edimma, the temple of Enlil,
*165. The Main Storehouse of Enlil,
The Gate of Uncut Barley
The Ninnu-canal of Enlil,
The Glorious Gate of Enlil,
The Eastern Gate,
*170. The Gate Facing Ur,
King of the land, Edara'anna.

## Stanza XII

The sleeping Wild Ox, let him rise![36]
The sleeping Enlil, let him rise![37]
The sleeping Dignitary, let him rise![38]
*175. Father Enlil, King of the Foreign Lands,
Dignitary, Lord of Nippur,
Among the rebellious, fattened bulls, let him rise!
Among the choice sheep of the linen-clad priest, let him rise![39]
Among the grist-fed goats, let him rise!
*180. Among the fat-tailed, banded sheep, let him rise![40]
... let him rise!
... of Nippur, the Bond of Heaven and Earth,
The sleeping exalted Dignitary, with the wind let him rise!
His words: "Wailing, wailing."

34. Var. The Dignitary, Wild Ox, is asleep; why does he not rise?
35. Var. Father Enlil, in his city, Nippur, why does he not rise?
36. Var. The goring Wild Ox, why does he not rise?
37. Var. Enlil, the goring Wild Ox, why does he not rise?
38. Var. The Dignitary, goring Wild Ox, why does he not rise?
39. Var. With the fattened sheep of the linen-clad priest, let him rise!
40. Var. Among the fat-tailed, banded sheep, why does he not rise?

### Stanza XIII

*185. The rising Wild Ox will look hither,
The rising Enlil will look hither,[41]
The dignitary is the rising Wild Ox, he will look hither,
Over Nippur, the Bond of Heaven and Earth, he will look hither,
Over Nippur, the Place of Fate-deciding.
*190. [. . . . .] gleaning by the walls.
You have overwhelmed us, you have destroyed us.

### Stanza XIV

The Wild Ox, his rising reached up to the sky,
Enlil is the rising Wild Ox, he reached up to the sky,[42]
The Dignitary is the rising Wild Ox, he reached up to the sky,
*195. Father Enlil, King of the Foreign Lands,
The Dignitary, Lord of Nippur,
The Lord, his word the sky cannot bear,
Enlil, his word the earth cannot bear,
The Lord, his unique hand the sky cannot bear,[43]
*200. Enlil, his unique foot (var. planted foot) the earth cannot bear[44]
The Wild Ox, his rising reached up to the sky.

### Stanza XV

You threatened, you threatened,
King of the Foreign Lands, it is you who threatened.
Who destroyed everything? It is you who destroyed!
*205. Who razed everything? It is you who razed!
Enlil, a well-founded house you turned into a reed hut,
The son of an honest man ran away(?),
Enlil, the (wearer of) fancy garments you killed by freezing,
He whose fields are wide fields, you killed by hunger,
*210. For the picker (of vegetables) from the earth, the earth stopped
      (producing),
To the drawer of water, the water hole cut off (its supply),
You threatened, but you exceeded your threats.

41. Var. The rising Father Enlil will look hither,
42. Var. Enlil, the Wild Ox, his rising reached up to the sky,
43. Var. The Dignitary, the grasp of his hands reached up to the sky,
44. Var. Enlil, the tread of his foot abutted the earth,

### Stanza XVI

You are exalted, you are exalted!
King of the Foreign Lands, you are exalted!
*215. In heaven, who is exalted? It is you who are exalted!
On the earth, who is exalted? It is you who are exalted!
Lord of all heaven, lord of the entire earth,
From the country of sunrise to the country of sunset,
In no country is there a king; only you exercise kingship,
*220. Enlil, in all the lands there is no queen, only your wife exercises
    queenship.
It is you, Enlil, who holds the rain of heaven, the water of the earth,
    and the halter of the gods.
Lord, you are the grower of legumes, you are the grower of barley.
Enlil, your glow boils the fish in the fresh waters.
You are exalted!

### Stanza XVII

*225–*231. (Broken)
    . . . that young man [is mourning],
    . . . that young girl is mourning.
    . . . "woe!" has increased, "woe!" has settled in,
*235.  . . . says "woe! There is trouble, woe! It is dark!"
    . . . in the bedroom, (she?) walks around in despair.

### The Eršemma

"Dignitary, turn around and look at your city!" let me say,
"Dignitary Enlil, turn around and look at your city!" let me say,
"King of the Foreign Lands, turn around and look at your city!" let
    me say,
*240. "Master of the Fulfilled Speech, turn around and look at your city!"
    let me say,
"Enlil, Father of the Nation, turn around and look at your city!" let
    me say,
"Shepherd of the Black-headed, turn around and look at your city!"
    let me say,
"The One Inspecting for Himself, turn around and look at your city!"
    let me say,
"The Warrior Who Leads the Troops, turn around and look at your
    city!" let me say,

\*245. "The One Who Feigns Sleep, turn around and look at your city!" let
me say,

"Enki, turn around and look at your city!" let me say,

"The Warrior Asalluhi, turn around and look at your city!" let me
say,

"The Lord Enbilulu, turn around and look at your city!" let me say,

"The Warrior Mudugasa'a turn around and look at your city!" let me
say,

\*250. "The Lord Dikumah, turn around and look at your city!" let me say,

"The Warrior Uta-ulu, turn around and look at your city!" let me say,

"Lord of Heaven and Earth, turn around and look at your city!" let
me say,

"Toward your city, Nippur, turn around and look at your city!" let
me say,

"From the brickwork of the Ekur turn around and look at your city!"
let me say,[45]

\*255. "From the brickwork of Sippar turn around and look at your city!"
let me say,

"The shrine Ebabbar, Edikukalama,"

"From the brickwork of Babylon turn around and look at your city!"
let me say,

"From the brickwork of Borsippa turn around and look at your city!"
let me say,

\*260. "From the brickwork of Ezida and Emahtila,"

"The brickwork of Etemenanki and Edara'anna,"

"From the brickwork of Isin, turn around and look at your city!" let
me say,

"The brickwork of Egalmah and Erabariri,"

"From the Ekiur, the Great Place, turn around and look at your city!"
let me say,

\*265. "From the Duku, the Holy Place turn around and look at your city!"
let me say,

"From within the Edimma turn around and look at your city!" let me
say,

"From the Ekamah turn around and look at your city!" let me say,

"From the Main Storehouse turn around and look at your city!" let
me say,

"From the Gagiššua turn around and look at your city!" let me say,

\*270. "From the shrine Egalmah turn around and look at your city!" let me
say,

45. Var. "From the brickwork of the Ekur, the foundation of Enamtila,"

"From the brickwork of Ur turn around and look at your city!" let
    me say,
"From the brickwork of Larsa turn around and look at your city!"
    let me say.
Your destroyed, flooded city,
In your destroyed Nippur, inundated by water,[46]
*275. In your destroyed, flooded city,
In your destroyed Sippar, inundated by water,
In your destroyed, flooded city,
In your destroyed Babylon, inundated by water,
In your destroyed, flooded city,
*280. In your destroyed Isin, inundated by water,
(In) your city whose harvested barley is weighed out (separately by the
    kernel),
The gluttonous man carries on without eating.
The wife of a young man there says "My husband!"
The son of a young man there says "My son!"
*285. The maiden there says "My brother!"
In the city, the mother who gives birth there says "My child!"
The young girl there says "My father!"
Young and old are raging,
In Nippur, young and old are raging,
*290. In Babylon, young and old are raging,
In Isin, young and old are raging.
Those standing in the streets were being chased away,
Their genitals, the dogs (carried) hanging (from their mouths),
Their scattered remains are set aflame(?),
*295. Their playgrounds have filled with storms,
The streets are not sated.

  46. Var. Your destroyed (city), inundated by water,

# Glossary

The glossary contains words from the Composite Text only; for material discussed in the notes the reader is referred to the index.

The numbers refer to lines in the Composite Text. Discussions, when called for, can usually be found in the notes to the first reference.

a: *ahulap* "woe!," 25 f.

a: *abu* "father," 1 (?), 73 (?).

a: *mû* "water," 221.

a-a: *abu* "father," 1–8, 39, 52, 93, 101, 116, 120, 186, 195.

a-a ka-nag-gá: "Father of the Nation" (an epithet of Enlil), 4, 52, 77, 130, 241.

a-ba: *mannu* "who?," 204 f., 215 f.

abul-mah: "Magnificent Gate" (a city gate of Nippur), 168.

abul-la i-bí urí[$^{ki}$-šè] (Emesal) = abul-la igi-bi urí$^{ki}$-šè: "The Gate Facing Ur" (a city gate in Nippur), 170.

abul-la ki $^d$utu-è-a: "Eastern Gate" (a city gate in Nippur), 169.

á-diri: "powerful" (?), 71.

a--du$_{11}$-ga (Emesal): *naqāru* "to destroy (a city)," *mahāṣu* "to smite (a city)," 273–280. The reliability of the equation with Emegir e$_{11}$ in Emesal Voc. III 65 is doubtful.

a-e: "oh!" (sound of wailing), 41–43, 87.

a--gar: see a-ta--gar.

a--gi$_4$-a (Emesal): *šanû* "to flood, immerse," *naqāru ša āli* "to destroy a city," 273, 275, 277, 279. The reliability of the equation with Emegir e$_{11}$ in Emesal Voc. III 66 is doubtful.

á-gur: "obstinate, rebellious," 177.

alim: *kabtu* "Dignitary" (an attribute of Enlil), 9, 155, 174, 176, 187 [194], 196, 238. Cf. S$^a$ Vocabulary K 29 f. (*MSL*, *3*, 62), Emesal Voc. I 5, II 23. See also e-lum.

a-li-ma-ha = alim (q.v.) -mah(a) (q.v.), 183.

am: *rīmu* "wild ox," 21–23, 153–155, 172–174, 185, 187, 192–194.

ama: *maštaku* "bedroom," 236.

ama-gal: *ummu rabitu* "Great Mother" (an epithet of Ninlil), 146.

ama-gan: *ummu (w)ālittu* "child-bearing mother," 286.

ᵈam-an-ki (Emesal) = ᵈen-ki: "Enki," 57, 82, 135, 246. Cf. Emesal Voc. I 38.

a--mar: see a-ta--mar.

am erín(-na) di-di: "Warrior Who Leads the Troops" (an epithet of Enlil translated *rīmu mudīl ummānišu*), 7, 55, 80, 133, 244; cf. Emesal Voc. III 2 and see p. 49.

amuru = muru: *burû* "reed mat," 24.

an: *šamû* "sky," 62 f., 65, 72, 192–194, 197, 199, 201, 215. Cf. also sub an-úr.

an = èm (q.v.), 32.

an$_x$(BÀD): *elû* "high," 70.

an- = àm-: (prefix), 29, 31, 33, 293 f.

-an = -àm: (copula), 29.

an-né--ús: "to reach as high as the sky," 192–194, 201–203. Cf. *CAD, E,* s.v. *emēdu* sub mng. 1c.

a-nu-da = an-úr (q.v.)-ta, 29.

an-úr: *išid šamê* "horizon," 29 f., 40, 65, 97, 124.

an-uraš: "Heaven and Earth," 144, 252.

a-ra-zu: *teslītu* "supplication," 143.

ᵈasal-lú-hi: "Asal, the Drenching Man" (Marduk), 9, 58, 83, 136, 247.

a-še-er (Emesal) = a-nir: *tānīhu* "lamentation," 41–43. Cf. Emesal Voc. III 73.

a-še-er--gá-gá (Emesal) = a-nir--gá-gá: "to set up a lamentation," 41, [42 f.]

a-še-ru = a-še-er (q.v.): 41.

a-ši-ir = a-še-er (q.v.): 41.

a-ta--gar: *mê rahāṣu/salû* "to inundate," 274. Cf. Emesal Voc. III 67. See also next entry.

a-ta--mar (Emesal) = a-ta--gar (q.v.): 274, 276, 278, 280.

bad: *nesû* "to be far away, remote," 14. (Read sumun: *labiru* "ancient?")

bàd-SI.AB.BA$^{ki}$: "Borsippa," 259.

bala: *dalû* "to draw (water)," 211.

bi- = bí-: (prefix), 37.

bi- = ba-e-: (prefix + infix), 103 f.

-da₄ = -ta: (postposition), 13–15.

dam: *aššatu* "wife," 16, 18 f., 220, 283; *mūtu* "husband," 283.

da-ma-al (Emesal) = dagal: *rapšu* "wide," 72, 209. Cf. Emesal Voc. III 96.

dè = "weak form" of du₁₁(-g) (q.v.), 237, ⟨238–253, 255, 257, 259, 262⟩.

de₅-de₅(-g): "to push," 118; to be translated by *šumqutu?*

di-di = "weak form" of du-du "cause to march, lead," see am erín(-na) di-di.

<sup>d</sup>di-ku₅-mah: *dajānu ṣīru* "The August Judge," i.e. Utu/Šamaš, 12, 61, 86, 139, 250.

dilmun, dil-mu-un, dilmun<sup>ki</sup>: *kabtum* "Dignitary" (an epithet of Enlil), 237.

dìm-me-er (Emesal) = diĝir: *ilu* "god," 114. Cf. Emesal Voc. I 1.

dìm-mi-ir = dìm-me-er (q.v.): 221.

diri(-diri[-g]): *watāru*, *(wutturu)* "to exceed," 34, 212.

du = túg (q.v.), 103.

dúb: *rābu* "to tremble," 62, 72.

du₇-du₇: *nakābu* "to gore," 172–174. On the orthography of *nakābu* see Goetze, *The Laws of Eshnunna* (1956), 134.

du₁₁(-g): *qibītu* "speech, promise," see umun du₁₁-ga zi-da.

du₁₁(-g): *qabû* "to speak, promise, say, threaten," 32–34, 202 f., 212, 237, [238–245, 253 f., 264–270], 271 f. This form is used in the *ḫamṭu* in complementary distribution with the *marû* form e; see NBGT II 9 f. (*MSL, 4,* 148).

du-ka = du₁₁-ga (q.v.), 33.

du-ku = dungu (q.v.), 29.

du₆-kù: "Holy Mound," 265.

dul: *katāmu, kuttumu* "to cover," 103.

dumu: *māru* "son," 17, 20, 284, 286.

du₅-mu (Emesal) = dumu (q.v.), [147], 207.

dungu: *erpu* "cloud," 29 f., 40.

dur-an-ki: *markas/rikis šamê u erṣetim* "Bond of Heaven and Earth" (an epithet of Nippur or one of its sectors), 156, 188.

du-ra-an-ki = dur-an-ki (q.v.), 182.

e: *qabû* "to speak," 25 f., 142 f., 235, 283–287. This form is used in the *marû* form in complementary distribution with the *ḫamṭu* form du₁₁(-g); see NBGT II 9 f. (*MSL, 4,* 148).

e = è (q.v.), 115.

é: *bītu* "house, temple," 25, 158, 160 f., 206. See also various temple names in the following entries.

è: *waṣû* "to come out," 114; *maḫû* "to rage," 288–291.

é-babbar: "White House" (a temple in Sippar), 256.

é-dàra-an-na: "House of the Heavenly Ibex" (Enki's temple in Babylon [?]), 171, 261.

é-di-ku₅-kalam-ma: "Temple of the Judge of the Nation" (an epithet of the é-babbar [q.v.]), 256.

é-dimₓ-ma: part of the é-kur (? q.v.), 164, 266.

edin: *ṣēru* "steppe," 38; *bītu* "shack," 44.

é-gal-mah: "Magnificent Temple" (Ninisina's temple in Isin), 263, 270.

é-ká-mah: "Temple, Magnificent Gate" (part of the è-kur? [q.v.]), 267.

é-gá-nun-mah: *ganunmāhu* "main storehouse," 268. See also ma-nun-mah.

egi: *rubâtu* "princess," [147].

é-ki-ùr: Ninlil's temple in Nippur, 161, 264(?).

é-kur: "Mountain House" (Enlil's temple in Nippur), 150, 254.

elam^{ki}: "Elam," 64, 96, 123.

el-lu-um-lu = sandhi form of e-lum (q.v.) mu-lu (q.v.), 115.

e-lum (Emesal) = alim (q.v.), 49, 73, 92, 107, 110 f., 145(?).

èm (Emesal) = níg: "everything, whatever, that which," 32, 34, 204 f. See Emesal Voc. III 36 ff., NBGT I 214 (*MSL, 4,* 137).

é-mah-ti-la: "Magnificent House of Life" (part of the é-zi-da, q.v.), 260.

é-MI-tum-ma-al: an epithet of the é-ki-ùr (? q.v.), 163.

èm-kú (Emesal) = níg-kú: translated *akallu* (sic!) "food," 178 f.; *akkilu* "glutton," 282.

é-nam-ti-la: "House of Life" (a temple in Nippur), 162.

^den-bi-lu-lu: "Marduk," 10, 59, 84, 137, 248.

en-du = èn-du (q.v.), 45.

èn-du: *zamāru* "dirge," 45.

e-ne: *ekijam* "where?," 25 f., 40; *šū* "he," 140 f.

en-edin-na: "the high steppe," 39.

e-ne-èm (Emesal) = inim: *awātu* "word," 197 f.

engur: *apsû* "the (subterranean) fresh waters," 223.

^den-ki: "Enki," 145.

en-nu-ug-gá: *maṣṣartu* "guard," 37.

èn-šè: *adi mati* "until when?," 1–8, 28.

en-zi: *ašarēdu* "choice, first rate," 178.

ér: *dimtu* "tear (of the eye)," 46 f., 89.

é-rab(a)-ri-ri: "House, Pillory which Clamps Down" (a temple in Isin?), 263.

erín: see am erín(-na) di-di.

ér--še₈-še₈: *bakû* "to cry," 44. See also ér and še-še.

é-sag-íl-la: "Temple, the Raised Head" (Marduk's temple in Babylon), 258.

e-sír: *sūqu* "street," 292, 296.

èš: *bītu* "shrine," 256.

ešemen: *mēlultu* "game," 295.

eškiri: *ṣerretu* "lead-rope, halter," 221.

eš-ki-ri = eškiri (q.v.), 221.

eš-še = èn-šè (q.v.), 2.

é-te-mén-an-ki: "Temple, Basis of Heaven and Earth" (the ziqqurrat of Babylon), 261.

é-tùr-kalam-ma: "Temple, the Corral of the Land" (Ištar's temple in Babylon), 258.

e-ú-nu-UK: "?," 28.

e-zé (Emesal) = udu: *ṣēnu* "sheep," 36. Cf. Emesal Voc. II 89.

e-zé èm-kú-e (Emesal) = udu niga(ŠE): *immeru marû* "fattened sheep," 178 f. Cf. Emesal Voc. II 90.

é-zi-da: "Well Founded Temple" (Nabu's temple in Borsippa), 260.

e-zin$_x$ = ezin$_x$ (q.v.), 1.

ezin$_x$(ŠE.TIR): *šubtu* (?) "dwelling" (?), 1.

ga-a-a-gu-ú = gá-gá (q.v.), 41.

gá-an-gu-ú = gá-gá (q.v.), 41.

gaba: *irtu* "surface, chest," 68.

gá-gá: *šakānu* "to settle down, set up," 40 f., 149.

gal: *rabû* "great," 10, 12; "adult, grown up, big," 26; "fancy," 208.

gal$_4$-la: *qallu* "genitals," 293.

gam (read gurum?): *qadādu* "to lie down," 36; *šumūtu* "to kill," 208 f.

gána: *mēreštu* "field, tilled land," 209.

ga-ša-an--ak (Emesal) = nin--ak: "to exercise queenship," 220. Cf. Emesal Voc. II 74 f.

ga-šà-an-keš$^{ki}$ (Emesal) = $^d$nin-keš$^{ki}$: "Lady of Keš," Enlil's sister, 147.

ga-ša-an-nibru$^{ki}$ (Emesal) = $^d$nin-nibru$^{ki}$: "Lady of Nippur," Ninurta's wife, 148. Cf. Emesal Voc. I 9.

ge: *kīnu, kunnu* "steadfast," 160.

ge (Emesal) = gemé: "slave girl," the Emesal and Akkadian terms are used in Emesal texts with the meaning "young girl, virgin," 45, 47 f., 233. This explains why Emesal Voc. II 71 equates them with Emegir ki-sikil "virgin."

-ge-en = -gin$_x$(GIM): (postposition), 29.

gi = gi$_4$ (q.v.), 116.

gi$_4$: *turru* "to restore," 126–128, ⟨129–139⟩, 140.

gi$_6$: *mūšu* "night," 14. gi$_4$-ri-da$_4$: *ina muši ullûti* "since that/those night(s)," 14.

gi$_6$(-g): *ṣalmu* "dark," 235. See also sipa sag-gíg-ga.

gi-di: *šulpu* "reed stalk," 39.

gig: *marṣu* "bitter," 27, 44, 89.

gi-ga = gig-a: *marṣiš* "bitterly," 46 f.(?).

gi$_{16}$-il-gi$_{16}$-il: *hulluqu* "to destroy," 189. Cf. Emesal Voc. III 59.

gina: *ginû* "baby," 26.

gi(-r): *dâku* (?) "to rampage," 21–23.

gìr-gi-lu: *girgilu* "girgilu (bird)," 88.

gìri-aša$_x$: see me-ri-aša$_x$.

gìri-gub: see me-ri-gub.

gìri-ús: see me-ri-ús.

giri$_x$(KA)-zal: *tašiltu* "splendor, joy," 43.

gi-sig: *kikkišu, huṣṣu* "reed hut," 206.

gu: *halluru* "legumes," 222. See also gu//še.

gu = gú (q.v.), 103.

gú: *kišādu* "neck," 103 f.

gú: "?", 118.

gub: *šuzuzzu* "to install, appoint," 36; *izuzzu* "to stand," 292. See also sub
   me-ri-gub.

gud: *šahāṭu* "to skip" (a line in a text), 158. Cf. also notes to *238.

gud-sún: "Wild Bull" (an attribute of Enlil), 49–61, 92–94, 119–121.

gud-niga(ŠE): *marû* "fattened bull," 177.

gukkal-guru$_x$(E.íB)-lá: *zibbānu* "fat-tailed, banded sheep," 180.

gul: *kalû* "to hold back, restrain," 41; *abātu* "to destroy," 204.

gur: see á-gur.

gu//še: "legumes and barley" = "fertility, prosperity," 222.

gú-zà--lá: *nenguru* (?) "to loll (lifelessly)," 91.

hun: *nāhu* "to calm down," 141.

hul-hul: *šulputu* "to devastate," 21–23.

hu-luh-ha: *galtu* "angry, terrifying," 1.

hu-mu = hun (q.v.) -ù, 141.

íb: *aggu* "angry," 1.

i-bí--du$_8$ (Emesal) = igi--du$_8$: *amāru* "to inspect," cf. Emesal Voc. III
   113 and see below.

i-bí-du$_8$ ní-te-na: "The One Inspecting by Himself" (an epithet of
   Enlil), 6, 54, 79, 132, 243.

íl: *našû* "to lift, bear," 197–200.

i-lu: *nubû* "wailing," 41–43, 87, 89, 184.

ì-lu = i-lu (q.v.), 41.

igi-du$_8$: "onlooker, observer," 25 f.

im: *zunnu* "rain," 221.

im-gu-ra = engur (q.v.)-a, 223.

i-ni-im = inim (q.v.), 109.

inim: *awātu* "word," [109].

inim--dé-dé (?): "herald" (?), 148.

i$_7$-ninnu: "Ninnu" (a canal in Nippur), 167.

i-ra = ér (q.v.) -a, 46.

ir--ši-še = ér--še$_8$-še$_8$ (q.v.), 44.

ì-si-in$^{ki}$: "Isin," 262, 280, 291.

iš-še-en-ni = ezin$_x$ (q.v.), 1.

itima: *kiṣṣu* "Holy of Holies," 21–23.

ka-na-ága, ka-nag-gá (Emesal) = kalam(a): *mātu* "the land (Sumer), the nation (Sumerians)," 90, 110, 117, 158, 171. See also a-a ka-nag-gá.

ka-na-da = ka-nag-gá (q.v.) -da, 116.

ká-še-nu-ku₅: "Gate of Uncut Barley" (a gate of the é-kur, q.v.), 166.

ki: *erṣetu* "earth," 63, 66–68, 98, 125, 198, 200, 210, 216, 221.; *ašru* "place," 144, 157; *ēma* "wherever," 33, 35. *uṭṭitum*, 207, 210.

ki = gi₄ (q.v.), 125 f.

ki-ága: *narāmu* "beloved," 146.

ki-gal: "Great Place" (or "Foundation Pit"? cf. *CAD*, B, s.v. *berūtu*) (an epithet of the é-ki-ùr, q.v.), 264.

ᵍⁱKID.MAH: see amuru.

ki-kù: "Holy Place" (an epithet of the du₆-kù, q.v.), 265.

ki--lá-lá: *šaqālu* "to weigh out," 281.

ki-nam-tar-tar: *ašar šimātu iššimmū* "Place of Fate-Deciding" (an epithet of Nippur), 157, 189.

kingal: *mu'irru* "commander," 150.

ki--ri-ri: *uṭṭitam utemmudu* "to run around, run away" (?), 207.

ki-ùr: see é-ki-ùr.

kú: *šūkulu* "to feed, fatten," 178 f.: *akālu* "to eat," 282.

ku₅: *parāsu* "to cut off," 281. See also še--ku₅.

kua(HA): *nūnu* "fish," 223.

ku(-ku): *ṣalālu* "to sleep," 37. See also ù-lul-la ku-ku.

ku₄-ku₄: *turru* "to turn into" (trans.), 206.

kur: *šadû* "mountain," 62, 64, 69–72, 95 f., 122 f.; *erṣetu* "foreign country," 218 f. See also kur-kur.

kúr: *nakru* "enemy," 16 f.

kur-gal: "Great Mountain" (an attribute of Enlil), 30, 40, 42–44, 52, 93, 101, 120.

kur-kur: *matātu* "foreign countries," 49, 52 f., 92–94, 119–121, 159. See also ᵈmu-ul-líl kur-kur-ra and umun kur-kur-ra.

lá: *maṭû* "to become reduced, little," 111.

la-la--gi₄-gi₄: *lalâ šebû* "to become satisfied, sated," 296.

larsamᵏⁱ: "Larsa," 272.

le-el = líl: *šāru* "wind, storm," 183. See also mu-le-el.

líl: *zaqīqu* "ghost," 295.

lu: *ma'ādu* "to increase, become numerous," 234.

lù: *dalāhu* "to trouble, stir up," 235.

lul: *sarru* "false," 8, 18(?), 56, 81, 134. See also ù-lul-la ku-ku.

ma = ma-a: *ajiš* "where?," 25 f.

ma = ma₄ (q.v.), 38.

ma (Emesal) = gá: *bītu* "shrine," 270.

ma₄: *(w)aṣû* "to grow" (intrans. and trans.), 38.

ma-al (Emesal) = gál: *bašû* "to be," 62, 64 f., ⟨66, 68–71⟩, 72, 95–98, 112 f., 122–125; *šakānu* "to set," 158 f.; *rašû* "to have, hold," 221. Cf. Emesal Voc. III 77.

mah: *ṣīru* "exalted," 73–75, ⟨76 f., 79–86⟩, 104 f., 213–216, 224; *rabû* "adult," 288–291. See also di-ku₅-mah, é-gal-mah, é-gá-nun-mah, é-ká-mah, é-mah-ti-la and ma-nun-mah.

ma-la(-g): "friend," 18(?). Cf. ma-li = *ru-ut-tum* (*CT*, *19*, 27, K. 2061:21) and ma-al = *ru-tú* (? *SBH*, 66 obv. 24).

ma-le = ma-al(+ e): "to alight," 29, 31, 33.

ma-mu-šú-a (Emesal) = gá-giš-šú-a: "Shrine, the Stool" (a shrine in Nippur), 269.

ma-nu-na = ma-nun-na (q.v.), 45.

ma-nun-mah (Emesal) = gá-nun-mah: *ganunmāhu* "main storehouse," 165. See also é-gá-nun-mah.

ma-nun-na (Emesal) = gá-nun-na: *ganūnu* "storehouse," 45.

mar (Emesal) = gar: *šakānu* "to place," 104. Cf. Emesal Voc. III 78.

ma-ra = mar (q.v.) -a: 104.

me-a: *ajānu* "where?," 29, 31, 33.

-mèn (Emesal) = -me-en: (suffix); 204 f., 213–216, 222 [224]. Cf. Emesal Voc. III 174.

me-na: *mati* "when," 27.

me-na-šè: *adi mati* "how long?," 28, 99–102.

me-ri (Emesal) = gìri: *šēpu* "foot," 113. See following entries and cf. Emesal Voc. II 197.

me-ri-aša$_x$ (Emesal) = gìri-aša$_x$(AŠ): "single, unique foot," 200.

me-ri-gub (Emesal) = gìri-gub: "treading foot," 200.

me-ri-ús (Emesal) = gìri-ús: "firmly planted foot," 200.

me-lám: *melammu* "glow," 223.

mu: *šumu* "line (in text)," 160a; "name" 49, 52 f., 62, 92–95, 119–122; *šattu* "year," 15.

mu (Emesal) = giš: *eṭlu* "young man," 44, 46, 232.

mu-bar-ra/-re--lá (Emesal) = giš-bar-ra/-re--lá: "to catch fire, be set aflame," 294.

mudna(SAL.NITA.DAM): *hīrtu* "wife," 146. Cf. Emesal Voc. II 73.

mu-le-el/-la = ᵈmu-ul-líl(-lá) (q.v.), 28, 100, 109, 116, 127.

mu-lu (Emesal) = lú: *awīlu* "man, master," 90, 103, 110, 142 f., 222. Cf. Emesal Voc. II 6.

mú-mú: "to grow" (transitive), 222.

mu-na-ka = mu-un-ak-e, 108. See translation ad loc.

mušen (Emesal?): *iṣṣūru* "bird," 87 f. Cf. notes ad loc.

ᵈmu-ul-líl (Emesal) = ᵈen-líl: "Enlil," 2–8, 39 f., 42, 52, 74, 93, 100, 109, 111–113, 120, 127, 130, [160], 162, 164, 166, 168, 186, 193, 195, 198,

200, 206, 208, 220 f., 223, 241. See also next entry and cf. Emesal Voc. I 4.

$^d$mu-ul-líl kur-kur-ra: "Enlil of the Foreign Lands" (an attribute of Enlil), 75, 101, 128, 220.

mu-uš-túg (Emesal) = geštug: *uznu* "ear," 107. Cf. Emesal Voc. II 183.

$^d$mu-zé-eb-ba-sa₄-a (Emesal) = $^d$mu-dùg-ga-sa₄-a: "Called with a Good Name" = Nabû, 11, 60, 85, 138, 249. Cf. Emesal Voc. I 52.

ná/nú(-d): *ṣalālu* "to lie down, sleep," 153–155, 172–174.

na-ám-ku₅ (Emesal) = nam-ku₅: "curse, oath," 35. Cf. Emesal Voc. III 52 ff.

nam-kúr: "hostility," 27(?).

nam-tar-tar: see ki-nam-tar-tar.

ne-èm-àr-ra (Emesal) = níg-àr-ra: *mundu* "fine flour," 179.

ní- (+ possessive pronoun): *ramān-* (+ poss. pron.) "-self," 62 f., 72.

nibru$^{ki}$: "Nippur," 22, 156 f., 176, 188 f., 196, 253, 289.

niga(šE): see gud-niga.

nigin, nigín: *sahāru* "to turn around," 237–255, 257, 259, 262, 264–272.

ni-ib-ru = nibru$^{ki}$ (q.v.), 182.

ni-iš- = nu-uš-: (preformative), 41.

nin: *ahātu* "sister," [147].

$^d$nin-ki: "Ninki," 145.

$^d$nin-líl: "Ninlil," 146, 161, 163.

$^d$NINNU: "Enlil" 154.

ní-ri: "awe inspiring," 69.

ní-te- (+ possessive pronoun): *ramān-* ( + poss. pron.) "-self," 6, 54, 79, 132.

nu = ná(-d) (q.v.), 183.

nu-uš-: (preformative), 41.

-nu: (suffix), 39.

-pa = -ba: (= -bi-a), 108.

$^{gi}$pisan: *pisannu* "basket," 106.

pú-sag: *šaṭpu* "water hole," 211.

rab: see é-rab-ri-ri.

-ri, -ri-: (affix), 13–15, 156–159, 188 f.

ri-ri(-g): *laqātu* "to pick," 210.

sá: "equal," usually translated by the verb *šanānu*, 112 f.

sa₄: see $^d$mu-zé-eb-ba-sa₄-a.

sa-an = sag (q.v.), 103.

sa-an-du-e = sag-du--è: "to confront," 115.

sá--du₁₁: *kašādu* "to reach," 33.

sag: *rēšu* "head," 103. See also sag-gíg-ga and sipa sag-gíg-ga.

ság: *saphūtu* "remains," 294.

sag-gíg-ga: ṣalmāt qaqqadi "black-headed," i.e., "people," 91, 111, 118, 121, 131. See also sipa sag-gíg-ga.

sal: muzzû "to oppress," 110(?).

sa-pa = sipa (q.v.), 102.

sar: šuhmuṭu "to chase away," 292.

si-du-a = šed$_7$ (q.v.) -dè: 2, ⟨3–27⟩.

si(-g), var. sù(-g): malû "to fill," 296.

sìg: narāṭu "to shake, tremble," 46 f., 63; sapānu "to raze," 205.

si-ge = sìg (q.v.) -e, 46 f.

sipa: rē$^{\text{ɔ}}$u "shepherd," 21, 36, 121, 131. See also next entry.

sipa sag-gíg-ga: rē$^{\text{ɔ}}$u ṣalmat qaqqadi "Shepherd of the Black-headed" (an epithet of Enlil), 5, 53, 78, 94, 102, 131, 242.

siskur$_x$(AMARxŠE.AMARxŠE): ikribu "prayer," 28, 142.

sù: redū(?) "to proliferate," 39.

su(-d/r/t): rūqu "remote, far off," 13, 15. See notes to 13 and see also šà-su$_x$-ud--ak.

sù(-g) see si(-g).

su-a-ì-im-du = sá-um-mi-du$_{11}$, 33. See also sá--du$_{11}$.

su$_8$-ba (Emesal) = sipa (q.v.), 37. Cf. Emesal Voc. II 12.

sukkal-mah: sukkalmāhu "grand vizier," 150.

sumun: see bad.

sur$_5$: šuqallulu "to dangle," 293; wrongly translated našû "to carry," ibid.

su-ta = sù (q.v.) -rá, 108.

ša = šà(-g) (q.v.), 108, 126 f.

šà(-g): libbu "heart, middle," 1, 106, 108, 160, 164, 266.

ša-ab (Emesal) = šà(-g) (q.v.), 126–141.

šà-èn--tar: ša$^{\text{ɔ}}$ālu "to ask (oneself = contemplate)," 105.

šà-gada-lá: lābiš kitê "linen clad priest," 176.

šà-mar (Emesal) = šà-gar: bubūtu "hunger," 207. Cf. Emesal Voc. III 84.

šà-su$_x$(BU)-ud--ak: "to make the heart fathomless," 108 f.

ŠE: see niga.

še: še$^{\text{ɔ}}$u "barley," 222, 281. See also gu--še and še-gu-nu.

še = ši (Emesal, q.v.), 89.

še = še$_8$ (cf. ér--še$_8$-še$_8$), 46 f.

-še-e = -šè: (postposition), 28, 99.

šed$_7$: pašāhu "to be pacified," 1.

šed$_x$(A.MUŠ.DI): kūṣu "frost," 208.

še-eb (Emesal) = sig$_4$: libittu "brickwork," 254 f., 257–261, [262 f.], 271 f.

še-gu-nu: "spotted barley," 144.

šèg-šèg: see šeg$_6$-šeg$_6$.

šeg$_6$-šeg$_6$, šèg-šèg: šubšulu "to boil" (trans.), 223.

še--ku₅: *eṣēdu* "to harvest," 281. See also ká-še-nu-ku₅.

šeš: *ahu* "brother," 285.

še--ša₄: *damāmu* "to mourn," 232.

še-še = še₈-še₈: *bakû* "to cry," 89.

ši (Emesal) = zi: *napištu* "throat," 87 f., 105; "life," 155 f. Cf. Emesal Voc. II 189.

-ši = -šè: (postposition), 28.

ši-še = še₈-še₈ (see še-še), 44 f., 48.

ši-iš-ku-ra = siskurₓ (q.v.) -a, 142.

šu: *qātu* "hand," 112.

šú: *katāmu* "to cover," 106.

šu-ašaₓ(AŠ): "single, unique hand," wrongly translated *tiriṣ qāti*, 199. Cf. also me-ri-ašaₓ.

šú-šú: *šapāku* "to pour out (the voice = shout)," 87–89.

šu-tab: "joining of hands, grasp," 199; translated *kepû ša šēpi* = "to bend the legs," *CT*, *12*, 46 ii 41.

tar: *parāsu* "to cut off, terminate," 210 f. See also ki-nam-tar-tar.

te: *minu, minam* "when?," "why?," 153–159, 172–174, 180.

ti: (*w)ašābu* "to dwell," 219 f.

ti = til (q.v.), 32.

ti- = dè-: (preformative), 181, 183.

til: *gamāru* "to finish," 35.

TIN.TIR.KI: "Babylon," 23, 257, 278, 290.

túg: *ṣubātu* "garment, cloth," 18(?), 103, 208.

tuku: "there is, belongs," 141.

tur: *ṣihru* "young," 283 f., 288–291.

tuš: (*w)ašābu* "to settle," 234; *šūšubu* "to install," 32.

tu₁₀-tu₁₀(-b): *kummuru* "to overwhelm," 191.

tuₓ-tuₓ(-b)(HÚB.HÚB) = tu₁₀-tu₁₀(-b) (q.v.), 191.

ú: *šammu* "grass," 38.

ù: *šittu* "sleep," 37. See also ù-lul-laku-ku.

u₄: *ūmu* "day," 13, 16 f. u₄-ri-da₄: *ina ūmi ullûti* "since that/those day(s)," 13.

u₆: *amāru* "to look," *hâtu* "to survey," 237 f., [⟨239–245⟩], ⟨246–252⟩, [⟨253⟩], [254], ⟨255, 257, 259, 262⟩, [264–272].

ú- = ù-: (preformative), 116, 126.

udₓ(ÙZ): *enzu* "goat," 179.

udu: *immeru* "sheep," 178.

ug₅: *mâtu* "to die," 18–20; *nēru* "to kill," 32.

ugaᵐᵘšᵉⁿ (ᵘNAGAᵍᵃ·ᵐᵘšᵉⁿ): *āribu* "raven," 108 f.

ú-ga = ugaᵐᵘšᵉⁿ (q.v.), 108 f.

uku-uš: *rēdû* "soldier," 149.

ù-lul-la ku-ku: *ša ṣalal sarrāti ṣallu* "The One Who Feigns Sleep" (lit. He Who Sleeps a False Sleep, an epithet of Enlil), 8, 56, 81, 134, 245.

umun, ù-mu-un (Emesal) = en: *bēlu* "lord, master," = lugal: *šarru* "king," 10, 12, 42 f., 57, 59, 61, 82, 84, 86, 133, 135, 137, 171, 175, 195–197, 199, 203, 248, 250, 252. See also below and cf. Emesal Voc. II 7–9.

umun--ak (Emesal): "to exercise kingship," 219. Cf. also umun.

umun/ù-mu-un $du_{11}$-ga zi-da: *bēlum ša qi[bissu kīnat]* "Master of the Fulfilled Speech" (an epithet of Enlil), 3, 51, 76, 129, 240.

umun/ù-mu-un kur-kur-ra: "King of the Foreign Lands" (an epithet of Enlil), 2, 50, 75, 128, 175, 195, 203, 239.

ur: *kalbu* "dog," 293; wrongly translated *nakru* "enemy," ibid.

úr: *išdu* "foundation," 65 f.; *sūnu* "lap, thigh," 104, 107. See also an-úr.

urí[ki]:"Ur," 271.

ur-sag: *qarrādu* "warrior," 9, 10, 12, 58, 60, 83, 85, 132, 134, 136, 138, 247, 249, 251.

uru, urú: *ālu* "city," 21, 25, 42 f., 237–245 ⟨246–253, 255, 257, 259, 262⟩, [264–270], 271–273, 275, 277, 279, 281, 286.

ús: *emēdu* "to lean," 107. See also an-ne--ús and me-ri--ús.

[d]uta-$u_x$-lu: "Cloudy Day" or "South Storm" (an epithet of Ninurta), 251.

[d]utu-è: *ṣīt šamši* "sunrise, east," 216.

[d]utu-šú: *ereb šamši* "sunset, west," 216.

$u_4$--zal(-zal): *šutabrû* "to go on (time,) to carry on," 27, 282.

za: *attā* "you (sg.)," 73–86, 114, 202–205, 212–216, 219, 221, 224.

zà-an-na: "farthest reaches of the sky, the entire sky," 217.

zà-ki-a: "the farthest reaches of the earth, the entire earth," 67, 98, 125, 217.

zé-eb (Emesal): see [d]mu-zé-eb-ba-$sa_4$-a.

zé-èm (Emesal) = sum: *nadānu* "to give," 16 f. Cf. Emesal Voc. III 118.

zi(-d): *kīnu* "well founded (house)," 206; "honest," 207. See also umun $du_{11}$-ga zi-da.

zi(-g): *tibūtu* "rising," 185–188, 192–194, 201.

zimbir[ki]: "Sippar," 255, 276.

zi-zi: *tebû* "to rise," 153–159, 172–174, 177–181, 183.

# Plates

*Plate 1*   YBC 4659 Text A Obverse

*Plate 2*   YBC 4659 Text A Reverse

*Plate 3*   CNM 10051 Text B Upper Edge

*Plate 4*   CNM 10051 Obverse and Right Edge

*Plate 5*  CNM 10051 Reverse and Right Edge

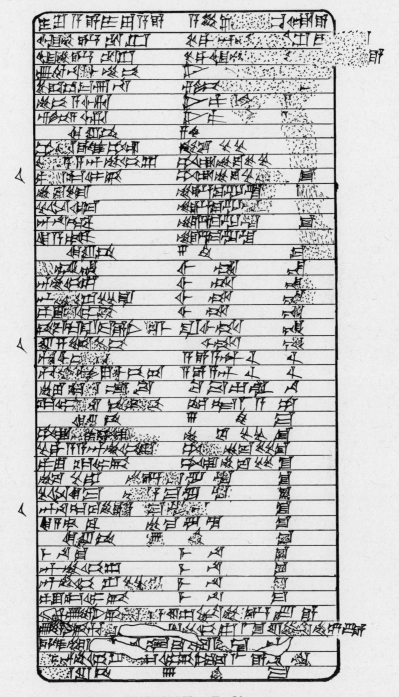

*Plate 6* VAT 7824 Text Ea Obverse

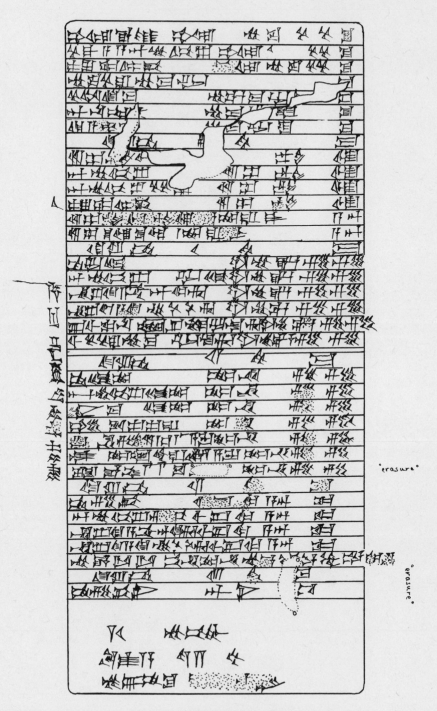

*Plate 7*  VAT 7824 Text Ea Reverse

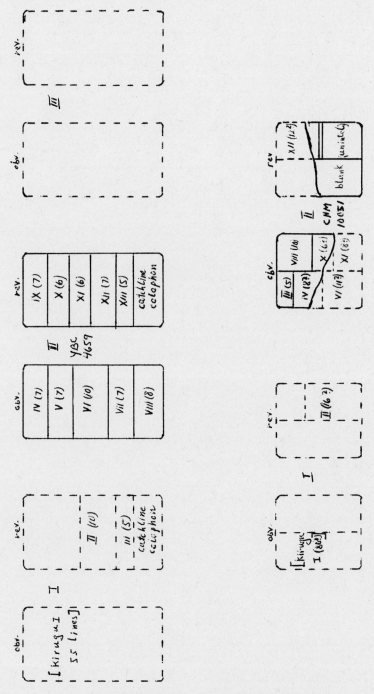

*Plate 8*  Recension A (Yale), Recension B (Copenhagen)

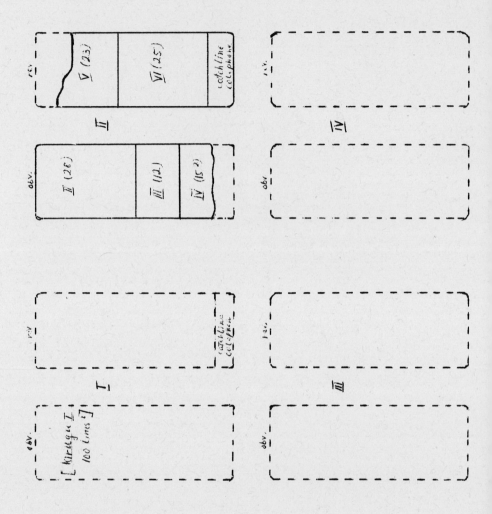

*Plate 9*  Recension C (British Museum)

# Selective Indices

## SUMERIAN

abulla, 111

ama$_5$, 130

AN.GI$_6$, 130

an-ta-lù, 130

aratta, 132

buru$_x$, 128

-da replaced by -ta, 69

/d-r/. *See* flapped /r/

/e/ elided in initial position, 102

*emen, 67, 82, 85

en-nu, ennuğa (various spellings), 77–78

en$_x$(ŠA)-du, 82

ér--gá-gá, 80

eš-ki-ri (=eškiri), 128

éš-kiri$_4$, 128

flapped /r/, 69–70 and n6, 77

/g/ interchanged with /h/, 119

/ğ/ spelled /n-g/, 78, 80

/gg/ nasalized, 74–75

girum$_x$, 77

giš, 81

giš-bar-ra, 142

glide, 80

gú-ru (= gud), 70

gurum, 77

/h/ interchanged with /g/, 119

i-lu-u-ak-ke, 80

i-lu-ú-ú-ak-ke-e, 80

im-gu-ra (= engur-ra), 129

i-si-iš--gá-gá, 80

ki-sum-ma, 104

ki-ib-bar (= ki-bala), 70

libir, 75

/m/ elided in intervocalic position, 82

-mú (= -mèn), 128

mu-sa$_4$-a, mu-sig$_5$, mu-šen, mu-še-na (all = mušen), 91

/n/ elided in initial position, 79

nasalization of /gg/, 74

/n-g/ as spelling for /ğ/, 78, 80

nigir, nimgir, 75

phonetic indicator (complement), 69, 103, 108, 113

/r/, flapped. *See* flapped /r/; interchanged with /l/, 70

sa, 77

šibir, 128

te-li (= diri), 70

tùn-tab, 121

/-u/ vowel at end of words, 80

ù-a (various spellings), 130

ù-un = (umun), 67

ur-bar-ra, 142

za (-a) -kam, 103

-zu, suffixed to geographic name, 134

## AKKADIAN

*akallu*, 114

*a-lí-lum*, 115

*alimu*, 47n2

*bēlum* (translating am), 47

*hiritum*, 111

*kepû ša qāti*, 121

*kūma ištar*, 103

*nakābu*, 112

*qabû* (translating tuku), 103

*sahāru* (translating gi$_4$), 101

*šakānu* (translating ús), 97

*saphussušu*, 142

*šimtam šāmu*, 108
*tarāṣu* (translating ašaₓ), 121

uk-*ba-ti-šu*, 115
*uṭṭitam utemmudu/luqqutu*, 123–24

GENERAL

Abū Salābikh, 45
am-e bára-an-na-ra, 6, 18
Ammi-ditana year 31 formula,
    45
Assur Calendar, 5, 6n6
Azitawadda, 126
balag, 2–3, 16
Civil, M., 81
Colophons, 11 ff.
*Curse of Agade, The*, 110
Dilmun, 45
Emesal, 5, 42–43
Emesal forms in Emegir and vice versa,
    67–68, 91
ér-šà-hun-gá, 5
ér-šèm-ma, 16
*Exploits of Ninurta, The*, 4
"Götteradressbuch," 135–36, 138
Hallo, W. W., 14, 81
Haplology, 111
"Harmonization" of text, 30, 104,
    122
Hendiadys, 141
Ipiq-Adad II of Ešnunna, 46
Jacobsen, Th., 72, 80–81, 96n13, 98, 106,
    132
*kalû* priests. *See* gala priests
*KAR* 15 and 16, 4
Kramer, S. N., 80n10, 83
Letter prayers, 5

Lines of text: omitted, 68, 102, 107;
    skipped, 47–48 *nn*, 109, 133
Malachi, 126
Mistranslation (Sumerian-Akkadian), 97,
    101, 114, 142
Musical(?) notations, 29
mu-tin nu-nuzₓ-ginₓ, 4
Naram-Sin, 110
ᵈnin-šà-ge-p-àda, 109
Nippur, 25 ff.; scribal school, 11; map of,
    109, 111
Psalms, 126
Refrains, 29–30
Rim-Sin, 46, 137
Royal titles, 46, 50, 109
ᵈšara, 109
Sin-leqe-unninni, 13
*SK* 25, 4–5
Sleeping Enlil, 107
Sollberger, E., 11–12
*STT* 155, 5, 18
Šulgi, 46n1
Šu-Suen, 46n1, 109
Tallqvist, K., 44
Tiglatpileser I, 109
Ur-Nammu, 109
Uruk Calendar, 5, 6n6, 18
Versions, discrepancy between, 106–07
Yahdunlim, 46
zi-u₄-sud-rá, 70n6